healing
journeys

healing journeys

Teaching Medicine, Nurturing Hope

Preface and Conclusion by Marilyn Winkleby, Ph.D.
Text by Julia Steele
Photographs by Kathy Sloane

Foreword by David Satcher, M.D., Ph.D.

Palo Alto, California
2003

Healing Journeys: Teaching Medicine, Nurturing Hope

About this book

All material for the program vignettes comes from the Stanford Medical Youth Science Program (SMYSP) 2000 summer program. Program photographs were taken during the 2002 and 2003 SMYSP summer programs. Consequently, photographs do not reflect the specific students described in the program vignettes. We have changed the names and other identifying information about all patients mentioned in *Healing Journeys*.

Library of Congress Cataloging-in-Publication Data
Hardcover ISBN: 1-879552-50-7
Softcover   ISBN: 1-879552-51-5

Preface and Conclusion by Marilyn Winkleby, Ph.D.
Text by Julia Steele
Photographs by Kathy Sloane, except pages 70-71 by Mitchell Craig and pages 210-211 by Marilyn Winkleby
Foreword by David Satcher, M.D., Ph.D.

Healing Journeys was set in Sabon 9.5/13.5 designed by Jan Tschichold in 1967; with Clarendon designed by Hermann Eidenbenz in 1953 and Trade Gothic designed by Jackson Burke in 1948. Printed on Huron Gloss Enamel 80# Text.

Design: Steve Jones - plantain studio, inc. / www.plantainstudio.com

Printing: Thomson-Shore, Inc. - Dexter, MI / www.tshore.com

Printed and bound in the United States of America

foreword

I grew up on a small farm in Alabama in the 1940s. At the age of 2, I developed whooping cough and pneumonia and came very close to death. My parents were prohibited from taking me to the nearby whites-only hospital. Instead, the only black physician in our region, Dr. Jackson, traveled 20 miles to treat me. He was not optimistic and told my family that he didn't expect me to live through the week. My parents had already lost two young children because they didn't have access to health care. They lived at a time and in a place where it was common for children to die. But I survived, and my mother told me the story almost every day of how Dr. Jackson had predicted I wasn't going to live. By the time I was 6, I was saying, "When I grow up, I want to be a doctor like Dr. Jackson." I wanted to make a difference for people who didn't have health care.

Our community consisted of five neighboring farm families. We had no running water or electricity and no television to give us a broader perspective of the world. We were a close-knit group that helped each other through hard times. I remember taking some of our crops and milk to other families when they did not have a good season, and vice versa. I also remember occasions when I ventured into town after saving my allowance to purchase an ice cream cone and being met with a sign that said African Americans were not served.

Fortunately, I have been able to journey a long way from our small community and widen my view of the world. I attended Morehouse College in Atlanta, an institution known for encouraging its students to make a difference. I continued on to Case Western Reserve University, where I received my M.D. and Ph.D. When I was a student at Case Western, there were only three or four black students, a fact that proved to me that there was a serious need for minority students in higher education and the medical sciences.

In medicine and in public health, we have dreams as a nation to eliminate disparities and ensure that everybody in this country has access to quality health care. These dreams are an extension of Dr. Martin Luther King, Jr.'s dream and they are critical to the future of our country. To accomplish them, we must make strong commitments. These commitments include responding foremost to the health needs of the most vulnerable among us—how we protect and promote the health of our nation reflects who we are as Americans. In the United States, we spend about 14 percent of our gross national product on health care, or $1.5 trillion a year. We spend more per capita than any other industrialized country, yet 43 million people in America have no health insurance at all. One in five children in the United States lives in poverty, and it is no secret that poverty promotes poor health. Disparities exist in a number of areas. A black infant, for example, is more than twice as likely to die in its first year of life as a white infant, and an Hispanic infant is one and a half times as likely to die.

When I was sworn in as Surgeon General, one of my top three priorities was to eliminate racial and ethnic disparities in health. We were able to make this one of the two main goals of Healthy People 2010, the nation's health agenda for the next decade. This goal was also the basis for the Department of Health and Human Service's Race and Health Initiative, which started in 1998 as an outgrowth of President Clinton's Race Initiative.

I believe strongly that the health professions need to more closely reflect the populations we serve. This is critical to provide accessible health care. We know that minority physicians are more likely to serve minority communities, more likely to treat patients who are poor, and more likely to live in medically under-served communities. An excellent example of this commitment to the under-served is my former student in community health at Morehouse School of Medicine, Dr. Regina Benjamin. After graduating from medical school, Regina chose to go to an under-served community in her home state of Alabama to practice. The community didn't have a doctor and greatly needed her expertise. She was often paid with food or other contributions when patients couldn't afford to bring money. She is still practicing in Alabama today and has become a leader in the community and in the field of family medicine. She is now the first black president of the Alabama Medical Association and the first black female board member of the American Medical Association.

I also believe very strongly that medical education ought to be an experience that takes place in an environment of diversity and that medical students must reflect this diversity. This is the only way to ensure quality health care that is sensitive to the needs of our increasingly diverse population. My own experiences growing up in Alabama certainly have influenced my approach to medicine, going back even to medical school. Since I grew up in an environment of racism and poverty, I think I am unusually sensitive to unequal or dehumanizing treatment. On my first day of OB/GYN rotations in medical school, students were lined up to do pelvic exams on "staff" patients. The patients were largely African American and gathered together for the exams in one large room. I refused to participate in what I considered an inhumane way to treat patients and, eventually, the student body was able to lobby to create more private and respectful conditions for patient volunteers. By reflecting the many and wonderful differences in America, our health professional schools can improve the way we as health professionals

8

relate to and treat our patients and communities. In the end, the benefit is more than clear: improved health for all Americans.

The Stanford Medical Youth Science Program (SMYSP) is working to make sure that the access that Dr. King championed is a reality. By supporting young people in need, SMYSP helps students who often feel shut out of the nation's educational system to aim higher and achieve success. By educating a more diverse group of health professionals, SMYSP helps minority populations who are often unfamiliar and inexperienced with the nation's health care system. SMYSP creates a sense of community in its graduates and encourages a philosophy of public service. The program offers a constant, familiar place of support. Like the close-knit farm community I grew up in, it is a place where students who are already resilient can help each other through the hard times. The end result is a program that has been remarkably successful in its goal of nurturing students. As its graduates continue on to become health professionals, SMYSP is helping create more diversity in the field of medicine, greater access to care for low-income populations and, ultimately, better health for our nation.

— **Dr. David Satcher, former U.S. Surgeon General**

preface

One day in the spring of 1987, two pre-med students came to my office at Stanford University with an intriguing idea. Michael McCullough and Marc Lawrence wanted to create a program that would link high school students in Northern California with Stanford's world-renowned resources. They envisioned a five-week summer program that would provide students with free, hands-on experience in medicine to further their interest in health careers. Michael and Marc didn't want a program for students who were on track for college; rather, they envisioned a program that would focus on bright, low-income students from impoverished communities and struggling families. The program would recruit students from rural and urban schools, students who, if they succeeded, would often be the first in their families to attend college.

The idea appealed to me. I had just completed my graduate degree in public health at the University of California, Berkeley, and come to Stanford to work, and I was already noticing a lack of diversity in my profession. The people I saw in hospital hallways and at medical conferences did not reflect the people in the communities around me. It was rare to meet a Latino doctor, or hear an African-American researcher presenting findings at a scientific conference. Money played a role, too: I met few health professionals from low-income backgrounds, although this was not surprising since ethnicity and income often go hand in hand in America.

Almost 20 years later, statistics show that there are still few students from minority and low-income backgrounds in the health professions. The inequality begins to develop early in the educational process. At the high school level, the dropout rate is approximately 50 percent for Native American students, 29 percent for Latinos and 14 percent for African Americans, compared with 7 percent for white students. The disparity is magnified at the country's four-year colleges. Among students who graduate from high school, only 0.5 percent of Native American, 16 percent of Latino, and 21 percent of African-American students earn a college degree, compared with 37 percent of white students.

By the time students get to medical school, the numbers have dwindled even further. In the University of California medical schools, only 5 percent of incoming students are under-represented minorities (primarily Latino) and only 3.5 percent are African American—in a state where 32 percent of the population is Latino and 7 percent is African American. The lack of diversity in our medical schools translates into diminished health care in our increasingly diverse communities: studies have repeatedly shown that physicians from minority and low-income backgrounds are more likely to specialize in primary care medicine and to practice in inner-city and rural areas where medically under-served populations are concentrated.

When Michael and Marc came to my office, I wondered how we could start a program like the one they envisioned. I asked them, "Do you know any interested students? Do you have a Stanford sponsor? Do you have any funding?" The answers were all "no." But Michael and Marc were familiar with Stanford. Before long, they found professors to give lectures and secured laboratories for practicums. They convinced Jeanne Kennedy and Sharon Beckham in Community and Patient Relations at the Stanford Hospital to create hospital jobs for the students and persuaded John Dolph, a well-known Stanford anatomy instructor, to teach an anatomy series. We wrote a successful grant to the Kaiser Family Foundation for $10,000.

We decided to reach out to students from East Palo Alto, a low-income neighboring community that existed in stark contrast to the affluence of Stanford. We were so late with our recruitment efforts that first summer that we had difficulty finding participants. Eventually, we met seven students who were interested, and Michael and Marc drove to East Palo Alto every morning to pick them up and bring them to Stanford, where they spent their days listening to lectures, meeting doctors, observing surgeries and working on cadavers.

In our pilot year, we met our basic goal of linking students with Stanford's resources, but we learned that we needed to do much more. For one thing, we needed to provide more thorough information about college admissions and financial aid. It was fine to encourage students to attend college, but they needed to learn how to make that idea a reality. We needed to create a home on campus that would allow participants to experience life as college students, so we turned the Stanford Medical Youth Science Program (SMYSP) into a residence-based program. We broadened our recruitment area, and mailed applications to more than a hundred high school principals, guidance counselors and science teachers in Northern California.

We found wonderful students. We met teenagers who had been through intense hardships: homelessness, sickness, family tragedy, war in their homelands. In our official first year of SMYSP, we had more than 300 applicants, which showed us that a tremendous number of talented students are interested in science and education. We selected 24 students. At first, I worried about them living together on campus, imagining broken curfews, homesick teenagers and complaints from parents. But the students were motivated and responsible. Michael returned to direct the program, and we hired a co-director and

12

eight counselors. All were Stanford undergraduates who were eager to mentor the students.

When we started SMYSP, we thought we were creating a program like many other academic enrichment programs—one that emphasized thinking critically, understanding the scientific process and working with faculty. But as time went on, we saw that the program went further: it created a nurturing environment that bred a sense of trust. Students told us how, after SMYSP, they felt secure showing their intelligence around their peers; how they were comforted to learn that they were not alone in their hardships; and how they became more accepting of each other's cultures by living with one another. They told us how meeting the program's staff of Stanford undergraduates proved to them that students from poor schools could be accepted at prestigious universities. And they became more and more excited about education, science and medicine as they worked with medical students, doctors and professors.

As the years went by, we learned that the greatest value of our program is that it encourages students to believe in themselves, to give back to their communities and to develop lifelong friendships. SMYSP graduates keep in touch with the nurses and doctors they worked with in the hospital. They hold college workshops for their peers when they return to their high schools. They invite SMYSP counselors to their graduation ceremonies and, as decisions about college loom, seek advice about the future. They stay in touch with each other and occasionally room together at college.

Over the years, many have come to us for guidance when they've had to leave college temporarily to care for a family member or help a sibling in trouble. They've asked for letters of recommendation—for college, for summer jobs, for the Peace Corps, for medical school. And, eventually, they began to suggest that we should write a book.

Healing Journeys is the result of that request. It is a book about how families, teachers, mentors and the program support students who face hardships. Most of all, it is a book about the students themselves—resilient young people who flourish when they are given opportunities.

Healing Journeys profiles 16 graduates who epitomize the spirit of the 333 young people who have completed the program over the last 15 years. The book also offers vignettes of the SMYSP experience, taking readers into operating rooms, lecture halls and the late-night conversations that fill the students' lives during the program. The title *Healing Journeys* itself is a testament to the fact that these students, having faced and overcome adversities to further their educations, have since chosen to dedicate themselves to helping and healing others as compassionate and involved leaders.

— Marilyn Winkleby

13

at the house:
opening the doors

Durand House sits on a tree-lined back road on the Stanford campus, across from a small park full of willow trees. The house is three stories high, a modern palace with pitched roofs and huge windows, set on a row of old-money mansions that have housed university fraternities for decades. The red-brick walkway leading to Durand's large front porch is lined with flowering bushes, and inside, the house is filled with dark wood and open spaces. There is a fireplace in the living room and the largest, ugliest couch anyone can remember seeing; it seats 10 comfortably and is done in a paisley pattern of orange and blue. The walls are covered with murals, including one in the dining room of a vibrant medieval parade created from thousands of shellacked gummy bears.

At midnight on a warm summer Saturday night, 10 Stanford student counselors are up and working in the house. They look apprehensive, exhausted, excited. In less than 12 hours, 24 high school students will arrive to begin the Stanford Medical Youth Science Program, and the counselors are eager to welcome them. The students who will arrive in the morning will come together united by three traits: a history of economic hardship, a passion for medicine and a fierce intelligence. At the program, their lives will become a whirlwind tour of hospitals and lecture halls as they're plunged into the worlds of science and medicine: before long, they'll be discussing genome sequencing and the basal ganglia of the cerebrum. They'll work in the state-of-the-art Stanford University Hospital and in the Palo Alto Veterans Administration Hospital, alongside doctors doing open-heart surgery, counseling AIDS patients and retraining paraplegics. They'll hear lectures by prominent researchers at the Stanford School of Medicine on everything from neuro-degenerative diseases, to gynecological oncology, to international health. They'll work with college admissions advisors who will counsel them on test-taking and financial aid applications. And, as the students who come to the program do every year, they'll bask in a message of individual worth, because they'll feel it every day—among students, doctors and professors who take time to talk to them, train them and teach them.

But all that starts tomorrow. Tonight is given over to last-minute preparations. The program's two student directors for the year, Tamara and Nkem, sit at a table in the dining room, going over the food list. Tamara, born of the Todichiinii Dine, or Bitter Water people, of northern Arizona, grew up on a sheep farm and is the first in her family to go to college. At Stanford, she is majoring in education. She has a calm, nurturing presence, and during the program she will take each of the students into her heart with the affection of a mother. At the end of the program, the students will vote her "most likely to keep us together." Nkem is a Nigerian who spent his adolescence living in South-Central Los Angeles; he has just graduated from Stanford with a pre-med degree and is getting ready to apply to medical school. At times, he is playful and laid back, full of jokes and encouragement delivered with a wide smile. But at other times, particularly when he is marshalling the students in the morning, he seems distinctly authoritarian, helped in no small measure by his physical presence: he stands over 6 feet tall and can bench press 415 pounds. At the end of the summer, he is voted "first to make a million dollars."

16

Co-director Grace is also in the dining room, working on the summer lecture series. Grace is of Chinese descent, and she has a steady reserve of kindness and an infectious enthusiasm for all things medical. She is the only counselor who is already in med school, having just completed her first year at the Stanford School of Medicine; she plans to be a pediatrician. At the end of the summer, she is voted "first to win a Nobel Prize."

The seven other counselors are moving furniture about, cleaning, setting up computers. The scene being played out is repeated each summer on the campus. Every year, SMYSP is run by 10 Stanford students, counselors who often come from low-income backgrounds themselves. Most are human biology majors who plan to go on to medical school. They are role models, confidants, mentors, friends. They pull the students into the program and then draw them out. Each night during the program, everyone gathers in the living room to hear a different student or counselor tell the story of his or her life, and within a week or two, there has been so much sharing that everyone is communicating with the ease of siblings. Though the SMYSP students speak many different languages (Spanish, Vietnamese, Hindi, Thai, Navajo, Yoruba, Tagalog and others), English and empathy link them together. The house helps, too. Durand has a kitchen, living room, dining room, den and numerous bedrooms. Its architecture lends a feeling of affinity; it is a home, not a dorm.

As the counselors work, the place comes together. Room assignments have been made; students bunk in groups of two, three or four per room. The counselors put a lot of thought into how students should be matched; the goal is to have the students live with someone different from themselves, someone they'll be able to get along with but also learn from. The staff has crafted welcoming posters for each of the participants, which are posted on the doors of the students' rooms. All of the girls will stay on the second floor, all of the boys on the third. At the entrance to each floor, masking tape has been laid down. "GENDER LINE!!!" it screams in red ink. "DO NOT CROSS." Boys are not allowed on the girls' floor and vice versa. This is a rule the staff takes seriously; the punishment for violating it is getting sent home permanently, though in the history of the program this has never happened.

On the second-floor landing, a large white board has a weekly schedule listing lectures, workshops, outings and hospital assignments. The first week is already written out; when the students arrive, they'll see notations for "hospital internship," "mentor night," "student talks," "neuro-anatomy lab" and more cryptic entries, like "todos time." Each day's schedule officially lasts 15 hours—the day starts at 8 a.m. and ends at 11 p.m.—and each year the students work furiously. Mornings, they're up at 6, laboring over research projects and taking sample SAT tests before they meet downstairs at 8 to head out the door. Forced lights-out at 11 are commonly met with a groan because there is more work to be done.

These are 16- and 17-year-olds, on the verge of adulthood and developing their own identities. They are at a volatile age. Most live in the midst of communities in turmoil, where there is the constant seduction of giving in and giving up. Every year, half a million

17

students drop out of America's high schools, and students who come from families in the bottom 20 percent of America's economy are *six* times more likely to drop out of school than students who come from families in the top 20 percent. SMYSP creates a safe space for students to talk about confusions and challenges in their lives. Once the initial bridges of trust have been built, stories pour forth: of migration, discrimination, addiction, gangs. But with the talk of fear comes talk of hope: of families who have sacrificed to find a better life, of counselors and teachers who have gone out of their way to encourage, of inspiration that has been found and employed.

By 4 in the morning, the counselors are drifting off to their rooms to try to get some sleep; the students are scheduled to begin arriving in just six hours, at any time after 10. By 9:45, the counselors are all back downstairs, the men dressed in suits and ties, the women in dresses, waiting by the door for the first of their charges to arrive. It is a beautiful sunny day. All of the doors to the house have been opened to let the warm air waft through. Music plays softly from a tape recorder in the corner of the living room. A little after 10, an old car pulls up. Out of it steps a Laotian family: an older man and woman, a 5-year-old girl dressed in a purple sequined gown and a teenage boy with a big grin on his face. As soon as they step out of the car, the staff yells in unison, "Welcome, Tom!" and then there is much laughter and applause. This is Tom, a sophomore from Modesto whose parents emigrated from Laos to the United States after the Vietnam War. The counselors hurry down the steps to help Tom with his bags.

Moments later, another car pulls up. This time, an African-American family steps out. "Welcome, LaTasha!" is the cry. LaTasha, a young woman from Stockton, is accompanied by her mom, her older brother and her beloved younger siblings: 3-year-old brother Eddie and 4-year-old sister Tyana.

Through the day, students continue to arrive, and each is greeted by the staff's chorused hello. By the late afternoon, all of this year's "SMYSPers" are at the house. Students unpack their bags, introduce themselves to one another, say farewells to their families, settle into their rooms, chat with the counselors. They are a reflection of the students who attend the program every year: bright, resilient. They work hard. At home, they rise early, cook, help take care of siblings. They take a full day of classes and spend the rest of their time on after-school jobs and homework. All have dealt with struggle. Of the 24 students at SMYSP this year, 11 are first-generation immigrants. Only four come from families that have not been split by divorce. Ten grew up without fathers altogether. One has a father in jail, another has a father who just got out of jail, and another has a father who died of a heroin overdose. One student has a brother who was shot to death by a gang. Another is adopted. Two have mothers who suffer from depression. One became a mother herself when she was 14 years old. And yet, despite all the hardships they have experienced and all of the worldliness they have been forced to acquire, they are still young people just beyond childhood, with the uncertainty, love of fun and need for acceptance shared by all teenagers. Weeks earlier, they wrote notes of introduction about themselves, which are posted, with their pictures, on a big welcoming bulletin board.

"Nyob zoo!! Hello!! I am the oldest of four children in my family." This is from Lee, a Hmong student from Fresno who immigrated to the United States in 1989. He is tall with long dark hair that falls over his eyes. "Knowing that I'm the oldest, I have to be a good role model for my younger siblings. Like my father always told me, 'You're the oldest, I'm counting on you.' So I don't want to disappoint my father, and I really try hard on everything I do. I've been interested in health and medicine since I was a little kid."

"I was born in the Sudan on March 12, 1983 (Pisces baby!!!), and arrived in the United States when I was 8 months old." This is from Yeshe, an Ethiopian girl from Oakland with a smart sense of humor. "Since I love children, I want to be a pediatrician.... When I was little, I used to watch infomercials on starving Third World nations, with children who are not only hungry but sick and need medical attention. So as a pediatrician, I plan to travel to all the Third World nations that need my help."

The students have written about other motivations in their lives. Enrique, a young man from King City with a sparse frame and quiet confidence, has written, "After noticing the struggles that my parents have gone through, I realized that education was the only way out. I'm the oldest in my family, and that's why I always try to set good examples for my younger brother and sister. I'm a very optimistic person and believe that anything can be accomplished if enough effort is put into it."

Candi is a young woman with large blue eyes. She is from Firebaugh, a small, agrarian town in the Central Valley famed as "the cantaloupe capital of California." Candi is the most religious of the students. "I have a strong Christian faith that is the foundation of my life and am blessed because I am not the expected person that many imagined I would have been," she has written. "I love school and love sports very much."

Marcus, a lanky African-American student from Sacramento, has written, "I am a very shy person at first, but as soon as I feel more comfortable with my surroundings, I am not so shy. I have a very large family which I love dearly."

As the light of the day begins to wane, everyone gathers in the dining room. Family members have left, and the group—10 counselors and 24 students—is preparing for the first of the many meals they will share together over the summer. The house cook has been chopping and cooking for the last two hours, and dinner is ready: students carry trays of lasagna and bowls of salad out of the kitchen and set them on the dining room tables. A sense of familiarity and camaraderie is already forming, fostered by the closeness the house affords. As the weeks progress, this house will become everybody's home: a place where students will sometimes be wearing pajamas and sometimes hospital scrubs; sometimes studying and sometimes dancing; sometimes washing dishes and sometimes chatting with Stanford professors; sometimes writing research papers and sometimes playing music; and always discovering more about each other, about themselves and about what their lives can be.

19

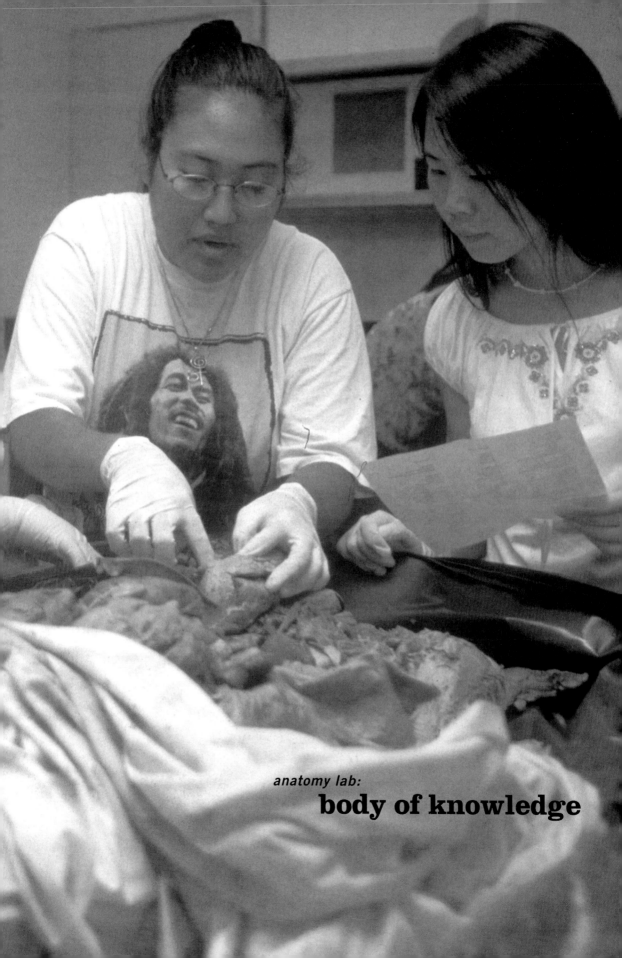

anatomy lab:
body of knowledge

The room is large and long, on the 10th floor of a San Francisco high-rise.
One wall holds a bank of tall windows that look out on a vista famed the world over:
the spires of the City by the Bay, the towers of the Golden Gate Bridge, and, beyond,
the green-gold hills of the Marin Headlands. With its size and locale, not to mention its
high-tech lights and flourishing hanging plants, the room could be a penthouse suite or
an executive boardroom, except for one thing: it is full of dead people.

The room belongs to the University of California, San Francisco medical school, and
every Friday afternoon SMYSP students come here for anatomy lab. Today, there are
some 30 corpses in the room, lying under pale green sheets that hide the flesh but reveal
enough of a form to identify that there is a body beneath. The air is soaked with the
acrid fumes of formaldehyde. In the corner, two cadavers lie exposed. They have nylon
stockings over their faces to mask their features, and their skin has the dull, gray look
of aged rubber. Groups of SMYSP students dressed in surgical scrubs are clustered around
the bodies, preparing to examine the human abdomen. A tall, blond man stands ready
to lead a tour through one of the cadavers. He is a medical student with the improbable
and charming name of M.D. Hope. With his floppy denim hat and easy humor, he
looks like a forgotten member of the M*A*S*H 4077th. "Okay, let's begin," he says as
he opens the pre-cut chest to reveal an assortment of organs.

Deftly, he reaches into the cavity and pulls out a purple mass about the size of a small,
tightly rolled sleeping bag. "Anybody know what this is?" he asks, holding the specimen
aloft, where the light catches the map of tiny red-blue lines zigzagging across its surface.
It is quickly and correctly identified as a liver by Vivian, a young Latina from Selma
with hair that cascades to her hips.

"Great," says the future Dr. Hope. "Now let's talk about the portal triad. See these
three passageways?" he asks, pointing to a section of the liver where there are three
tube-like openings. "Here's where the liver takes in portal vein blood, which it detoxifies
before it sends it on to the heart. Here's where it takes in arterial blood, which supplies
the cells of the liver with oxygen. And here's the bile duct, where the bile that the liver
produces is sent to the gall bladder to be stored." The students lean in for a closer look.
"Now, when you drink too much alcohol and get cirrhosis, this causes portal hypertension
because the passageways corrode and blood can't get through the liver. That leads to
anastomoses, a condition where the blood is forced to detour and use alternate veins.
Those veins aren't used to carrying a large amount of blood, so they're forced to
expand. They can rupture and create internal bleeding, which can be lethal." He looks
around at the group and says, "Another good reason not to drink too much."

But it will be years before these students can walk into a bar and order a beer, since the
average age of these budding physicians is 16. With the bodies, the students are intent,
enthusiastic; they have no qualms about examining them. "Can some brave soul try to
locate the large intestine?" Hope asks. Anthony, a young Fijian man from Sacramento,
reaches in to find it. Gently, he moves other viscera aside until he locates it, and then he

22

pulls it forth to show the group. "Okay," says Hope, "now, where's it going to stop?" Everybody laughs. "Don't worry," Hope assures him. "I won't make you go all the way to its end." But Anthony smiles, and it's easy to get the sense that, in the interest of science, he wouldn't mind a bit.

The group talks about the functions of the large intestine and the small intestine. Hope points to the small intestine's three key points: the duodenum, the jejunum and the ileum. "The duodenum is really where the action is," he says. "It's where the digestion kicks in, where acid is neutralized, where enzymes break down food, where vitamins and minerals pass into the bloodstream.

"Now here"—he pulls a long, thick tube out from the belly—"are the jejunum and the ileum, which form the bulk of the whole small intestine. This is another area where vitamins and minerals pass into the bloodstream. See these veins all over it? There are lots of places in the wall of the intestine where nutrients can travel out into the blood."

Several of the students reach in to examine a piece of the 25-foot-long intestine. They have already explored the thorax and the upper and lower limbs, and they are developing an ease with these cadavers as they come to know their physical intricacies.

"You see that small, finger-like projection?" Hope asks. "That's the appendix. It can get inflamed, and sometimes it will get very bad and burst."

"My appendix burst," volunteers Michelle, a self-described "Tex-Mex" student from Fresno.

"Really?" says Hope, glancing up from the body with a quizzical look. "That can be a dangerous condition."

"I survived," she says matter-of-factly.

"Okay, I've got another question for you," says Hope. "When someone feels pain from their appendix, why don't they feel it deep inside the body where the appendix is located?"

"Because nerves are tied to the skin?" someone guesses.

"Great," says Hope. "Now, what's this?" he asks, pointing into the lower portion of the chest.

"The diaphragm," says Tom.

"And what's it made of?" asks Hope.

23

"Muscle," says someone else.

"Exactly, and it's very strong. You want it to lower and create a vacuum to give the lungs space to expand. Now look at these muscle layers here on the chest wall. Why do we want those?"

"To protect the organs," volunteers Marcus.

"To cushion any blows," offers Candi.

"To help the body move efficiently," ventures Lee.

And so it goes for the entire afternoon. The students work their way diligently through the torsos, finding and examining the gall bladder, the spleen, the kidneys. The complex intricacy that creates the simple miracle of the human body is encountered time and again as different functions are delineated and discussed. Late in the day, the lab ends. The students pull off their rubber gloves, talk about what they have just learned and get ready to head out for the drive back to Stanford.

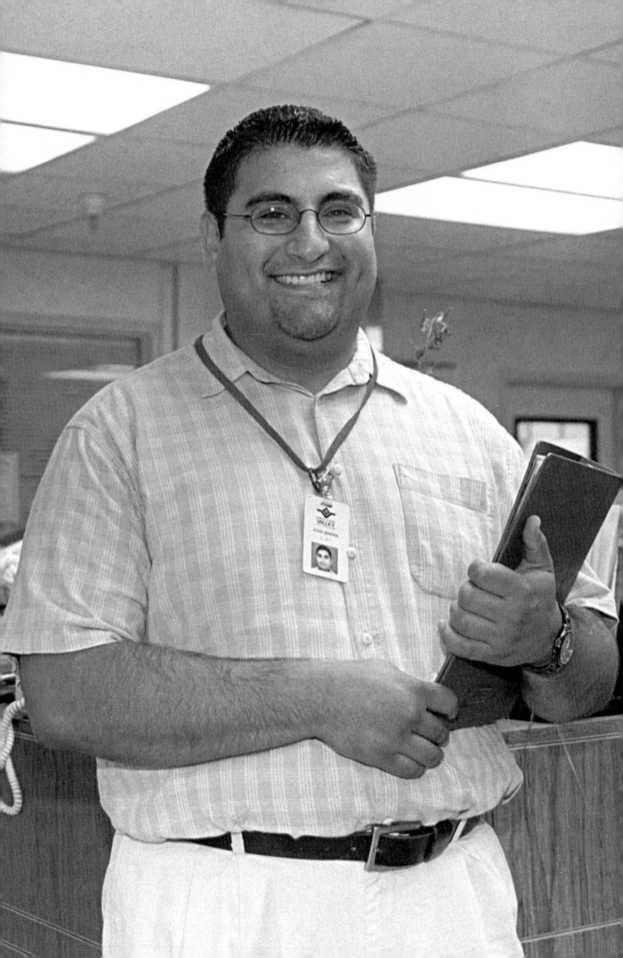

juan
ibarra

"The best trees grow on the steepest hills."
— Burundi proverb

Graduates of the Stanford Medical Youth Science Program are now scattered throughout the world. They have been everywhere from Ghana, to Vietnam, to Fresno, doing everything from building wells, to administering vaccinations, to delivering babies. Juan Ibarra, who went through SMYSP in the summer of 1990, is a quintessential alumnus: smart, humane, committed to a life of healing. He is stocky and tall, with short black hair and small eyeglasses that lend him the air of an aesthete. Charity and calm radiate from him; he has the countenance of a thoughtful, kind-hearted wrestler, true to the nickname that has stuck with him since the second grade, when he ran with a gang called the Little Stockton Pee Wees: El Osso, or The Bear.

Juan is now a public health specialist in his late twenties. He lives with his sister Sylvia, her husband and their two children in Redwood City, a town on the peninsula south of San Francisco with an identity that is almost as much of an oxymoron as its name. Redwood City is home to a working-class Hispanic population and, thanks to Silicon Valley next door, a number of high-rolling high-technology companies. Today, *carnecerias* and taco stands sit beside dot-com headquarters along the main thoroughfare of El Camino Real as the King's Highway is transformed into an artery of the Information Superhighway. The houses just across from Sylvia's were recently torn down and replaced by the new headquarters of an Internet company. Its huge neon sign casts a light through Juan's front window while, as his young nephews race around exuberantly shouting in Spanish, he talks about the tumult, tragedy and blessings that have marked his life.

He begins at the beginning, at his family's *ranchito*, in a small agrarian community located in the Mexican state of Michoacan, inland from the country's western coast and not too far from the world-famous metropolis of Acapulco. There he was born, the last of the 10 children who lived, to Luis and Aurora Ibarra, on land his family had inhabited for generations. When he lived there, the land was used to raise farm animals, like cattle and pigs, and crops like alfalfa and garbanzos. One of Juan's first memories is of going out into the fields to pick garbanzos and popping their elliptical pods into his mouth, eating the delicious legumes on the spot, fresh and green. It was a family tradition to get together to roast garbanzos: relatives would gather to cook, salt and eat the beans. Houses on the ranchito were made of mud, with no plumbing. Bathing was an adventure accomplished by hauling buckets of water from the river, leaving them in the sun to warm and then pouring them over yourself while standing in the "shower," a large metallic tub. For centuries, schooling on the ranchito was done at the church, and it was here that Juan's parents and older siblings received their formal educations. The school was rigid, authoritarian and only went to the sixth grade. Anyone wanting to continue on in education had to leave the ranch and move to town for high school—an expensive, uncommon feat.

Long before Juan was born, his father Luis started traveling to the United States, coming into the country seasonally to work under the auspices of an American program begun in the 1940s to recruit cheap Mexican labor. Luis worked in the fields and on the railroads, one of the millions of manual laborers who formed the backbone of California's burgeoning economy. Little by little, he saved and made plans to bring his wife and children to California with him—permanently. Juan was an infant when he took his first trip across the border, and by the time he was 2, the family had migrated north for good, settling first in Chino, where there were strawberry fields forever and plenty of jobs for people with strong backs and humble expectations.

The family lived the life of migrant farm workers, moving from Helena to Fresno to Five Points and beyond, following the crops, tied to the harvest cycles. They returned to Mexico for the Christmas holidays every year, and another of Juan's earliest memories comes from that time: breaking piñatas at a community festival. "The piñatas in Mexico are very different than the ones in California," he explains. "They are more like pots, clay pots. You hit them and it hurts like hell. You can imagine these little puny kids trying to break these things." Persistence was rewarded when the stash in the piñata came tumbling forth: huge oranges and a shower of candies unique to Mexico, with flavorings like tamarind and mango.

When Juan was 5, the family settled in Stockton, and it was here that he began his official education, in a kindergarten several blocks from home. It was an unnerving time. "I was really attached to my mom, really attached," remembers Juan. "I was the youngest, her favorite—in Spanish you call it 'ensentido'—and she was overprotective of me. So going to kindergarten was scary and difficult." Gradually, Juan's anxiety of being left alone in a foreign place subsided, and by the first grade, he'd even come to like school—or at least the social parts of it. Juan and his buddies in the Little Stockton Pee Wees would ditch catechism, even ditch school sometimes to go to Safeway and steal candy, and they often picked fights with other kids in the neighborhood. "They used to joke around with me because I was a husky kid and say, 'You're big, you can defend the ring,'" remembers Juan. "Actually, I was deathly afraid of being involved in a fight. But there was an expectation as a young child: you should defend yourself; you should fight. It was all part of the culture and the beliefs of my brothers and uncles."

Things changed in the fourth grade. Juan joined the choir and started singing in church on Sundays (though he still resisted religion, a "huge problem" with his mother). He realized his English was lousy and started to pay more attention in his bilingual education classes; when he did well there, he started to take his other classes more seriously, too. But the main reason for Juan's turnaround, his greatest influence at the time, was his first serious mentor: his brother Raoul.

"Raoul is four years older than me, the third youngest. He was very... militant. I can't think of any better word for describing it," says Juan, adding wryly, to prove his point, "He was in the Marines later in life."

Raoul motivated Juan. He would cover the wooden walls of the family's house with math problems for Juan, written out in chalk, and the two would go through them together, with Raoul explaining to his brother how to find the area of a circle or the angle of a triangle. Juan was entranced. By the time Juan was in the fifth grade, Raoul was thinking about college, and he became more rigorous. He and Juan set their schedules: after school, they exercised at the YMCA and then they studied. If Juan had any questions as he was doing his homework, Raoul would answer them. When Juan had finished his work, he would stay by his brother's side and read whatever books he could find. "Encyclopedias were a big thing in my life," he remembers. "I loved getting my hands on them, because you'd just turn the page and there would be something new to discover."

29

By this time Juan was so enthusiastic about school he was reluctant to take the annual two-month family sojourn to Mexico, fearful that he would miss out on something great or fall behind. When the others left, he stayed behind with his sister Sylvia. "I said to the others, 'Aren't you worried about missing school?' But they went. Most of my older sisters and brothers didn't really have a big interest in education. The five youngest all graduated from high school. But the five oldest were working in the fields by the time we came over from Mexico, and they never went back to school."

On the night of November 3, 1986, when Juan was in the eighth grade, his family suffered its most terrible blow. The family was still living in Stockton, in a garage that had been converted into a two-room apartment. Juan was sleeping with his brother in

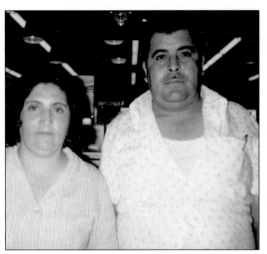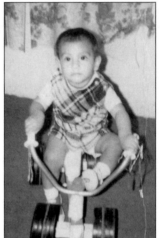

a. Juan's parents Aurora and Luis. "We were new immigrants from Mexico when this picture was taken," Juan recalls. "It was taken at Savemart on the east side of Stockton, which was our favorite grocery." b. Juan at age 1. "The bike was my first birthday gift," he says. c. Juan at 7. "Our first Christmas in our new home on the south side of Stockton."

one of the two rooms when he awoke to the sound of his sister's screaming. He looked at the clock, saw it was around 3 a.m. and thought that he had perhaps imagined things, or maybe that he'd heard cats fighting. Then he heard the noise again and realized something was very wrong. "I got a feeling in my body of being frozen, paralyzed," he remembers. Juan's brother crept out of bed and went to check on what was happening in the other room. But the door was locked, which only heightened Juan's fear. "My mother had a habit of reading the Bible late at night, and she always left the door open for us in that back room," he explains. "It was always, always open. Then I saw my sister screaming and wailing, and I knew something horrible had happened. My brother went in the other room, and then everything just exploded."

In the other room, a nightmare existed: an intruder had broken in, killed both of Juan's parents and attacked another brother, who was able to get away and out a window to get help.

While they waited for the police, Juan's brothers and sisters kept him away from the horrific scene. Gradually, a response team showed up: the police arrived, the ambulance came, journalists appeared. Eventually, the family was escorted out of the house to the

30

hospital. "I walked by the living room, and that's when I noticed all the cameramen, reporters, police, paramedics," says Juan. "It was just too much to process. I didn't feel much but fear. I didn't want to see, but I did want to see." The funeral brought new traumas. "The memory of the drive and the fear that I was feeling as we got closer to the funeral home is still fresh. It was the longest drive that I could ever imagine, the anticipation of seeing my parents again."

Talking now about the crime, many years later, Juan says the family never really recovered. The counseling they all went through did not help their grief. "We all lacked the skills to deal with it in an effective manner," says Juan. "I loved my mother so much, and I was so attached to her that I really couldn't comprehend it. We were a very religious family,

a. Juan at 10. "I was in the third grade," he says. "I started to go working in the fields with my parents at around this age." b. Juan at 13, with his sisters Angela and Maria and brother Alfonso. "This was the first Christmas we spent without my parents," Juan remembers. c. Juan at 16. "This was for a passport photo. I was taking my first overseas trip on my own to go on an Earthwatch study in Cancun, Mexico."

but my faith"—which had been weak to begin with—"was shaken. The Christmas after the murders, I said, 'I don't understand why God would take our parents.' My family was very upset and said, 'What do you mean? You don't believe in God?' It was a huge conflict."

In his 20s, Juan found a psychologist to work with and also began to open up to friends about what had happened to his family that night. But in the immediate years after the crime, Juan didn't talk to anyone about what had happened. "I just put all my energy into school and disregarded everything else," he remembers of the time. He finished up the eighth grade and moved west, to live with Sylvia in her home in Redwood City. He stayed away from the trial, though he does remember a lawyer coming to the house to ask the family to choose between a sentence of death or life without parole for the man who had killed their parents. To avoid the more drawn-out process of imposing the death penalty, the family chose life without parole. To this day, Juan knows virtually nothing about the man who committed the murders.

Moving to a new community and a new school is hard on any adolescent, let alone one whose family has just been torn apart by violence. The adjustment to Redwood City was difficult for Juan, who left a "huge, multiethnic network" of much-loved

31

friends behind in Stockton to start ninth grade at Sequoia High School. In the wake of the trauma and in the absence of friends, scholastics became more and more important. Juan excelled in math and science. "That passion was always there," he says. "My brother instilled a love of math in me. In the ninth grade, I was taking geometry with 10th-, 11th- and 12th-graders." Science was the same way. "I remember in the fifth or sixth grade, I had this science book, *How to Do Experiments*. It was full of things like, for example, laying a yardstick on a flat table and laying a newspaper on one end and banging it. Part of the yardstick would break off, and how it broke off illustrated principles about pressure. I loved doing things like that." During his high school years, Juan spent a lot of his time at the public library; whenever he got there, he invariably headed first for the section with books about experiments. He got very involved with a group called MESA (Math, Engineering and Science Achievements) and took field trips to NASA, to the University of California at Davis to see solar panels, even to Edwards Air Force Base in Southern California.

By the 10th grade, Juan had started to make friends: he'd go to the library with them, play badminton and tennis. He was talking to his teachers more. "I started feeling a little bit more included," he remembers. Juan found mentors, or they found him. His friend Jorge Uliz, a dynamo who was a year ahead of Juan in high school and involved in everything, was the president of MESA; he encouraged Juan to take on the club's presidency after him. Ms. Kaufman, an Australian woman who taught Juan math, encouraged him to apply to SMYSP and gave him the application forms. Today, when Juan thinks back to the many mentors who have helped him through his life, he muses on the responsibility that individuals have to reach out to mentors.

"In high school, I was always reaching out," he says. "If I saw something that was particularly interesting in a person's life, I wanted to know more about it. Mentoring was a continual reaching-out process, either by them or by me. It's almost like a spider web. You must have that willingness to reach out and talk to other people who are vastly different from you but who share an interest in developing themselves and improving their situation in life.

"No one critical mentor changed my life entirely, but many people had an influence. My parents had a huge influence. They were still working in the fields when my dad was 53 and my mom was 52. They were murdered at 3 o'clock in the morning, but they would have been going out into the fields at 5 o'clock that morning to provide for us. Not working was never an option for them. Their struggles to provide for us, their determination, protectiveness, leadership—that exemplified and demonstrated a way of being in the world that taught me a lot."

Juan entered SMYSP in 1990, in the summer after his sophomore year. He remembers the program as a wonderful, surreal experience. "I came to this perfect, serene place where everybody got along, and, for me, it was such an abnormal experience. I had food every day. I mean, I could just walk downstairs and get food. There was a cook! It was a fantasy land. I felt like I was living in a castle." Any initial feelings of alienation soon wore off. Juan loved the sense that he was meeting others like himself, highly motivated students who wanted to learn more about medicine. "I identified with the people in the program in such a powerful way, in a way that was much stronger than anything I had experienced before," he says. "These were incredible people who had persevered through difficult circumstances, and being together with them in the intimate context of the program was very inspiring. We were all triumphing over something." At the same time that he relished meeting similarly focused people, Juan also reveled in the diversity he encountered, and he broke cultural molds with the same determination and force with which he had attacked the piñatas years before. With a smile, he remembers meeting a Vietnamese student at SMYSP who was one of only two male dancers in Ballet Folklorico, a Mexican dance group. Until then, Juan had always thought Vietnamese had no interest in dancing, let alone in the dances of Juan's own culture.

Juan spent his summer working in the operating room: "One of the things I remember best from that time was watching a surgeon doing open-heart surgery. I think it was a triple bypass. They had a huge metallic machine with a little handle that somebody was cranking, and they were using it to open up the patient's chest. I had to run out and get some blood and bring it into the operating room. When I got back, the surgeon looked at me and hinted for me to come over. I looked at what he was showing me: it was a heart that he had completely in his hands, and it was still beating." Juan's experiences in the OR and his stints in the "chaotic" emergency room formed the bulk of his daily journal entries, a required part of the program. He wrote about the fear he experienced, about the shock of realizing how fragile life can be and how people can suffer or in an instant be physically impaired for the rest of their lives. He wrote, too, of how encouraging it was to see all that medicine could do for people in states of shock and trauma.

Juan also appreciated the program's "intense" lectures, listening to Stanford professors talk about their specialties and learning about things like anatomy and epidemiology as well as non-traditional medical subjects, like integrative medicine and ways of healing. "Before then, I'd had such a narrow view of biology," he says. "I thought, 'You're a doctor and that's it.' It was fascinating to see different disciplines and to see them used to conduct research. I remember a lecture on interdisciplinary approaches that looked at research on the wavelengths of bird calls during mating: it used math, a little engineering, biology, all kinds of things." Over the summer, Juan absorbed the key message of SMYSP: that it is safe to trust the broader world and to embrace the many opportunities that lie within it. When he left the program, it was with a reinforced conviction that he belonged in the health care field; thoughts of becoming an engineer dissipated in the wake of Juan's realization that his heart was in healing. He also left the program with a renewed appreciation for his own background and triumphs. "I extracted a greater sense of motivation and pride from my life," he recalls. "I was no longer ashamed of my background. On my college essay, I wrote about my experiences working in the fields. After that summer, and being with so many unique people who had overcome real hardships to achieve great things, I was proud of those experiences."

During Juan's junior year, he went to visit an older friend from high school who had gone on to Stanford and was living on campus. "He invited me over, and I saw his dorm and thought, 'Wow, what a crazy place.'" Juan saw people playing guitars and arguing politics, read bulletin boards covered with notices from all kinds of campus organizations, including women's groups and gay groups. It was a revelation. "Before that, when I thought of a dorm, I thought of it as just a place with beds," says Juan. "I was fascinated."

33

Juan applied to Stanford and was accepted, a significant feat given that Latinos made up only 8 percent of the university's undergraduate population, and many of those students came from upper- and middle-class backgrounds. Though it had been only four years since he'd left Stockton, Juan had come a long way from a city where just over half of the students who entered the educational system actually graduated from high school. What had started with math problems written out on bedroom walls had now led him into some of academia's most hallowed halls. He spent four and a half years on the campus, living in Casa Zapata, the Latino theme dorm, and studying a new, interdisciplinary major: human biology. "I took traditional biology, developmental psychology, population genetics, really anything that looked at the human body. Cultural medical anthropology, for example—which I'd never even heard of!—where we looked at other cultures and how they deal with illness and healing. I loved it."

Juan's closest friends in his first year on campus were friends from the SMYSP program who had also been accepted into the university. While he was on campus, he stayed close to the program, attending reunions; talking to parents, participants and staff; even helping to raise money for SMYSP by talking to potential donors about his experiences as a high schooler in the program. Juan also made program history when he became the first participant to become a program director. In his junior year, he was a co-director, and then, just before he graduated, a director.

During his time at Stanford, Juan was also involved in CHE, Chicanos in Health Education, a program through which he mentored younger students who were interested in medicine. He would spend hours with students, talking with them about what classes they needed to take, helping them develop their schedules. "I wanted to make sure people knew what to expect and get them to try new things. I had been deathly afraid of leaving my family when I moved to Stanford, but going through the experience of dealing with loss, I learned to adapt to new environments, get used to new things and welcome those opportunities. I'd tell all of the people I mentored, 'Don't be afraid of change. Change can be good for you.'"

Juan took his own advice when he finally divulged his greatest secret to his family: that he is gay. "I knew about myself even when I was a young child, that I had same-sex feelings of attraction and wasn't heterosexual," Juan says. "As far back as I can first remember, that was always a part of me. I don't think it was an orientation that I acquired as I grew. In college, my sexual identity became a lot stronger. People started wondering, 'Hey, how come you never have a girlfriend?' It was a constant issue. My family already knew I was different. I verbalized ideas that were pretty radical within my family, like asking, 'How come all the women in this family just cook, and the culture doesn't encourage them to go to school?' I remember when we watched the movie *Philadelphia*, I was arguing that the lead character, who had lost his job because he had AIDS, deserved justice, and my brother was very shocked that I was defending a gay man. But I always took the side of protecting the rights of marginalized people, which included people who identified as gay."

Juan gradually withdrew from his family. He was often overwhelmed by sadness and anxiety. "In college, I was so afraid of coming out and being ostracized by my siblings. I had already dealt with the loss of my parents, and I thought if I lost the rest of my family, that would do me in. I got so anxious if I went home at spring break or Christmas. It was a very painful time in my life. Finally, my sister confronted me. And I had to defend myself. The whole situation had been like a time bomb. After she found out I was gay, she entered an emotional crisis herself, thinking, 'Here's the youngest member of the family with a promising future ahead of him, and now he's telling us that he's gay, and his life is ruined.' Soon after, everybody else in the family knew. They were very distraught. Eventually, by going through counseling, I got stronger. But I'm still struggling with it all in my family."

One of the biggest conflicts concerns the impact Juan's sexuality may have upon the next generation of his family. "People from low-income communities who attend a school like Stanford and then go back to their communities get flak about that. Your old friends put you into a little box, aren't comfortable when you start talking about new ways of thinking, of questioning. When they found out I was gay, my family's reaction was, 'Damn it, it was that Stanford University experience. We knew you shouldn't have gone there.' Now all my nieces and nephews are going to get flak for that because my family is so conservative. Having a gay uncle who went to Stanford means that a school like Stanford is definitely not going to be an option for them."

Juan graduated from Stanford in 1996. He looked for a job where he could work on community health education and found it in a small clinic in the nearby town of Sunnyvale. There he was able to reconnect with his roots, for the clinic treated indigent Latino laborers. Seven years after he'd completed the SMYSP program, Juan was back in his community, using his training to help families like his own. He did a little of everything: drawing blood, administering vaccines, translating for doctors and reading TB skin tests.

After he'd been at the clinic for a year, Juan heard about and applied for a job as a communicable disease investigator with Santa Clara County. While he waited for his application to traverse the county bureaucracy, he took a six-month job working as an HIV-prevention coordinator in San Jose. The job involved doing counseling within the community; Juan spent his time in places where young, gay Latino males congregated, providing information on condom use and safe sex practices. It was a perfect job for a young, gay Latino man going through the coming-out process. Juan developed a "second family" of men who were grappling with issues of self-esteem and community recognition. The job gave Juan a greater sense of confidence and identity—and it also introduced him to his long-term partner.

Juan did get the call from Santa Clara County, and he took the job as a communicable disease investigator in San Jose, in the shadow of a large public county hospital, doing what he calls "shoe-leather epidemiology." He worked to assess the incidence of TB infection in the county of Santa Clara and counsel sufferers of the disease. Indeed, Juan's empathy for those who are suffering seems unwavering, and he talks calmly yet passionately about the need for all health workers to be understanding and aware. "Cultural competence is a significant issue in public health," he says. "For example, when I was a medical assistant, there was a young woman from Columbia with an ear infection. I had to take her vital stats, ask her how she was doing, translate for the doctor. I saw she had a small piece of cotton in her ear, and I asked if she was bleeding. She said no. I felt that maybe she felt some shame. I didn't want to offend her, so I was very careful with my tone of voice when I asked her what the cotton was for. She told me she had

35

taken some penicillin and put it on the cotton and then taped it to her ear. She said that she learned to do this when she was a child. It took some skill and sensitivity to explain that the body could not use medicine in this way and to make sure that she really understood and believed that she needed to take the antibiotic orally, not topically. And if somebody hadn't taken the time to deal with her sensitively, she wouldn't have been comfortable enough to talk about what she was doing—and she would have kept on doing it."

That he is good at what he does has not gone unnoticed: Juan was named the Santa Clara Public Health Department employee of the year, despite the fact that he had only been in the department for two years, and this was the first time such an award had been given.

What of Juan's own continued growth? In the fall, he will begin a joint master's degree in social work and public health at San Diego State University. He is drawn to public health because of the personal challenges the work provides and because he believes public health training will allow him to help make medicine a better field. But, he says with a smile, "Whatever happens, I know times change and you can't really be comfortable in your set ways. You must challenge yourself to grow and understand and contribute as much as you can, and help other people who are walking similar paths."

36

infectious disease:
contagious passion

Since SMYSP aims to mimic aspects of college life, lectures are a key part of the program. Every Monday, Wednesday and Friday morning, students walk across campus to Stanford's main quadrangle, where dozens of classrooms sit anchored by the university's cathedral. There, they hear some of the nation's most innovative professors and doctors talk about the work they're doing. Topics covered at this year's program range from retroviruses to cloning. On the first day of lectures, the students trek over to hear from Dr. Gary Schoolnik, a specialist in infectious diseases based at Stanford Hospital.

Dr. Schoolnik is tall, white-haired, soft-spoken. Just before 9 a.m., he ambles into the classroom, switches on an antiquated slide projector sitting in the middle of the room and asks for the lights to be turned off. The room goes dark, and Dr. Schoolnik's first slide appears on the screen at the front of the room. It reads: "'It is within the power of man to eradicate infection from the earth.' —Louis Pasteur."

"I study infectious diseases, which are a huge human health issue," Dr. Schoolnik tells the assembled students with calm authority. "In the last 50 years, three infectious diseases—tuberculosis, malaria and AIDS—have killed more people than all wars and natural disasters in recorded history." He pauses to let the magnitude of his statement sink in—though these students are already aware that the medical terrain of their country is changing. The chronic diseases caused by poor diet, smoking, drinking and insufficient exercise are being joined by a new scourge of infectious disease in America: sexually transmitted diseases, HIV/AIDS, hepatitis, tuberculosis, pneumonia. The students see these diseases in their families, their schools and their communities.

"I'm afraid Pasteur's statement is overly optimistic," Dr. Schoolnik says. "But I would like to begin this morning by telling you about one major disease we have eliminated: smallpox." Dr. Schoolnik flashes to a slide of a young man in the advanced stages of the disease. Several students gasp at the sight of the man's body, which is covered with the pustules of smallpox.

"Smallpox is a very old disease," begins Dr. Schoolnik. "We have a 4,000-year-old Egyptian mummy of a person who we know had the disease." Methodically, vividly, he traces the history of one of medicine's greatest success stories. He describes the pioneering 18th-century work of Edward Jenner, an English country doctor who developed groundbreaking theories on immunity and inoculation after observing that milkmaids who developed pustules on their fingers from milking cows never got smallpox. He details the creation of a vaccine against the disease and describes the World Health Organization's momentous undertaking in the 1960s and 1970s to eradicate smallpox once and for all. "By 1975, the disease was left in only Ethiopia, Somalia, India, Bangladesh and Nepal," he says. The students are rapt as he describes how the war raging between Ethiopia and Somalia was suspended to get the vaccine in. He ends his history with a slide from 1976 showing the last person in recorded history to get the disease. "But," he says, "as we all know from reading the newspapers, the story of smallpox is not over. The virus is still alive. Those concerned about biological warfare and acts of bio-terrorism think it should be completely destroyed; those who worry at the prospect of annihilating any living thing and who think that the virus might have some use for further study think it should be kept alive."

From the story of smallpox's containment, Dr. Schoolnik turns to the tale of his own work, which focuses on infant mortality. He shows a map highlighting the places in the world where children die most frequently. Much of Africa and the Middle East are highlighted, as well as India, Bangladesh, Bolivia and Haiti.

"Infants are susceptible to many infectious diseases," he says. "Some of the worst things they suffer from are diarrhea, respiratory diseases, measles, tetanus, malnutrition and malaria. Ten percent of all children who are born die in the first year of life. I study diarrhea, which is a dangerous disease in children because they lose too much fluid, get dehydrated and go into shock. Children get into a vicious cycle where they have severe diarrhea, which leads to reduced food intake and malabsorption of food, which leads to malnutrition, which leads to poor resistance to infection, which leads back to severe diarrhea." Dr. Schoolnik shows a graphic detailing the four stages in the deadly cycle. "You can see how devastating it is," he says. "My own work has focused on the state of Chiapas in Mexico, where the diarrhea rates are very high. The infant mortality rate in Chiapas from diarrhea had been estimated at 32 in 1,000 live births."

Dr. Schoolnik shows slides of cloud-shrouded green hills; small, simple houses; and strong-looking women dressed in multicolored skirts. "Chiapas is beautiful," he says. "Perhaps some of you know it?" Enrique nods; so do Oscar and Ivan, two other Mexican Americans in the SMYSP class.

"It has been one of the most important things in my life to have had the opportunity to work there," Schoolnik continues. "It has allowed me to appreciate a different way of thinking about the world. The people I work with are Mayans, and almost all of them are corn farmers. They have traditional healers in their communities who take care of many of their health needs. The germ theory of disease is a foreign concept; they tend to look at disease as having a spiritual root. When a child has diarrhea, they go out into the night and try to find the pieces of the child's soul that have been lost.

"When we first arrived in Chiapas, we spent a lot of time in the community, explaining what we were trying to do. We formed a collaboration with a local clinic and set up a fairly modern laboratory, and then we began collecting stool samples from babies. The women in the village were wonderful: they made a commitment to help us, and every day they would let us know which children were sick with diarrhea. Once we had the stool specimens, we applied DNA probes and identified all of the organisms responsible for creating the diarrhea." In the process of the research, Dr. Schoolnik and his team made a grim discovery: the death rate among infants in Chiapas from diarrhea was three times higher than they had believed, approximately 102 in 1,000 live births.

The scientists on Dr. Schoolnik's team isolated the *E. coli* bacterium that was causing the infants' diarrhea and took it back to the lab at Stanford for in-depth studies on how the germ functioned. They knew how the babies got the E. coli into their bodies: mothers harbored the organism in their intestines and—because of poor hygiene—passed it on to their children when they were preparing their food. But the scientists didn't know how the organism actually functioned once it was inside the body, so the detective work began in earnest. The breakthrough came when a postdoctoral student named Jorge Giron discovered the mechanism that the E. coli used to attach to the lining of the human stomach. From there, Stanford scientists were able to isolate the 14 genes in the germ that enabled it to attach to the stomach.

"We wanted to see what would happen if we knocked those 14 genes out," says Dr. Schoolnik. "Would that prevent the bacteria from sticking to the stomach lining and effectively neutralize them? It seemed to us like it should. We did some genetic engineering and some gene splicing and created an organism that was exactly the same but missing the 14 genes. Then, to really test the altered bacteria, we had to give them to human volunteers."

Dr. Schoolnik and his group recruited 60 people: graduate students, medical students and members of the community. All volunteers were hospitalized. Then some were given a drink that contained the raw E. coli that had been brought back from Mexico, and some were given a drink that contained the genetically altered E. coli.

The scientists weren't the only ones monitoring the experiment: using the slide projector, Dr. Schoolnik shows clippings from newspapers, with headlines like, "Science is on the Run at Stanford" and "When Duty (and Nature) Calls." Next, he shows pictures of four young men with the flush, strong look of healthy college students. "These four were some of the people who participated in the experiment," Schoolnik says. "Two of these guys got the altered E. coli, and two of them got the unaltered. We measured their stools for 48 hours after the bacteria were administered. And the two who got the unaltered bacteria were terribly sick." He shows a shot of the two, post-experiment, sitting up in their hospital beds, smiling weakly. They look exhausted. "Now these two," he flashes to a slide of the other two students, who look fit and fine, "got the E. coli with the genes removed. And they had no diarrhea."

Dr. Schoolnik ends his lecture with a few thoughts about the new world of genetic modification and current efforts to use his research to create a vaccine that will stop diarrhea and reduce infant mortality. Then he asks for questions.

"What attracted you to the field of infectious disease?" asks Elizabeth.

"In 1947, when I was 5, my mother was in the hospital dying of typhoid fever," Schoolnik responds. "My father was a doctor and a microbiologist. He'd read an article in the newspaper about a new therapy for typhoid, where the patient would be injected with a toxin that would kill the bacteria. He wrote to the scientist named in the newspaper, and the scientist sent my father a vial of the toxin. He injected it into my mother, and by the next day she was perfectly well."

From the story of his mother's miraculous recovery, Schoolnik switches gears. "Being a scientist involves much more than being in a lab," he says, his voice soft but gaining in intensity as he looks at each of the students before him. "To treat something, you must see the whole picture of what is going on. Infectious diseases don't occur just because of dangerous organisms; they also occur because of poverty. Poverty can undermine the best efforts to control infectious disease. In Chiapas, for example, most of the land is owned by a few rich people. There is a low literacy rate, poor housing, bad health care, and there has been a lot of guerrilla warfare in the state. It's one thing to create a vaccine, but it has to be administered. After our project ended in Chiapas, Stanford medical students manned a new clinic there for three years. But when the fighting between the rebels and the soldiers got bad, we had to pull the students out—and so the people in the area lost access to that medical treatment." Dr. Schoolnik shows another slide with a circular graphic, another cycle of sadness and waste. At the top of the image, a young boy named Luis is infected by tetanus bacteria because he is barefoot and has stepped on a thorn. He is barefoot because he has no sandals. He has no sandals because his father is poor. He was not vaccinated against tetanus because the health team does not have the resources to vaccinate poor children.

Schoolnik knows that the students before him are more aware than most of the hardships of poverty. He ends his talk by stating the principles that have come to guide his work. "Scientists must work with economists and politicians on these issues," he says. "They must address poverty and the availability of medical care. Education of women is another issue: the most potent thing that we can do to control infectious disease is to educate women. Ultimately, eradicating disease is closely linked to creating social justice."

irene
linetskaya

"After a storm, fair weather; after sorrow, joy."
— Russian proverb

Irene Linetskaya has an irrepressible energy, a zany sense of humor and a natural beauty; when she speaks, her words come tumbling forth, punctuated by giggles and embellished by her expressive hands. There is no immediate hint of her history in her demeanor, though a clue to her early years can be faintly detected beneath her American accent; there is an occasional staccato to her words, a tempo and lilt that give away her Russian roots. She was born in Kiev in the Ukraine, 60 miles from the Chernobyl nuclear power plant. That fact meant little when she came into the world in 1977, but changed everything in 1986, when there was an explosion at the plant. Her parents were engineers and, more important to Irene's identity, they were Jews.

"In Russia, it's just so ingrained to hate Jews," says Irene. "My mother was at the top of her class in high school, but they wouldn't let her into the university; she ended up doing a correspondence course to get her training. I remember my brother, who was seven years older than me, coming home with bloody noses, beaten up because he was Jewish. I was blond, so nobody knew I was Jewish, and I wasn't allowed to tell anyone. But I was always scared that people would find out."

Anti-Semitism was not something to take lightly in Russia. Less than 40 years earlier, when the Nazis arrived in Kiev, they dug a huge pit in the center of town. Then they rounded up 33,000 Jews, lined them up, took their teeth and glasses, and shot them at a pit called Babiy Yar. Before the Nazis showed up, Irene's beloved grandmother— already a tough, resourceful woman at the age of 18—had gauged the mood of history and urged her parents and eight brothers and sisters to get out of Kiev. But her parents— Irene's great-grandparents—had not believed the threat was great enough to warrant uprooting their entire lives. "No one will touch us," they told their daughter. She disagreed and put three of her sisters and herself on a train to Siberia. She never saw her family again; they all died in the massacre at Babiy Yar. In Siberia, the sisters spent four years working in a brick factory. Irene's grandmother met a man and married him. "I asked my grandma once how they got together," recalls Irene, "and she said, 'His family had chickens, and that fed my sisters.' My grandma spent her whole life supporting people. She's always the wall everyone leans on."

Irene's own father died of cancer when she was 2. Her mother remarried, this time to a violent alcoholic who is currently wanted in Russia on murder charges. Home became a terrifying place for Irene, and she spent more and more time with her grandparents. Her grandmother's first husband had died before Irene was born, and when Irene was 2, her grandmother remarried. Her new husband adored Irene, and the feeling was mutual. "He was my best friend, even though we weren't blood-related," says Irene. "He was Polish. When he was a young man, he was coming home through the fields one day when he saw the Nazis shoot his wife and baby. So he left Poland and came to Russia, and there, years later, he met my grandmother."

On April 26, 1986, Irene was at a birthday party when a reactor in the Chernobyl nuclear power plant exploded. While Kiev residents knew the basics of what had happened from the outset—there had been an accident at the plant—they weren't told much more by the government, which wanted to keep the danger of the situation obscured. Irene remembers finding a mushroom "the size of my head" growing up from underneath the pavement by her home, but everyone was still drinking the milk and water and eating

46

food grown in the area. Finally, several months after the accident, the authorities decided to send all the children in the city away; Irene was put on a bus and told she was going to camp.

She was gone through the summer. By the time she returned, her mother had died of cancer, her stepfather had left, and her brother was living alone in the family's apartment. Irene moved in with her grandparents. "Every day, my grandmother would cook for me and my grandpa, and then she would take a number of buses across the city to go and look after my brother. She's not the cute little type of grandmother, my grandmother. She's really tough." As if to prove this point, Irene notes that her grandparents lived in an apartment right across the street from Babiy Yar.

Despite all of the turmoil, Irene describes herself as a confident and independent child who loved her school, which she remembers as "excellent, strict, intense and science-based. Physics started in the fourth grade!" she recalls. Her biggest problem in school, she says, was that she was constantly in trouble for her gregarious, non-stop talking.

Two years after the Chernobyl explosion, things changed again. Irene's grandfather was now very ill with cancer, but her grandmother didn't trust Russia's medical system enough to let him go to the hospital. She herself had been diagnosed with Parkinson's disease, and the state was threatening to take Irene away and put her into an orphanage. And then—for these were the days of Gorbachev and *glasnost*—came a lucky break: the borders opened up, and Russian Jews claiming religious persecution were allowed to emigrate. Once before, just before Irene was born, the family had been poised to leave Russia, but at the last minute the government had closed the borders. Irene's great aunt made it out and moved to Oakland; it was she who now sponsored the family to come to the United States. "I think the real motivation was me," says Irene, looking back. "My grandparents were so old at that point, I don't know if they would have left if it weren't for me. But it was lucky that we came to the States when we did, because two years later the whole Soviet Union fell apart."

Irene, who was then 11, her grandparents, and her mother's brother, Uncle Boris, spent a year working their way toward the United States. Her brother, who had enlisted in the Russian army, stayed behind. The four took the train to Austria, where they stayed in one little room with a dripping ceiling and got their paperwork in order. From there, they went to Italy and traveled by bus to a small beach town. "It was a real resort town, and it was transformed by the hundreds of Russian refugees who were sent there," remembers Irene. "The townspeople just *hated* us. We were getting some money, but not enough to pay for both food and housing, and it was really cold. I was sick for months and lost a lot of weight. It wasn't an easy time, but I was a kid and I adjusted. I made friends even though it was a transient community."

Most refugees stayed in the town only a month or two until they received the papers they needed to travel to Israel or the United States, but Irene's family had to wait 10 months for their papers. Finally, they received the go-ahead and flew from Italy to California. In Oakland, Irene's great-aunt found them an apartment in the city.

"Soon after, a fortunate thing happened to me," says Irene. "My grandmother had another, much older sister who had moved from Russia to Canada in the 1920s. By the time we arrived in the West, she was living in the Bay Area, too, in a neighborhood that

47

had a great school. And since the neighborhood where we were living in Oakland was iffy and the school there wasn't great, she invited me to live with her and her family." Irene moved in with her distant relatives and started seventh grade. None of her new family spoke any Russian, so she was forced to learn English in a hurry.

Another key moment in her life also came during this time, when she saw her first pediatrician. "In Russia, doctors were a nightmare. We were all terrified of doctors," says Irene. "But my American doctor was young and sweet and considerate. And I fell in love with her profession. I was only 12, but I decided right then to become a doctor."

On the weekends, Irene traveled to Oakland to be with her grandparents. By this time, her grandfather was very ill. A year after they arrived in the United States, he died.

a. Irene, age 2, with her mother, brother and a friend in the family's apartment in Kiev. b. Irene, age 4, playing a snowflake in a Ukranian folk dancing class. "My mom made the costume from scratch," she remembers. "She made most of my clothes herself, often out of curtains." c. Irene at 5, on her birthday.

"Although I was devastated to have lost my best friend, it was a huge relief," remembers Irene, "because he had been suffering for so long."

Irene's grandmother moved from Oakland to San Francisco to live within the larger Russian community there. Irene moved to the city to be with her and started eighth grade at a school called the Hebrew Academy; she stayed there all through high school. "I think it was a perfect way to transition to American society," she says. "The school was small—there were only 17 people in our graduating class. I was in the middle always, between the dorky kids and the popular kids. Everyone felt comfortable with me because I make jokes and am easy to talk to. One thing that was challenging: I was an atheist in a super-Orthodox school. But I've always done my own thing."

Little by little, Irene's family adapted to the United States. Her Uncle Boris learned English, got a good job and got married. Her brother finished his stint in the Russian army, and Irene sponsored him to come to the United States. Irene herself had now mastered English, and with her dedicated and disciplined studying, she began to earn straight A's. She also started working to earn money for the family, putting in 20 to 30 hours a week, first as a babysitter, then as a salesclerk in a women's clothing store.

48

"It kept me out of trouble," Irene says. "And at school, I thought, 'Yes, I can do this!' A lot of kids in my school were going to college, so that was definitely part of the plan for me, but I just didn't know how to approach it. Then, in the eleventh grade, my biology teacher said, 'There's a program at Stanford for students who want to be doctors.'"

The more Irene learned about the Stanford Medical Youth Science Program, the more convinced she became that the program was meant for her, and she for it. "When I went through SMYSP, I was as plugged into it as they come," she remembers. "I was so excited. It was the first time that I was really challenged academically, the first time I was in a college setting, the first time I was working in a hospital. I felt medicine was my calling, but my high school jobs had kept me so busy that I'd had no time to volunteer in a hospital,

a. Irene at 13, again on her birthday, her first in the United States. b. Irene at 17. "This picture was taken during the SMYSP on-campus interview day," she says. "It's me next to some tree on the quad at Stanford." c. Irene at 24, in the dorm during her first year at Harvard Medical School.

so I didn't really have any firsthand knowledge about what being a doctor entailed."

At SMYSP, Irene was given a job in the cancer radiation therapy department of the Stanford Hospital. In her words, she "freaked out." "I said, 'You can't put me here; my whole family died of cancer.' But I was told to give it a chance. The first day, they put us in the waiting room to play with the kids, and there was this little boy named Max. He was about 3, he had no hair, and he had a brain tumor that was growing out of control. He went to radiation therapy twice a day, where they played him Disney tunes throughout the treatment. He would lie on the table and bop his feet up and down. It was so sad, but the prognosis was full recovery. Being surrounded by cancer was a tremendous challenge for me, but I stuck through it."

There were other influential firsts at SMYSP for Irene. "The diversity was a huge thing. I'd never experienced that much diversity. At first, I was seeing every color of the rainbow, and that was new for me and I was a little nervous. But we became such a strong community, such good friends. When you meet someone from a new ethnicity and become so close, you don't look at that ethnicity as foreign anymore. And it was so powerful to hear people's stories. After hearing some people talk, I felt like I was the

49

luckiest person alive. I saw that other students were real victims of abuse, while I was really a victim of circumstance."

Another key first at SMYSP was finding a direct mentor. Irene became close friends with Juan Ibarra, the first SMYSP alumnus to direct the program. "I remember walking with Juan and talking about how our parents died. I talked to him a lot about college, and he was so encouraging. He said, 'Don't worry about the money.' And coming from a person with a background so similar to mine, a person who'd been orphaned, who didn't have any money of his own, that meant a lot. He told me to just focus on getting into college. And all the counselors were so encouraging. They all said, 'Don't worry, Irene, you're going to get in here if you want to.'"

Irene left SMYSP with a renewed conviction that she should—and could—become a doctor. Her dreams took on a tangible force, and her plans began to mold to reality. "I came back with so much energy," she says. "SMYSP helped me know specifically why I wanted to be a doctor and how medicine made sense in my life. It just opened up my mind. I started studying biology really hard. I was on the college track: I got the Stanford application and got the whole thing done long before senior year had even started."

Irene sent off her college applications—to Stanford, several University of California schools and Rice University—and then waited, anxious and trying not to be. On December 16 when she got home from her Rice interview, her grandmother said, "Oh, you've got some mail."

"And it was the small envelope from Stanford," remembers Irene. "I almost died. If you got the small envelope, it meant you probably weren't accepted. I was afraid to open it. I put it on my bed and sat on it for hours. I couldn't open it. Finally, I had to. And it said, 'Congratulations.' I started screaming, and my grandmother said, 'What! What's going on?!' I told her and she said, 'Are you crazy? Of course, you got accepted.' I got a great financial aid package, so I knew I could handle it. And I think it was really my story that got me in, because my grades and SAT scores were like lots of other peoples'. SMYSP brought out my strengths and gave me confidence and taught me to be proud of my story."

In her last year in high school, Irene was also sponsored to travel back to Eastern Europe to march in memory of all of those who had perished in the Holocaust. She was one of more than 6,000 young people who gathered in Poland to walk in the "March of the Living," staged to commemorate the end of the war 50 years earlier. "We walked a windy path in the snow in the Polish countryside, from the Auschwitz concentration camp to the Birkenau camp. We spent a whole week traveling around gray, dreary Poland, going from camp to camp. From Poland, we traveled to Israel. The contrast was startling—Israel was brilliant green, and there were red poppies blooming everywhere. It was a wonderful, enlightening trip. It reinforced my pride in being Jewish. When I first came to San Francisco, it took time to adjust and to believe that I could tell people openly about being Jewish and not have to fear being beaten or ostracized. After the trip to Israel, when I first went to Stanford, I tried to immerse myself in the Jewish community. But it didn't feel quite right. My community at Stanford was always my friends at SMYSP."

At Stanford, Irene majored in human biology with a focus on community health.

Her entire time at the university was marked by community involvement: her own experience with discrimination, as well as the lessons she'd learned from her grandmother and at SMYSP, drew her to marginalized communities. She found out about an organization called Alternative Spring Break, which sponsors college students to do volunteer work, and spent three spring breaks with the organization. In the first year, she learned about children's issues in East Palo Alto, visited a bilingual education school and a YWCA doing child abuse prevention work, and traveled to Los Angeles for a conference on children's issues. The next year, she led an HIV and AIDS outreach project in San Francisco, which visited 17 different organizations working with HIV and AIDS patients. She and her group did needle exchanges, handed out food and visited people with the virus from many ethnic communities. "People were incredibly gracious and generous with their time and their stories. We were so grateful to be there." The next year, Irene led a similar HIV and AIDS outreach project, this time in New York City.

"It was hard being poor at Stanford," Irene says. "Dealing with the paperwork and loans made me nervous because I was on my own. But then, I was always on my own. When I first came to Stanford, I had bouts of feeling sorry for myself, thinking, 'Oh, other people can do all these great things, but I'm poor and I can't.' But, finally, I said, 'Yes, I can do interesting things, too, and why not?' That's when I found Alternative Spring Break. And, of course, SMYSP was always there."

In the summer after her sophomore year, Irene became a SMYSP counselor. "It was amazing to be in the position where people were looking up to me, and I was able to give advice based on my personal experience. I could do the same things that Juan had done for me and assure kids that college was not a problem. The most depressing thing about being a counselor was getting 438 applications for 24 spots. You *knew* the impact the program would have on students, but you couldn't extend it to all of them."

In her last year at Stanford, Irene spent four months in Ecuador, learning Spanish while working first in an orphanage, then in a hospice for terminally ill patients. Just after graduation, she spent a month volunteering in a small village in Nicaragua, improving her Spanish. She then put the language to use working in an HIV clinic in the Mission district of San Francisco; the clinic was, she says, the most inspirational medical setting she has ever encountered. In the fall of 2001, Irene was admitted to Harvard Medical School. Her first year at the school was "fantastic," she says, flashing her uncontainable smile. At Harvard, she is studying to become a community physician; she spent her first med school summer carrying out a patient education project in an HIV clinic in Dakar, Senegal.

Irene's effervescence and commitment to social justice have fused to give her an optimistic sense of compassion and a spirited determination to heal others. Her approach to life is eminently festive: she is as comfortable talking about zodiac signs as she is about exotic viruses. "I don't want to work in a private clinic," she says, musing on where she will go after she graduates from Harvard. "I want to work somewhere like Shriners Hospital, which treats low-income, seriously ill kids. Something big with poor people coming in for advanced care. Or a small HIV clinic. And I want to spend a significant part of my life working abroad. Addressing the health care needs of the poor, both in the United States and abroad, will be my focus in medicine."

51

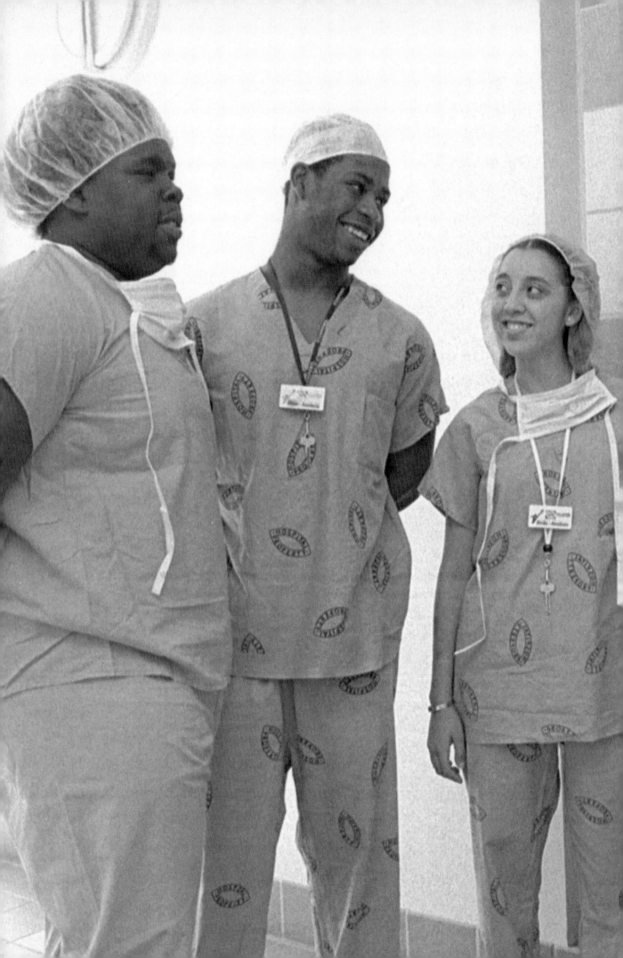

3RD FLOOR

↑

Patient Unit 3C
Building 101

← ain Lobby
CU
rgery

at the hospital:
on the job

The Palo Alto Veterans Affairs Hospital lies close against the foothills behind the town. It is a large facility with clean, cubist lines, full of light and glass; it radiates modernity and efficiency. Near the hospital's entryway, a huge American flag is flying; outside the front doors, veterans in wheelchairs are scattered about, enjoying the sunshine and an occasional cigarette.

LaTasha and Candi are here for the first time. Like every student who attends SMYSP, they will spend two days a week interning in a hospital setting. Some students are assigned to the VA; others work just down the road at the Stanford Hospital, another state-of-the-art medical facility. At both hospitals, student internships take place in operating rooms and emergency rooms; in oncology, anesthesiology and dermatology departments; in the morgue, in delivery rooms, in X-ray labs, in hospital chapels—basically, in every department. There, students do everything from assisting doctors and observing procedures to acting as impromptu translators and filing hospital charts.

LaTasha and Candi have been assigned to the physical therapy department of the VA. They were dropped off in front of the hospital at 8 a.m. with contact names and directions to the department, courtesy of the program counselors, who each year spend dozens of hours coordinating the internships and getting required clearances from the hospitals. Candi is wearing a flowered sleeveless top and khaki pants; LaTasha is in a pink T-shirt and black slacks. They look like very professional 16-year-olds.

When they arrive at the department, LaTasha and Candi meet Kristin Collins, who does physical medicine and rehab. Kristin is a calm, friendly woman with large star earrings dangling from her ears. On her wrist, she wears two Chinese bracelets: one, she tells the girls, to repel negative energy, the other for courage and strength. A small pin on her ID tag identifies her as a member of the Air Force Reserve.

Kristin tells the students about the department where they will spend the next five weeks. "Here we handle spinal cord injuries," she explains, "primarily long-term spinal cord injury patients." Since most spinal cord injuries are permanent, rehab in the department tends to focus on staying active and building strength in a wheelchair. Kristin hands photocopied packets of information to LaTasha and Candi. They are labeled "Introduction to Spinal Cord Injury."

"In general, the younger our patients are, the more traumatic the cause of their injury," says Kristin. "Some elderly patients just fall and injure their spinal cords. For the younger ones, it tends to be high-diving or skiing accidents that cause their injuries, or car accidents—although that's better with the new seat belt laws."

As the three talk in the department's large communal office, they hear snippets of conversation from other therapists consulting on the phones, phrases like "massive cerebral hemorrhage," "not enough blood to the brain," and "crushed vertebrae."

54

"We have three full-time physical therapists here and one half-time," Kristin explains. "We also get students who come for clinical experience." She asks what areas of medicine the girls are interested in studying. LaTasha says she's interested in physical therapy and feels she got the perfect summer assignment. Candi says she's interested in being a pediatrician one day, but at this point she "wants to learn about all of it."

"Okay," says Kristin, "then let's go see some patients." She takes the girls on rounds. The first patient they see is an elderly man with a white beard and a large torso. He has had a stroke and is having problems with his mobility, including difficulty rolling over in bed. As Candi and LaTasha watch, a friendly young woman with lots of freckles works with him to get him to roll over. She offers encouragement and reassurance, and after a little while, is able to get him to summon the strength to roll his body over.

After watching the therapists work with several bedridden patients, Candi and LaTasha spend the rest of their day in the department's "gym," a large room with stretching and strength-building devices. A poster on the wall shows a very old man lifting weights; he has a phenomenal physique. "Growing old is not for sissies," reads the text below his picture. In the gym, the girls prepare hot pads to put on patients' muscles. They learn to move patients out of their wheelchairs and into exercise machines. They ask the patients about their lives, their injuries, their families and their time at the hospital.

While LaTasha and Candi are in the physical therapy department, Elizabeth is in the diagnostic radiology department, watching a patient get a CAT scan. Marcus is in the VA operating room, watching a doctor remove a prostate cancer. Chantha is in the Stanford OR, watching a surgeon excise a lymph node from a man with lymphoma; the node will be used to make a vaccine that doctors hope will boost the patient's immune system and fight the disease. All over both hospitals, medical miracles are taking place and the students are right in the thick of it.

In the evening, the group gathers for a key ritual of the program: Todos Time. In Spanish, "todos" means "all," and every night at 9:30, the students spend a half-hour talking about any and all subjects: lectures they heard that day, things that happened at the hospital, patients they've met, procedures they saw performed. Sometimes the topics stray from medicine: one night in the summer, they discuss dreams they are having when they sleep; another night they talk about violence and its origins; another night, about spirituality. Today, with everyone just back from the hospital for the first time, the talk is about where they've been and what they've seen.

Enrique is assigned to the operating room at the VA. "I followed around an assistant nurse," he says. "I talked to a patient who was going in for open-heart surgery, and then I talked to him again when he came back out. I watched an operation where they took two biopsies. The smell of burning flesh is not great, but I was surprised how quickly they could cut through bone."

55

Oscar is in the OR, too. When Enrique mentions cutting bone, he grimaces. "I was watching an open-heart surgery and I was fine when I saw the general anaesthetic being applied," he says, "but when they cut, I felt terrible. The doctor used a saw and it was like 'BZZZZZZZZZ.' I almost fainted."

Natalie also spent the day in the OR. "They were really relaxed about it all," she says of the doctors she watched. "I couldn't believe it. We were about to cut somebody open, and they were talking about Rice Krispie squares."

Tom is working in the morgue. "It rocks!" he says. "You guys don't know. It's so fun. Sam, who runs the place, is weird, but he's funny. He tells us to ask as many questions as possible, and we call each other by our first names only. We'll get to dissect organs and sew up bodies."

Ivan is working in the morgue, too. "The doctor is just so used to it all," he says. "He was in there working, and there was a head sitting on the tray right next to him."

LaTasha is one of the last to talk about her day. "I was so excited when I found out that I would be able to work in the physical therapy department," she says. "We're in the spinal cord injuries unit. We observed the patients and met all kinds of different people, and they opened up and shared. I met a guy in a wheelchair who'd been shot by kids seven years ago. I met a guy who'd been injured in a motorcycle accident." Echoing the sentiments that seem to fill the room, she adds, "I wasn't bored a minute."

kao
vang

"Cultivate a heart of love that knows no danger."
— Cambodian proverb

Kao Vang was born in 1979, in a refugee camp in Thailand. It was during the summer, sometime in June probably, although no one really knows for sure. When he came into the world, he had a brother waiting for him; his sister had died of an illness before Kao was born.

Kao's parents had escaped across the border from Laos to reach the refugee camp. They were Hmong, fleeing the mayhem of the Vietnam War, which had spilled over into the mountains where they lived. Before the war, Kao's grandmother used to tell him, life had been simple for his family. In the mountains, there was no electricity, no technology, no formal education. Prestige came from clothing; a person could spend a whole year making a single elaborate outfit. Life revolved around working in the fields. Families grew beets, green vegetables and rice. They raised pigs, chickens and oxen. Kao's mother, the only girl child in her family, toiled non-stop; his father had more time to himself but greater familial responsibility due to the misfortune of having a father who was an opium addict. Kao's father spoke Hmong, Lao and a little Thai; his mother spoke only Hmong. When Kao's parents were children, they had no contact with anyone outside their Hmong community.

But isolation became impossible in Southeast Asia in the '60s: just after Kao's parents married, the Vietnam War broke out. Suddenly, surviving meant not only working hard, but evading conflict and capture, too. Instinct became a strength relied on to stay alive: over the centuries, the Hmong had developed an intimate and extensive understanding of the terrain in which they lived, and during the war, that understanding saved them.

Before long, the American Central Intelligence Agency decided it wanted access to that knowledge. The CIA recruited Hmong men and sent them into Vietnam to guide American forces through the landscape. When he was in his early 20s, Kao's father was recruited to lead guerrilla attacks and to scour the mountains for American planes that had gone down; if American troops were found alive, the Hmong were to save and hide them and give them safe passage. Kao's father spent two years with covert forces in Vietnam and then returned to his wife in the mountains.

When the Americans began to retreat, the Vietnamese government began to retaliate against the Hmong for the part they had played in the war. Kao's parents heard about a camp that refugee Hmong families had set up across the border from Laos, in Maejarim, Thailand. Kao's parents, along with some 50 other family members, stole into the forest and began walking toward the camp. It took them six days to reach it.

They were in the camp for three years, and it was there that Kao was born. The camp was safe but crowded, and there was never enough to eat. Houses, built by the refugees, were made of bamboo and scrap metal, with thatch roofs. The camp was damp and hot; sanitation was minimal. In a few grassy areas where the jungle had been cut back, families could grow their own crops. Eventually, the camp grew large and established enough to be recognized by the Thai government as an official refugee camp. After that, UNICEF was present to make sure that food and medicines were available.

Families applied for visas to leave the country, and slowly these were granted. Kao's parents were among the last to get their paperwork; many of their relatives left the camp before them. Kao's mother's family went largely to France, his father's to America. Leaving the camp was a heartbreaking experience marked by more uncertainty.

60

"In the back of their minds," says Kao, who has heard the stories of those days from his relatives, "it was always, 'Will we ever see each other again?' It was a time when you felt lucky that you weren't being chased or hunted down, but when you still dreaded the unknown future that you would have to face."

Kao's uncle, Lao, had mastered English; he got a job working for UNICEF as a translator. Another uncle had already moved to America, to Minnesota, and, via Lao, he was able to get messages to Kao's father—messages that said, "Don't worry, things are okay in the United States. People are friendly. Tell your wife and children not to be scared about coming." As they prepared for the move, Kao's parents experienced another first: life in a classroom, where they were both taught rudimentary English.

Eventually, the family received news that they were going to Vermont. They had been sponsored by an American family and would receive government assistance to help them survive financially. Kao was a year old when he arrived. He remembers the family in Vermont as "very nice, open and eager to get to know my parents. They helped my dad learn more English. When we arrived in America, my mom was overwhelmed. But my dad was excited and thought, 'Wow!' The flying, and the beautiful buildings and the level of organization—he'd never seen anything like it before. I remember him telling me about going to a department store and seeing an elevator for the first time. In Laos, they relied on nature to meet their needs. In the United States, they found everything was ready-made and you just had to go to the store."

That, of course, assumed that you had the money to pay for things—and money was a constant struggle for the family. Slowly, as Kao's father grew more familiar with the United States, as he learned English and more about the culture, he began to find work. His brother in Minnesota suggested a move to the Midwest, and he was able to find sponsors willing to help Kao's family: "two wonderful ladies," as Kao describes them. "One of them, Susan, employed my dad as a custodian. The other lady, Barbara, loved education, so she read to me a lot and took me to school."

Still a young child when he moved to Minnesota, Kao remembers being bundled up in a little penguin snowsuit to guard against the cold. In it, he was sent to kindergarten, where he found that he loved school. "I had a wonderful teacher, Mrs. Walter, and I was the only Hmong student she'd ever had, so she always took a special interest in me," Kao recalls. He enjoyed math and anything to do with outer space. The one subject he didn't like was English: "I hated it, and I still hate it. When I went home from school, there was no one to talk to in English. No one could understand. When my brothers were older, we would talk in English, but when we were little, we always communicated in Hmong."

In the early '80s, Minnesota was hardly a hotbed of diversity, but Kao and his family felt welcomed. "I don't remember anyone making me feel uncomfortable," says Kao. "I think society was more accepting of our differences than they might be now. We were fortunate to emigrate when we did, though in truth there weren't a lot of Hmong around, so I was forced to fit into the existing structure. I just watched Americans and copied the way they talked and dressed. My dad was always teaching me manners.

"When I was very young—6 or 7—I was quiet, more of a watcher than a doer. I didn't really become a doer until I had to take on more family responsibility. I remember

61

playing in the snow, playing with my older brother and my cousins. We would pick berries in the country, play tag, climb trees. But at school, it was different. I was on my own there and focused on my studies."

Kao's family continued to grow; his mother had five children while they were in Minnesota. "I was a great baby sitter," Kao says today with a smile. "That's why I can't wait to have children of my own. I remember waking up in the night whenever one of my little sisters was crying." But while the new children brought great joy, they took a toll: Kao's father now had seven children and a wife to care for, in a land that was still very foreign to him and where he was working as a custodian for not much more than minimum wage. "In Laos, you need a lot of children to help you manage the fields," says Kao.

a. Kao's grandmother (left) and great-aunt in the refugee camp in Thailand in 1977. b. Kao (left), age 5, in Minneapolis, Minnesota, with his older brother Xong and younger sister Hlee. c. Kao at 20 with his fourth-grade teacher Ernestine Brown and her husband during his second year at UC Davis. "This was my first collegiate conference presenting my research project," he says. "I invited some of my teachers."

"But the society here is different, and there was really no one here to tell my dad that. It was always hard for him to be dependent on other people. He wanted to be independent, but having so many children and so little education made it harder."

As Kao grew, he took on more and more responsibility for his family. By the time most boys were beginning to read, he had become the family's de facto interpreter. When his parents dealt with the world, increasingly he helped to ease their way through the process: helping his dad apply for jobs, helping his mom read the newspaper.

When Kao was 8, his father decided to move the family to California, a move he was convinced would bring them greater independence. He traveled to Crescent City, a small town on the coast in Northern California. When he found a job as a custodian, he sent for the family.

Crescent City differed from Minnesota in many ways. For one, the weather was better, not like the tropics of Laos, but warmer nonetheless. Kao remembers sunshine and trips to a nearby beach. The family had a little more money, since Kao's father was being paid a little better. Most importantly, there were other Hmong families in the town. "There were almost half a dozen families there," remembers Kao, "so there were

62

young people to play with after school. I began to open up a lot more and engage with other people."

Crescent City was a fishing town, and Kao's father used to come home with his own fresh catch of the day. Kao worked at school and improving his English. "A few of my Hmong friends were very centered academically, and they were always competing against each other," he says. "They really challenged me to learn more English, so I was fortunate. And people at the school were very accepting. The teachers were always encouraging."

The family stayed in Crescent City for two years and then moved south to the larger city of Stockton to be near to Kao's mother's brother. There they had their first real taste of discrimination. "I remember going with my dad to fill out job applications, and

The Vang family in Stockton. "All of my family members are in the picture, except for my father, who is taking it," says Kao, "and one of my sisters, who is married and out of town. In the picture are myself, my mom, my older brother, my four younger brothers and my four younger sisters."

people would ignore us. Sometimes if you asked for directions, people would say, 'Go back to where you came from.'"

Kao started the fourth grade. "I was at an age where I very much wanted to fit in. The friends I made were cutting classes, vandalizing property. A part of me knew it was wrong, but I still wanted to hang out and see it. But that year, I learned that sometimes you have to take a stand and go against your peers. I was very fortunate that my fourth-grade teacher, Mrs. Brown, took an interest in me. She helped me get into a comprehensive program for gifted children, and I was able to change." Ernestine Brown had already been teaching for more than 20 years when she met Kao, and she knew a gifted child when she saw one. She remembers Kao as a "very exceptional student. He was so bright. I tried to give him everything I could above and beyond the regular work to keep him challenged, but it still wasn't enough. I thought, 'This child really needs more.'"

Mrs. Brown arranged to have Kao tested by the school psychologist. When the results came back, the psychologist thought there must have been some sort of mistake: surely this quiet, shy little boy who spoke English as a second language couldn't be as

63

smart as the tests suggested. But he was. Mrs. Brown met with Kao's father. "What should I do?" he asked, and when Mrs. Brown suggested transferring Kao to a school for gifted students, he agreed. But it wasn't the end of the relationship between Kao and Mrs. Brown. In high school, Kao returned regularly to her fourth-grade class to tutor students; she remembers he was particularly helpful to Hmong children in the class who were struggling with their English. When Kao presented his first science paper in college, he invited Mrs. Brown and her husband to come to the event, and they made it a point to take the day off and be there. "I can't say enough about the young man," says Mrs. Brown today. "I have his picture up in my office, and when people ask about it, I say, 'That's one of my fourth-grade students I admire.'"

When he was in the fourth grade, Kao also went to the hospital to translate for his relatives for the first time. "It was very scary," he remembers. "It was all adults and it was such a fast-paced environment, but it didn't take long for me to get comfortable with translating. There were a few doctors who encouraged me, but others wouldn't even talk to me. They would just say, 'We don't need an interpreter.'

"In Stockton, there is a great need for people who can communicate in both Hmong and English. There are a lot of Hmong people who all have lots of children and live in small two-bedroom apartments on monthly incomes of about $1,200. They're having so much difficulty adjusting to this culture, and sometimes it's nice for them to have someone they can look up to who's telling them it will all be okay. People see Stockton as a city where only poor people live, a place with a lot of ghettos. Living with that stereotype, you can look at yourself and think you don't have a lot of value. But because I am from Stockton, I have a different view. That poverty also develops a bond. We all want to better ourselves."

By the time he was a teenager, Kao was getting calls every week from families who needed help filling out applications, finding jobs, settling disputes or getting a doctor. "There's a huge gap between my parents' generation and my generation, and everyone in our family group—our clan of about eight families—thinks of me as a caretaker. Sometimes it's a big, overwhelming responsibility. It's hard to be in a position where you have to make sure all the kids are doing well in school and all the older ones are being cared for as they should be. The weekends were the worst," he says. "I remember whenever anyone was going to have a baby, they would call me to go to the hospital with them. They would consult me from the moment they found out they were pregnant until the actual delivery." Kao would always stay for the delivery, present just behind the curtains while a new member of his ever-expanding de facto family was born. But being so closely connected meant seeing interactions that were troubling.

"There was a time when my dad had to go to the dentist. He had Medi-Cal insurance. The dentist gave my dad one shot of local anesthetic and started to pull out his teeth. My dad told me he was in a lot of pain, and I told the dentist. But the dentist said he knew he had given my dad enough anesthetic, and started to pull another tooth. My dad pushed his hand away, and the dentist just said, 'This guy is a nut,' and walked out of the room. Up to that point, I had thought of medical people as kind individuals who wanted to help others. That dentist made me think differently. It made me begin to stop trusting people."

Other disturbing incidents occurred, sparked by the fact that in the medical arena, Hmong and Western beliefs and practices are often in conflict. "In medicine, there's a big difference in the cultural values between the Hmong and the Western doctors," says Kao. "Everything is seen as a whole for the Hmong people, and you can't invade the body. The Hmong believe, for example, that if you remove a gall bladder, maybe your spirit won't be able to come back. Sometimes Hmong families may be afraid to tell the doctor what medicines or home remedies they have taken. So the doctor has to make the effort to reassure the families and let them know that their information is important and confidential. I've experienced situations where the doctor comes in, can't understand the families, ignores the interpreter, and just touches the patient and prescribes medicine.

"Late one night, I was at home, and I got a call that my uncle was very sick. I call him 'uncle' because he was the same generation as my dad, but he was actually a cousin. His mother had used some Hmong medicine—herbs and acupuncture—to help him as well as she could. I called the paramedics from my house and headed over. The paramedics got there first. When they saw the herbs, they assumed he was using illegal drugs. At that point, they seemed less enthusiastic about helping him; they put him on a gurney and threw their bags on top of him. When I got to his house, they were putting him in the ambulance. He died that night. On the death certificate, it said 'undetermined' under cause of death. Seeing how they treated him and his family made me say, 'This isn't right.' They didn't make an effort to help or to understand. Because I did so much interpreting, I saw a lot of that. I remember when my younger sister was very sick— they thought she probably had meningitis—and the medical professionals told my dad not to interfere. They threatened my dad and said that if he interfered, they would have all of his children taken away."

In contrast to the challenge of negotiating the medical arena, school was a great escape. "School was a place where I could be by myself and not worry about all the emotional times with family, a place where I could be calm," says Kao. When, in the fifth grade, he'd transferred to the school for gifted students, he'd found the classes "were very challenging and went way beyond the traditional curriculum. In junior high, I again learned a lot. The classes were very diverse, with lots of Asians and Hispanics and African Americans. The teachers were interested in us, and having so many bright people around really made me focus. That extended through high school. I was with the same group of people; we had structure and we all wanted to learn.

"In high school, I had a terrific biology teacher, Mr. Bisagno. I was scared of him at first—he was big and very stern and old-fashioned, and he expected a lot—but he took an interest in my education. One day he called me in and told me about the Stanford Medical Youth Science Program. He gave me the application and a map showing how to get to Stanford for the interview. He even offered to drive me there."

Kao filled out the application and then waited. When he was invited to the campus for an interview, he was predictably nervous. "It was very memorable, the whole interview process. It was my first time on the Stanford campus, and the prestige of it, the reputation and the luxury: it was scary! But also, I was impressed that a place like this could make time for someone like me. So it was exhilarating, too. My dad was there, and it was something to see the joy on his face."

Kao Vang

Kao was accepted into the program and entered in the summer of 1995 with Mr. Bisagno's words ringing in his ears: "Just be glad that you're there doing something that you never thought you could."

"SMYSP was one of the most enlightening things that could have happened to me, and it did a lot for me," he says of the program. "It allowed me to explore the medical field. It was the first time I was living with a whole house of others like me who shared the same interests: medicine, science and college. We all wanted to do better for ourselves; we were all open-minded and willing to set aside old impressions. Seeing how the counselors interacted with one another gave us energy to interact that way ourselves. The bonds I formed, and the friendships, and the exposure to different cultures will always remain with me. Being in that atmosphere really shaped the way I perceived what I would do in the future."

Kao volunteered in the vascular surgery department of the Veterans Administration Hospital. The experience helped him to become a little more trusting of doctors again. "When I went home after SMYSP and started interpreting again, I didn't see just the patient's side. I began to understand the physicians' side, too, to look at the responsibility and the limited time that they have.

"I never thought about what it means to be Hmong until I was in high school. Some other minorities are much more ready to confront authority, but passivity is very typical of the Hmong people. I always accepted things as they came. There wasn't anyone to tell me, 'This is wrong.' When my dad went to the dentist, and when my uncle passed away, I was still submissive. Finally now, I'm becoming comfortable with advocating for the patient. But only now I'm beginning to develop the thick skin to really challenge things. At SMYSP, we were encouraged to do that.

"In high school, people often told me I would be a great leader, but I took that as praise rather than as a challenge. By the end of high school, I began to realize that it was a challenge to do something with my life."

Kao was accepted at the University of California, Berkeley and at UC Davis; he chose Davis because the campus is closer to home and, he says, he preferred the quiet "cow town" atmosphere of Davis to the more liberal and lively Berkeley scene. He has remained remarkably committed to his family and has had three siblings living with him at various points in his college career: a sister who is also a UC student, a brother in high school and another brother in junior high. "It's good for them to be living with me, to have a role model," he says. "And it's good for me to watch them grow." Kao's newest roommate at Davis is Chor Vang, a 1999 SMYSP graduate from North Highlands, who is now a pre-med student at Davis. The two met at a SMYSP reunion.

To pay for his education, Kao won one of America's most prestigious educational awards: the Buck Scholarship, which funds all the expenses of college and graduate school. "All the seniors in my high school knew about it," he says of the Buck award. "It was thought to be the mother lode of all scholarships." Kao didn't think seriously about applying for the award until he got an application in the mail from the SMYSP staff, with a note urging him to apply. He talked to a few teachers, and they encouraged him, too.

"So I applied," he remembers. "The application was so straightforward. It just had standard questions and asked for a 250-word essay. I remember that seemed like a short essay to award such a big scholarship." Kao sent off the application in December of his senior year, thinking it was "a big shot in the dark." In March, he got called for an interview. "We went to the Buck estate in Vacaville," he remembers. "It was about 90 minutes from Stockton. My dad drove me. He'd taken me shopping for a suit, and I bought one that was made from black wool. It was very hot! I was nervous, but one of my teachers, Mr. Caldwell, had given me a mock interview, so I was less apprehensive than I could have been."

When Kao arrived at the estate, he was given 20 minutes to write another essay, this time on who he would choose to have dinner with if he could go back in time and meet anyone. He decided on his maternal grandfather. "I wrote that we would eat rice," he remembers, "and that I would ask him where my mother got some of her traits."

After writing his essay, Kao was ushered into a room where about a dozen people were waiting for him: the Frank H. Buck Board of Directors and their spouses. He sat down "on a very deep couch," and they began asking him questions. "They asked about myself, how I felt, about my family, about the Hmong culture. At the end of the interview, I got into a nice conversation with someone who asked me how, if I was a family doctor, I would handle an underage patient who wanted an abortion. I told her I would consider it my job to make everything as comfortable and easy for the patient as possible. I told her it wouldn't be up to me to convince the patient, but rather to respect the patient's wishes and confidentiality."

It was almost four months before he heard anything about the scholarship: one Saturday in the summer, Kao was returning home from work when his sister ran out to meet him, waving an envelope. "Congratulations," read the letter inside. "We welcome you to be a new Buck Scholar..." Looking back years later, Kao says, "at that moment I began to understand the meaning of 'I can do anything and become anyone in the future.'" He told his parents and then he called Mr. Bisagno, who, along with his wife, took Kao to dinner. "That night, Mr. Bisagno told me, 'All your dreams and wishes can come true now. You just have to push forward.' And he was right. I've been blessed in ways I could never imagine. The scholarship has taken away a lot of stress about money and allowed me to be more involved in the community."

And yet, despite the achievement, Kao nearly decided against going forward. "I almost didn't go to college," he reveals. "Right after my high school graduation, someone very close to me passed away. It was a newborn baby. I was following the course of the pregnancy right along and was at the hospital with the mother. Because of the cultural clash and various misunderstandings, no amniocentesis test was done. When the baby was finally born, she passed away after a few days. And I was thinking, 'What's the point? I might as well not go to college, because despite all of the new technology and the advancements in the field, medicine couldn't even save this life that I loved very much.' But my roommate-to-be—he was Russian—called me up to say hello, and after talking to him, I felt a little better. So I found myself again.

"In college, I became involved with peers who have passions to make society a better place for everyone," says Kao. "Seeing my peers doing that, I really began to understand that I'm in charge of my destiny. If I were still in my original country, I would be working in the fields all day, without education. Feeling how fortunate I am makes me want to

Kao Vang

make change for the better." Through Upward Bound, a national outreach program, Kao has tutored and spoken at high schools in Davis, Stockton and Sacramento. He also tutors high school students through a program he helped to found called Southeast Asians Furthering Education, or SAFE.

"SAFE is doing pretty well," he says. "I know there is a lack of outreach efforts to certain populations, and that's a place where I can really have an impact. I believe people like me have a responsibility to help our younger brothers and sisters, to tell them, 'This is what you do to be successful, to get educated.' We used to assume that the younger ones who were born in the United States would be doing better, but in fact they are more involved with gangs and drugs than with academics. There aren't enough people like me to be role models, people who've been through the system but who also understand their communities and their culture."

Kao has just graduated, and he remains committed to becoming a doctor, still largely out of a desire to treat Hmong patients—a desire to finally be the healer, not the middleman. But he is modest and cites daunting medical school admissions statistics as he notes that, Buck Scholarship aside, becoming a doctor is still not a certainty.

For the time being, Kao is working full-time, improving his scientific research skills. He is part of a five-year study looking at using diet as a non-invasive way of managing asthma. "I learned the people approach of medicine, and now I'm concentrating on the scientific approach," he says. "Then if I go to medical school, I will do a better job." He is also thinking of starting work on a master's degree in nutrition biochemistry next fall. "With that background behind me, after the five years, it will be a natural transition into medical school. I'll also be clearer as to how to use my medical education. And if I don't get into medical school, then I think I'll probably start teaching and transition into helping the next generation," he says. "Either way, it will work out very well."

tropical medicine

Dr. Kelly Murphy is a clinical assistant professor of surgery in Stanford's emergency medicine department. He is direct, pragmatic, the kind of down-to-earth guy who looks like he's only worn a tie four or five times in his life. He has spent the last five summers in Papua New Guinea as part of a team doing medical outreach work in some of the country's more remote villages. One afternoon, he comes to the SMYSP house to present a slide show detailing some of the cases and conditions he and his colleagues saw and treated in the Pacific Island nation.

Murphy's slide show offers the students a snapshot of illness and treatment in the developing world; even for students from some of California's poorest neighborhoods, it is a sobering picture. Dr. Murphy shows image after image of people who are suffering, particularly children. "There are sick children everywhere," he says. "There are fungal infections, there's malaria, lots of dehydration." A picture of a particularly ill child appears on the screen. "This child would have been in an intensive care unit in the United States," Murphy says.

"There is no electricity, no running water. No one has any money, and there are only the bare essentials. The main source of food is sago, the filtered pulp of a palm tree, which is boiled into a paste, then wrapped in banana leaves. If there are bananas or eggs, those go to the children. Crocodile hunting in the river is a source of meat."

Dr. Murphy shows pictures of the terrain: it is lush and wet, with spaces for spartan, thatched houses carved out of the landscape. There are pictures of the wide, gray river that connects the villages in the region, and even a picture of a rooster "who sounded like he had TB and started crowing every morning at around 3:30 under the house we lived in," says Murphy. But mostly the pictures are of illness. "This area has one of the highest infant mortality rates in the world," Murphy tells the students. "The nearest real hospital is in Port Moresby, 800 miles away. One mother whose child had congenital hydrocephalus walked the 800 miles, carrying her child all the way, but by the time she got there, it was far too late."

Dr. Murphy shows slides of common tropical ailments: tropical ulcers, infested by flies and host to maggots' eggs; and yaws, large sores that can eat all the way to the bone. There are pictures of leprosy and elephantiasis. And there are diseases more familiar in the West, like cancers. One girl, just about to die, has a nose almost destroyed by a skin cancer; a man with a swollen neck has lymphoma.

"The whole experience of health care is relative," says Dr. Murphy. "There was no way we could dramatically improve the health conditions in these areas. Our goal on these public health interventions in Papua New Guinea was really to think about the impact of health care in a basic way: to talk about hygiene and to dry up wet areas to cut down on mosquitoes and malaria. We would set up an informal school or clinic where we taught basic pathology, and village health aides came from all around for training.

72

"Now this," Dr. Murphy flashes to a slide of a serious-looking young man, "is Spedi. He was the first village health aide we trained." He flashes to another slide. "Here we are teaching Spedi to examine the belly. Malaria in this area is chronic, and it causes an enlarged spleen, so you can check for that in the belly to diagnose the disease. Now here," he says dryly, flashing to a picture of a blue tarp laid out on the grass and covered with vials and bandages, "is a picture of our hospital supply room." Dr. Murphy finishes up his slide show with a few more cases: a boy who lost his finger to a crocodile bite, a man with elephantiasis in his leg.

When the visual portion of the lecture is done, Dr. Murphy asks for questions. Marcus raises his hand and asks, "How do you deal with seeing so much suffering?"

"Well, you just get used to seeing weird stuff," Dr. Murphy replies. "You get used to it, and most of the time you can treat it. That's why medical work is so wonderful. We were able to cure all of the infections we saw with just a little bit of medicine. Also, we try to look at things very objectively. We take notes on everyone we see, and we check on everyone each year when we go back.

"There is some stuff that's hard to take, especially seeing kids who are very sick with illnesses that you know you could cure if you were home—but because of where you are, there isn't anything you can do. Those cases are very, very frustrating."

"How do you get your funding to do this work?" asks Michelle.

"Well, it's a very low-budget project. We get some money from corporations, some from groups here on campus. Drug companies give us medicines that are close to expiring but which are still good. All of the doctors on the project foot their own bills, which amounts to some $5,000 to $10,000 a person. The medical students who go along get subsidized."

"What was it like living in the villages?" asks Vivian.

"There are a lot of cultural barriers. It's a very patriarchal society, and the men and women are kept strictly segregated. It's taboo for a male doctor to touch a woman. We would have to have a meeting of all the village elders to make sure it was okay for us to give treatment."

"Did you have any cultural sensitivity training at all?" asks Tamara.

"Not really," says Dr. Murphy. " It was difficult to work within the system sometimes. A 5-year-old male child has more authority than an adult woman in this society. That's hard to see."

"What about attempts to incorporate traditional remedies?" asks Tamara.

"There's an anti-malarial medicine they make by grinding up the seeds of a certain type of papaya and drinking the powder in a tea," says Murphy. "In every village, we sat down and asked them about how they treated certain things, and then we compared practices between villages. We looked to what could be used when we were gone. And the people are definitely open to change. When the World Health Organization first went into these regions in the 1950s, cannibalism was still practiced. People used to eat the brains of their vanquished enemies and also of their relatives. WHO doctors discovered that this caused a brain infection in those who had eaten the brains. They brought this information to the village elders, and they said, 'Okay, we won't do this anymore.'"

After Dr. Murphy leaves, the students break up into groups to discuss what they have just seen. Most are nonplussed. They talk about the severity of the cases and compare them with health conditions in their own communities. They wonder openly whether they'd have the courage to go to Papua New Guinea themselves. Some express concerns about contracting malaria. Others wonder at the living conditions (these are, after all, teenagers, not saints). But their universal admiration for the medical team is evident. And some students seemed thrilled at the prospect of practicing relief medicine in the developing world. "It's so amazing," says one of them. "I hope I'll be able to do something like that one day."

katrina
hunter

"The spring makes the stream flow."
— African proverb

Katrina Hunter is soft-spoken, with a gentleness in her voice that should never be mistaken for frailty. She is filled with strength. When she was 5 years old, both her mother and her brother died. When she was 12, an accident left her father permanently disabled. Through high school, she cared for her bedridden father, cooked for her brothers and worked to keep money coming into the household. She spent hours each day taking buses across town to and from one of Sacramento's best public high schools, determined not to let misfortune dictate her future. It didn't: in her senior year, she was accepted at every college she applied to, including Harvard and Stanford, and she won a full scholarship to pay for her education. Later adventures followed, including a semester in Egypt, where she became fluent in Arabic and converted to Islam.

Katrina was born in Chicago in the late '70s. Her early years were the happiest of her life: when she hears anything by the Doobie Brothers or Rick James, she is instantly transported to a time when she was surrounded by friends and a large, devoted family. "Do you remember the theme from that show *Bosom Buddies*?" Katrina asks with a laugh. "That always takes me back."

Katrina's parents, Bonnificia and Thomas, had been sweethearts since adolescence, married in their late teens, and became parents a year later when their son Anthony was born. Bonnificia and the baby moved in with Thomas' mother while Thomas went to DePaul University. During the week he studied urban planning; weekends, he came home to see his family and work in his uncle's mechanics shop. A year after Tony was born, Thomas Junior arrived. "He had a lot of medical conditions right from birth," says Katrina. "The RH factor and jaundice and his legs pointed outward, and he had to wear steel leg braces to correct that." A third son, Jonathan, arrived four years later, and six years after Jonathan, Katrina was born.

Thomas was working for the city as a social worker in the projects, making sure that people had food for their children or help with drug or alcohol addiction. It was a good job and the family was thriving. Katrina's oldest brother Tony took care of her, and Thomas Junior, she says, "was like my second daddy. He used to protect me. He would be the one to wake me up and feed me in the morning. My youngest brother Jonathan was the pest of the family."

Katrina describes her father as "very proud and very disciplined." Her mother was Catholic, "very religious. I remember watching her singing in the choir just before I fell asleep in the church pew. She used to tote me everywhere. She'd dress me up like a little doll, and we'd go to my grandmother's house and all go shopping. She'd take me to school in the morning: we'd be in the car, and I'd be sitting on her lap."

When Katrina was 3, her mother started working in a medical lab and taking classes at the University of Chicago. "She actually wanted to do medicine," says Katrina. "She got a job in a histology lab. I'm not sure what her job title was, but we still have slides she brought back from the lab. Having all these slides around: that was my first memory of anything to do with medicine."

Katrina, just 5, was about to learn a lot more about the field. Among his health concerns, her brother Thomas had a heart condition, a form of cardiomyopathy. He was taking medication for it, but one night in April 1983 he suffered terrible arrhythmia. The family called an ambulance, but by the time it arrived, Thomas had died. The death took a huge toll on Bonnificia. "My mom couldn't deal with it," remembers Katrina. "She went downhill. Her heart would beat so hard that the muscle couldn't work and the heart would shut down. She had the same condition as Thomas, but she didn't know it. The doctors figured that the stress triggered it."

A month after her son's death, Bonnificia went into the hospital herself. She was on a list for a heart transplant, but in the early '80s, that procedure was still very experimental. Katrina visited her mother in the hospital; just before she graduated from kindergarten, she went to the hospital to show her mother the new dress she would wear for the ceremony. "When I showed her my dress… that's the only time I remember seeing her sad," says Katrina. "About a week after that, my father told us she had died.

"A year or two after she died, I started to understand more. When my father would tell me that she'd been on a list for heart transplant, I started to understand what that was. After my brother and my mother both died, the doctors were very worried about the rest of us, so they did all these tests: genetic tests and also echocardiograms. One of my brothers has symptoms of cardiomyopathy, but they don't affect him. My other brother has a heart murmur. They tested me, too, and I was fine."

But emotionally, no one in the family was fine. "We were all affected differently," remembers Katrina. "My father didn't let himself be consumed with self-pity. He went into survival mode, thinking he had three other kids to care for. My oldest brother became withdrawn. Jonathan became a delinquent. He had to be put into a continuing-education school because he just couldn't make it in high school—he was always in trouble. Me, I was too young to fully understand everything. I remember watching a show called *The Bionic Woman*: she was this robotic woman who didn't remember her mother, and somehow her mother came back—it turned out she had been in a witness protection program or something. I remember thinking maybe that would happen to me, that my mother would come back."

Seven months after his wife's death, Thomas moved his children to California. His mother had moved to Sacramento, and Thomas, remembering that his wife had always wanted to go to California, decided to move west, too. The family arrived in Sacramento in February 1984. They spent that month living with Thomas' mother and looking for a house to rent. "We moved about five times, trying to find the right place," remembers Katrina. "Everything was much more expensive in California."

Katrina started school. From the beginning, she did well. "I was close to all of my teachers," she says. "I remember I had a problem with talking too much in elementary school; that was the only thing that would get me in trouble. Then my teachers would sit me down, and sometimes I felt they were hard on me. They would be disappointed if I did something wrong. It made me work harder, especially when they called my father. When I came home, I couldn't do anything until I finished my homework. And my father would even give me more homework to do."

Katrina's father was "almost a perfectionist," she says. "He grew up in a house full of girls. He used to say, 'I saw what happened to my sisters and your mother. They got married and had children young.' He felt my mother had so many dreams, and because she got married and had kids so young, she wasn't able to carry them out—though I never heard any complaints from her about that. But he never wanted that to happen

79

with me. He wanted me to be independent, so he taught me to do everything, from fixing cars, to mowing the lawn, to electrical work.

"When I was in elementary school, I took a test—a listening test of some kind—and I was approved to take up a musical instrument. I took up the violin, because some of my friends were taking violin. They dropped out after the first week, but my dad wouldn't let me drop out, so I stuck with the violin from the fourth grade through high school."

In the seventh grade, Katrina's violin teacher, Ms. Southard, gave her private lessons. Katrina mastered Vivaldi's *Four Seasons*; she also loved to play Southern fiddle tunes. She learned to play the cello. "Ms. Southard wanted us to be flexible," she says, "and she would put me on cello because my fingers are long. In eighth grade, she brought me

a. Katrina in November 1977, when she was 6 months old and celebrating her first Thanksgiving. b. Katrina (top row, far left) at the Developmental Institute Preschool in Chicago, class of 1980.

a newspaper article about an African-American girl from Florida who won hundreds of thousands of dollars in scholarships. That was the first time I remember somebody being really adamant about me getting scholarships and going to college."

Katrina thrived through junior high. One of her key memories from the time is of a group session at school: "They would get groups of kids together, and we would meet our career counselor every week. In my group, we were all African-American girls, and we all came from lower socioeconomic households. We were asked about things happening at home. And I'm thinking, 'My brothers are acting up and I lost my mother.' But I heard some of these girls say the most amazing things, things I've never heard before. They had mothers who were drug addicts and prostitutes, fathers they never knew. I thought I had it bad! Hearing these kids—and we were just 12 years old—after that, I didn't think my problems were worse than anyone else's."

In seventh grade, Katrina met her best friend, Knieeka Jake. Knieeka was also living with a single father. "She's my friend to this day," Katrina says. "We started going to church together. We cooked for our families together. I remember when we were in high school—I think we were sophomores—we each cooked our first Thanksgiving meal. We called each other the whole time, you know, 'How's *your* turkey doing?'"

Knieeka gave Katrina a friend to talk to. Before that, there were times she felt isolated living in a house with three men. "Like when I had my first period, I thought, 'Who do I tell?' I remember having to tell my father because I needed some feminine products. So I wrote him a note and put it in the glove compartment of the car. My dad drove me to school every morning, and I told him, 'Dad, there's a note for you in the glove compartment. I want you to read it, but I want you to wait until I'm gone.' That's when he started giving me an allowance."

When Katrina was in the eighth grade, her father was injured. "He was a teacher in Sacramento, and during the summer he would volunteer to take special-education kids on projects," Katrina explains. "One of their projects was to clean up this old

a. Katrina at 2. b. Katrina at 12, when she was in the seventh grade and living in Sacramento. c. Katrina in her dorm room at Northwestern University, just back from Egypt.

cemetery. My father wasn't told that in certain areas there were headstones under the grass and dirt. When they went to shovel in one place, they shoveled into a block of cement. After that, my father couldn't stand. They had to rush him to the hospital, and his back just deteriorated.

"The city decided that they wouldn't cover him with health insurance, even though he was employed by the city. So my father started using his credit cards to pay his medical bills. But he couldn't do that for long, so he decided to sue the city for help in taking care of his back. A lawyer friend of my dad's took on the case. But it dragged on, and my father wasn't getting treatment. His back was getting worse. Some disks slipped, and after a while he couldn't move anymore."

Katrina got ready to go to high school. Her father wanted to enroll her in a private Catholic school; Katrina wanted to stay with Knieeka and her other friends, who were going to public school. She took the entrance test for the Catholic school. "I tried to fail it," she remembers, "but I didn't." In the end, she was able to convince her father to let her go to John F. Kennedy High School. "It was in a different district, but it was one of the best public schools in Sacramento," she says. "My cousin lived in that district, and I used her address." Since Katrina's father could no longer drive, she took the bus every

81

day, a trip that took up to an hour each way. "My father was very worried. I didn't go anywhere after school unless it was an extracurricular activity, and I would always let him know."

They were all conscious of the potential for violence in the city. "We were aware of gangs, and it really didn't matter what part of Sacramento you were from," Katrina says. "When you went to school, you were with everyone, and you were judged by what was acceptable to the gangs. Some of my friends had fathers and brothers who were in on this stuff and brought it to their homes. My brothers even tried to bring it home, but my father wasn't going to allow that."

When Katrina wasn't at school, she was at church. "Knieeka's father was a preacher in an apostolic Pentecostal church in Sacramento, and I started going to that church. I remember when I came home after I got baptized, I didn't want my father to see I was wet, because he wouldn't have been happy. My family on both sides are Roman Catholics. But after a while he got used to the idea, and he was okay with it because it kept me safe."

Katrina met her greatest mentor in high school: Jean Crowder, the career counselor at Kennedy High. "She was determined not to let my economic situation be a factor in whether or not I would succeed," says Katrina. "She pushed me to try things, put ideas in my head, took me places. She had lists and lists of different scholarships and programs. She was constantly on the phone with college recruiters and advisors."

Crowder told Katrina about SMYSP and suggested that she apply. At that point, says Katrina, "I had already decided that I wanted to be a doctor. I wanted to help people. I liked science. And it was all my dad could talk about. He told me how my mom always wanted to be a doctor."

Katrina was called for an interview and Crowder drove her from Sacramento to Stanford. Katrina was nervous and convinced she wouldn't be chosen for the program. Crowder, by contrast, was very calm. "She said I'd be called and I'd go," remembers Katrina, "and she was right. My dad was bouncing off the wall, he was so excited."

Katrina's nervousness extended through the first days of the program. "My brother dropped me off, and I was thinking, 'Any minute, something's going to go wrong.' I only had about $20. It was the first time I'd really been away from home. I remember thinking, 'I'm here all alone.' But I got over that because I realized everyone was basically alone. My strongest memory of the program now is of the day we graduated. I was bawling, and I couldn't believe it was all over."

During SMYSP, Katrina worked in the post-anesthetic care unit at Stanford Hospital. "One of the nurses told me that the time just after surgery is critical because it's not clear how patients will react to the anesthesia," she says. "She said I should talk to the patients. I particularly remember a conversation with a very old lady. She had the bluest eyes I'd ever seen, and her hair was very long and white like cotton. She told me she'd been a nurse, and talked about her life in the 1930s and '40s. She was fading in and out of consciousness. Just before she faded out, she said, 'I think I'm going to die today.' She grabbed my hand and said she loved me. I called the nurse and they wheeled her away. I found out later that she was fine."

Katrina looked in on other SMYSP interns at the hospital and saw the workings of a number of departments: "There was so much going on. I remember watching a brain surgery. They'd cut a triangle out of the skull, and, as they worked, they looked at the brain by using a small camera and a monitor. I was just fascinated by what I saw. Things that you never think about, like temperature changes in the room. It would be 40 degrees around the operating table and 80 degrees in the rest of the room, because if you're doing any kind of a transplant, you need to keep it cool for the organ. I saw one woman having an abdominal hysterectomy. I'm watching the surgeon stick her hand in the woman's belly, and I'm thinking, 'I can't believe this woman is somewhere in dreamland while all this is happening.' Someone else was having their spine worked on, and the doctors were using a machine that was sawing through bone; I had to stand behind a screen because there were fragments of bone and marrow flying around the room."

At the hospital, Katrina learned about medicine; at the program, she learned about herself. "The program made me see that if I wanted to go on to college, I could. It was because of SMYSP that I felt I could apply to schools like Stanford. Before, I thought, 'Poor Trina, her mother and brother passed away, her father's sick, she has to work.' But afterwards, I thought, 'There are so many people who have faith in me. I can do anything.'"

Another important thing happened during the SMYSP summer: one of Katrina's uncles from Chicago called to say that he was going to be in California and he'd visit her at Stanford. At that point, no one back in Chicago knew about Katrina's father's illness. "He was a proud man, and every time he talked to them, he would say he was fine," she says. "So when my uncle called me, I said, 'No, why don't you go and visit Dad in Sacramento.' I wanted him to see how sick my father was and how bad things had gotten. And he did. He went home and told the family. After that, my uncle made a few trips to California just to make sure things were okay."

Katrina entered her junior year in high school. "I was more confident in all my classes," she says. "I registered for honors and advanced placement (AP) classes. I was in an honors AP biology course with Knieeka, and we were dealing with recombinant DNA and antibiotic-resistant bacteria, and doing our own research."

Though her uncle's involvement had helped to ease the burden on Katrina, things at home were still difficult. By the time Katrina returned from SMYSP, her father was completely bedridden. Katrina spent her free time taking care of him and running the household. Her brother Tony had joined the Navy; her brother Jonathan was spending most of his time away from the house. Crowder suggested that Katrina contact the county and ask if they would pay her as an in-home care provider. They agreed to give Katrina minimum wage to take care of her father. "I also did tutoring all through high school," she remembers, "anything I could do to make some money. Half of our income came from my mother's survivor benefits, and half from what I earned."

When Katrina was a junior, Crowder told her about the Buck Scholarship, the same scholarship that Kao Vang had won. Katrina applied and was invited to Vacaville for an interview. Once again, Crowder did the driving. "Vacaville is maybe 30 miles from Sacramento," she remembers. "When I got there, I saw the Buck mansion at the end of the street and I thought, 'What am I getting myself into here?' There were six people interviewing each student. They asked me about SMYSP and whether we worked with cadavers. When I said yes, they asked me, 'What was it like?' And I thought, 'What will I tell them? If I'm honest, it might just gross them out.' But I decided to be honest. Words came flying out of my mouth. I told them when you're sitting down at Thanksgiving, cutting up the turkey, it's just like that. And I'm thinking to myself, 'What am I saying?' That's the one thing about the interview I remember. They just stared at me. They seemed very indifferent. So I thought, 'That's it. I'm not coming back.' Ms. Crowder had waited for me the whole day."

Katrina was wrong about the Buck people's indifference. Six months after the interview, she learned that she'd been selected for the scholarship. "When I found out I got the scholarship, I called and asked how they got their money, because I wanted to make sure it was stable for the four years," she says. "They told me in a nice way to mind my own business." Katrina applied to do biochemistry and biology at eight distinguished universities. She was accepted at all of them and decided to go to Northwestern near Chicago.

"I decided on Chicago because of all the family there," she says. "I felt it would just be a matter of time before my father would follow, and then he would have other family members to take care of him." Knieeka also decided on Northwestern, and the girls set off together. Crowder took them on a trip to Target and bought them irons, towels, backpacks and all the other things she felt they'd need.

"When I left for Northwestern, my brother Jonathan moved into the house and he was supposed to take care of my father," says Katrina. "But he was rarely at home, and I remember my father calling me once and telling me, 'I haven't eaten today.' It was 6 in the evening, and he hadn't eaten because my brother hadn't come home. Finally, just as I'd hoped, my father said, 'I have to go somewhere where someone can take care of me.' I told him to come to Chicago. His lawyer told him that he needed to stay in Sacramento at least another few years to win his case, but my father said, 'It's just not worth it,' and left. He settled the case, and they gave him enough money to move.

"When my grandmother saw him, she broke down and cried. She had no idea that he was so sick. He moved in with my uncle, and he has a doctor now. He's still not working, but they think they're going to be able to treat him. He's able to walk now with a cane."

Katrina and Knieeka roomed together at Northwestern. Katrina remembers, "The first thing I did was buy two packs of chocolate chip cookies. I ate them all on my own, and no one could tell me I couldn't. That was my rebel period," she says with a laugh. "When I was in high school, my father wanted me to focus completely and solely on school. I didn't have any boyfriends. The first time I had ever been out late at night was when I went to college." Crowder continued to check on the girls: she sent them care packages from Sacramento and one summer traveled to Chicago to visit them.

In her classes, Katrina felt prepared. Thanks to all the time she'd spent crisscrossing Sacramento on city buses, she'd gotten herself an excellent high school education. "My first year at Northwestern, I didn't think the work was too difficult," she recalls. "In my sophomore year, I was taking sciences: in classes I was getting B's and C's; in the labs I was getting A's. My lab professor told me the general classes were really 'weed out' classes to see who could get through them and go on to medical school. In the past, if I wanted something, I just did what was needed to get there, but during sophomore year, I realized I wasn't willing to do the work to get into medical school. I loved the labs and the research, but as time went on, I realized that there were lots of ways to help people, that I didn't need to do medicine."

Katrina was rethinking things outside of the classroom, too. She and Knieeka had joined a Pentecostal church in Chicago and, says Katrina, "When we weren't in school, we were mostly in church.

"I started to have problems with a lot of the teachings of the church, because I found that some of them weren't based on the Bible," she remembers. "It started to get away from spirituality. I was getting a lot of, 'You can't do this, you can't do that.' One of the rules was that you couldn't wear pants. But we were in Chicago and it was 20 below. We were freezing. I couldn't find anywhere in the Bible where it said you can't wear pants. I read it cover to cover looking just for that. I researched the history of clothing! I brought all the stuff I had looked up to my pastor. When I did that, my pastor told me that I was possessed by the devil. People were praying for me, trying to cast out demons, and I was thinking, 'This is just crazy.' The pastor basically told us that if we didn't wear skirts, we were no longer members of the church. I couldn't accept that, so I left."

Katrina started to go to non-denominational Varsity Christian Fellowship meetings. "I started to think I needed to take the message of Christianity abroad," she says. "I thought the best place to do that would be in the Muslim world, so I started to study Arabic. I decided to go to Egypt to take classes in Arabic culture at the American University in Cairo. I had declared a minor in Middle Eastern studies, and my advisor said I could use those classes. I contacted the Buck Scholarship people, and they said they would pay for it.

"My dad thought it was just ridiculous. But at that point, because I had been working in high school to run the house, I was feeling pretty independent, so I just told my father I was going. I was 21." Katrina got on a plane. It was her first time leaving the country. En route to Cairo, she had a 10-hour layover in Frankfurt; sitting in the airport, she felt anxious and worried about being alone. Then she got on a Lufthansa flight to Cairo. It was a preview of what was to come. "The menu was all Arabic food," Katrina says. "No one spoke English except one woman from Yemen. She actually thought that I had to go to Cairo to go to school because I couldn't go to school in America. She thought blacks in America weren't allowed to go to school! We had a long conversation on the plane. Flying over, I could see a lot of the countryside; it was beautiful. Then we landed in Cairo. The buildings were centuries old. It was amazing."

Katrina settled in at the American University. She studied two kinds of Arabic, the formal and the colloquial, and became fluent in both. "My best friends in the dorm were the Egyptian cleaning women, and they spoke no English," she says, "so we always spoke in Arabic."

Katrina had arrived convinced that she wanted to be a Christian missionary. She had the telephone number for the Cairo office of the Varsity Christian Fellowship, and she kept calling and leaving messages. No one called her back. "I never got through," she says. "At that point, I'd been reading the Koran. I found that reading the history of both religions was a major thing for me. After reading and studying, I converted. I think I was searching for something a little deeper and more spiritual than Christianity, and I actually found everything that I needed in Islam. All the problems and questions were answered there.

85

"In Islam, I was taught that it's not evil to have doubts and questions. As I learned more Arabic, I realized how little I'd known. In Islam, everything has a purpose, a reason. There is a place for the rational in the religion. For me, it offered order."

At the university, Katrina developed a close friendship with an American woman who was also studying Arabic and who had converted to Islam. "I would go to the mosque with her," says Katrina. "She never talked to me about Islam, and I never asked. But I really converted in my heart while I was there. I did it officially when I came back to the United States."

It was not an easy thing to do. The conversion marked the hardest year of Katrina's life. "My God! That was a difficult time," she says. "My father was okay with it. He's very rational and he thought I'd made a rational decision. But my Christian friends… that was so hard. I'd thought these people were my friends forever. One spit on my shoe, and one yelled at me and told me she had no respect for me anymore."

Knieeka was away, traveling in Europe when Katrina returned. She arrived in Chicago a week after Katrina, but was only in the city for a day before she had a flight to Mexico for a Spanish language program. "I picked her up from the airport, and I told her about my conversion in the car. She couldn't really take it seriously," says Katrina. "But after that, we talked about it a lot by e-mail. In the end, she accepted it. But it was hard, because she was in Mexico and I was in Chicago."

Katrina grew lonely and despondent: "I did a lot of reading and thinking during that time. I started doing badly in school. It was supposed to be my senior year, but I dropped a lot of classes. My advisor was calling, wondering what was going on. I was afraid the scholarship people would drop me. I can't believe how the Buck Foundation— I call them the Buck people—stuck around through it all. A lot of people wouldn't understand when you're dropping classes and starting to get C's, but the Buck people were always there for me.

"I had to stay in school an extra year. My family was very concerned about me. They were calling all the time to see how I was doing. My father and uncle were supportive: they told me, 'You can always come to us.' Gradually, I started to feel a little better. The school paper started calling me because they were interested in my conversion. And I met my husband at that time. He's Muslim, too. He was born in New York City, and he converted when he was in high school."

Katrina's husband lived in Fort Lauderdale, and when Katrina finished her degree at Northwestern, she moved to Florida to get married and start a master's program. She didn't attend graduation, but she did get a request for an invitation to the ceremony: Jean Crowder called to ask for one. "So I typed up a really nice one and sent it to her," says Katrina.

She is now working on a master's in mental health counseling. "Remember I told you about that group session we had in junior high?" she asks. "That was when I decided I wanted to help someone in that way. First, I figured I should go the doctor route. Later, I figured psychology would be a way to help people and make a living. But I'm still thinking about other things. I'm thinking about doing a master's of social work, and I'm also looking into a Ph.D. in psychology."

86

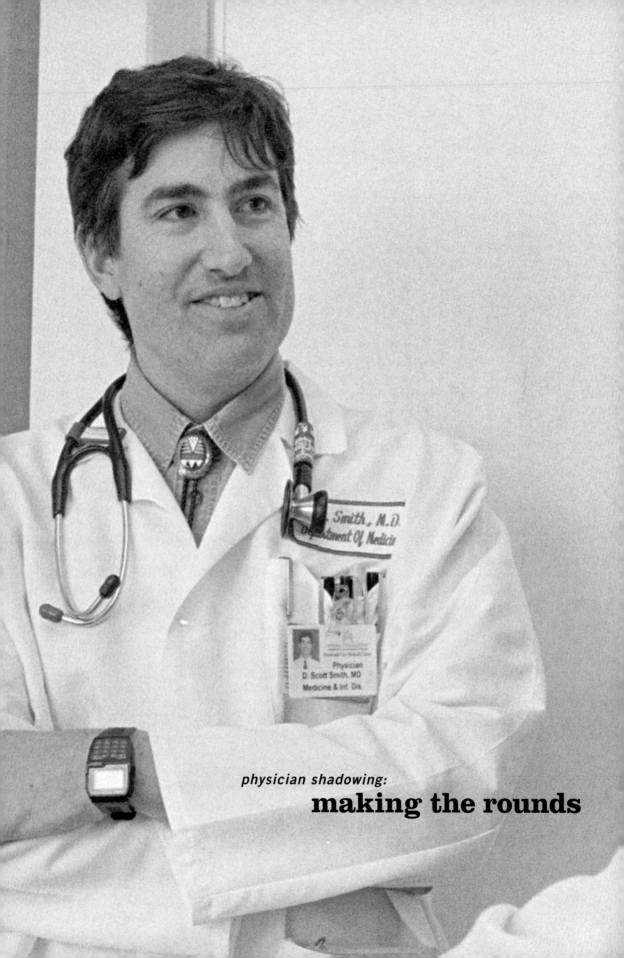

physician shadowing:
making the rounds

Dr. Darvin Scott Smith is an internist at Redwood City's Kaiser Permanente Hospital. He is tall, young, enthusiastic about his practice and devoted to his patients, with the attentive concern and encyclopedic knowledge that everyone wants in a doctor. He sees patients with all kinds of ailments, but his passion is tropical medicine, which he studied at Harvard. At the hospital, his specialty is AIDS; every week, he runs an HIV clinic, where which he cares for more than a hundred patients.

Oscar has come to SMYSP after just completing his junior year at Healdsburg High School. He is from Guanajuato, Mexico, and has been in America for less than two years; his English is still a little hesitant, and his Mexican accent is strong. He lives with two older sisters in California; his five remaining siblings, as well as his parents, are still in Guanajuato. Oscar misses his family a great deal, especially his two youngest sisters, who were 4 and 5 when he left, but he hopes to stay in America until he is a doctor. He is a very intelligent young man, and even with the newness of his English, he is rapt in medical lectures and frequently raises his hand to ask insightful, complicated questions.

Oscar has come to Kaiser to spend the morning shadowing Dr. Scott Smith. Physician shadowing is another key part of SMYSP, affording the students a chance to be virtual physicians themselves for a day. They don the mantle of the profession—a white coat—and then spend hours meeting patients, listening to them recount their medical histories, watching the doctors do physical examinations and sometimes participating themselves, hearing the hypotheses and diagnoses offered, and listening as treatment plans are sketched out. For all of the students, it is their first time being on the other side of the doctor-patient equation, and for many, it is an experience that further convinces them that they want to be doctors themselves.

When Oscar arrives at the hospital, Dr. Scott Smith is just about to see his first patient of the day. He greets Oscar with a handshake and quickly gives him one of the many starched coats hanging on the back of his office door. "We'll do real introductions after we see this patient, Rosa," he says. "I want to hear all about you.

"Now, I've checked with Rosa, and she's happy to have you accompany me on the examination. She's a 32-year-old woman with asthma and she's pregnant, which is making her asthma worse, so that's why she's here. So let's go in and see her."

Rosa, a robust Latina woman, is waiting in the small examining room. Her young daughter sits in the corner, swinging her legs and looking nervous. Dr. Scott Smith makes introductions, taking time to put everyone at ease. Oscar and Rosa chat briefly in Spanish, which seems to make them both less apprehensive. The doctor then asks Rosa to take some deep breaths so he can listen to her lungs. "They sound clear," he tells her after she has taken a few breaths. "I can't hear a wheeze, and that's good." He passes his stethoscope to Oscar, who also listens to the breathing. Everyone in the room smiles when, the initiation rite concluded, he hands the stethoscope back.

90

Next, Dr. Scott Smith listens to Rosa's heartbeat, which is strong and constant. "We have to wait about five more weeks before we can hear the baby's heart with a stethoscope," he tells Rosa. "Now," he says, looking down at her chart, "could you tell me about your exposure to tuberculosis?" Years before, Rosa had a positive TB reading; though she was asymptomatic at the time, she took medicine for the disease, anyway. Dr. Scott Smith, who is seeing Rosa for the first time, wants to make sure there is no chance she is still infected, and he asks her to have her medical records sent to him so that he can review her history thoroughly.

After some final advice about the asthma and encouraging words about the pregnancy, the examination is concluded. Oscar and Dr. Scott Smith retire to the doctor's office, where he quizzes Oscar about his background and interest in medicine. Oscar explains how he came to the United States with his father. "My first idea was to stay for a short time and then go home," he says, "but I changed my mind and stayed to get an education. It was very hard at first—I didn't understand a word the teacher was saying. Even in my algebra class, it was hard to follow! But I stuck with it and now I have all A's." Oscar speaks in such an unassuming way that his words have no tinge of boastfulness. Dr. Scott Smith compliments Oscar on how quickly he has mastered the American school system—two years ago, Oscar barely knew English; now he is studying at Stanford for the summer.

Dr. Scott Smith's next patient has arrived. She is an older woman in a baby-blue blouse covered with embroidered flowers. For the last three months, she has been snoring—so loudly that she wakes herself and her husband up at night. Dr. Scott Smith asks her a number of questions: no, she says, she's had no headaches, no pains, no weight loss or gain. She's never smoked and she just had her thyroid checked. Dr. Scott Smith looks at the tympanic membrane in her ears and at the uvula in the back of her throat, and he and Oscar listen to her lungs. In the end, Dr. Scott Smith diagnoses sinusitis as the likely cause of the snoring. "It may be a temporary thing," he tells his patient. "If it is your sinuses, it's an easy thing to give you a decongestant. Here's a prescription, which may make you a little sleepy. The main thing is to look out for fever and headaches; if you develop either, come back and see me."

After the examination, back in Dr. Scott Smith's office, Oscar asks the doctor why he asked the questions he did. "Weight can be a problem because it can press against the throat and cause snoring," he explains. "That can cause anoxia, where the oxygen actually gets cut off; it'll wake people up. Also, headaches are another sign you may not be getting enough oxygen."

The nurse stops by to say that it looks like the doctor's next patient hasn't shown up. He decides to show Oscar a slide show he has created and keeps on his desktop, *Tropical Diseases in Northern Climates*. It is a collection of photos of the exotic equatorial maladies that have shown up in an unlikely place: here in his office on the 37th latitude.

"There's so much travel now that these diseases are being distributed in places they never existed before. We're seeing leprosy, illnesses like these." His slides are pictures of his own patients: close-up shots of suffering in different parts of the body, images showing flesh that is blistered, distorted. When a picture of a man with a swollen leg comes up on the screen, Oscar identifies his ailment as elephantiasis; when an image of a woman with a large blister on her lips appears, Oscar guesses—correctly—that it is herpes. Dr. Scott Smith is impressed. When the slide show is over, he stands up. "Okay," he tells Oscar, "we've got a really interesting case over in the other wing of the hospital that I want to show you." Dr. Scott Smith looks enthusiastic, like a kid with a new discovery to show a friend. "This is a woman who came in with *necrotizing fasciitis* on her leg. That's flesh-eating bacteria. Have you heard of it? They had a bad outbreak of it in Oakland a couple of weeks ago—turned out the bacteria were in some black tar heroin that came in from Mexico. Twelve people were exposed to it, and six people died.

"The case we have here is an older woman who is a professional gardener. She got a cut on her leg that the bacteria got into, but she was lucky and got here fast, so she'll live and even keep her leg."

The patient, Delores, is in a bed on the seventh floor of the main hospital. When Oscar and Dr. Scott Smith arrive, there is already a surgeon in the room, checking her infection. The sight is astonishing. The back half of the woman's leg is completely gone; the flesh has been eaten down to the bone. The flesh remaining on the leg looks ragged. The surgeon, a young New Zealander with close-cropped, peroxided hair, is gently examining the calf. "Do you feel pain there?" he asks, pressing a spot, and then another, and another. "There? There?" The woman is remarkably sanguine, given the circumstances, and answers calmly.

Dr. Scott Smith, Delores' primary-care physician, puts on a pair of rubber gloves to aid in the examination of the leg and asks how she's doing. She tells both doctors that she is happy to be alive. Dr. Scott Smith introduces Oscar, who remains by the door, reluctant to intrude and somewhat taken aback by the severity of the wound. Dr. Scott Smith chats with Delores and the surgeon a little longer and asks Delores if the plastic surgeon has been in to see her yet. When she says no, he tells her, "Well, you'll see him soon. He's hard to miss: he'll be the tanned, relaxed-looking guy." Then he and Oscar leave and head back to the office for the next appointment. As they walk, Oscar asks how long it took from the onset of the infection to create the wound. "I'd guess about two to three hours to create that abscess," says Dr. Scott Smith. Oscar is clearly surprised at how rapidly the disease can progress. "It's a very dangerous condition," confirms the doctor. "It starts with a sore red spot that hurts like crazy—the pain is all out of proportion to the initial lesion. One of the interesting things is that this form of bacteria is actually very common. It's the same one that causes strep throat. When it gets into a cut, it can go crazy. We put this woman on antibiotics to stop the infection, and when her leg has healed more, then the plastic surgeon will do a skin graft."

Dr. Scott Smith's next patient is suffering the scourge of another frightening affliction, HIV. The doctor will be seeing this patient for the first time; he is a young man who has just discovered he is carrying the human immunodeficiency virus. While they wait for his arrival, Dr. Scott-Smith talks to Oscar about the virus. He brings out a complicated plastic model about the size of a football; it is a model of a CD4 cell being infiltrated by HIV. Dr. Scott Smith explains how the virus hijacks the T cells inside CD4 cells and gradually takes over the entire cell, transforming it into a machine to replicate the virus and finally killing off the T cells—and the body's immune system—altogether. He talks about his patients and how he cares for them, describes the new drugs on the market and how they inhibit and block the virus at different stages. "The next big drug we're hoping for is a fusion inhibitor, which may stop the virus from attaching to CD4 cells altogether. We know that there are some times that nature stops it. We know that about 5 percent of males of European descent have a gene known as CCR-5, which blocks the virus from entering cells."

"Is it possible they could use gene therapy to give the CCR-5 gene to HIV-positive patients to help the body stop the production of the virus?" asks Oscar.

Dr. Scott Smith is delighted by Oscar's suggestion. "You should be a scientist!" he says with a grin.

The patient is now 20 minutes late, and Dr. Scott Smith is worried that he may not show up, that he has decided he's not emotionally prepared for his first visit with a doctor since his diagnosis. Dr. Scott Smith decides to call the patient's home number to see if he's there. He gets the answering machine and leaves a carefully worded, nondescript message asking the patient to please call him. Just after he hangs up, the nurse pops her head in the door to say that the patient has arrived. Dr. Scott Smith looks pleased. He asks Oscar to wait in his office: "Since this is my first time seeing this patient, I think I'd better go in by myself at first. I'll ask him if he feels comfortable with you coming in a little later."

Dr. Scott Smith is gone for about 20 minutes. When he returns, he gives Oscar a quick rundown on the patient. "His name is Eric. He's 26, a young gay man, and having a hard time with this. He's told me he's suicidal. I've given him information on support groups and told him about several clinical trial groups I can get him into, but I want to see him back again soon, to make sure he's all right.

"He says it's fine for you to come in while I finish up his examination, so just let me grab some information here that I want to give to him and then we'll go back in." Dr. Scott Smith pulls together a stack of pamphlets and flyers from around his office, and then the two walk across the hall to the examining room.

Eric is a large man, tall and heavy-set. He is dressed in black leather that's decorated with chains and studs, and his motorcycle helmet rests on a chair in the corner. He has pale skin, a large mustache and a faint smile.

93

Dr. Scott Smith introduces Oscar and then goes through the reading materials with Eric, detailing the specifics of different support groups and medical trials. "Okay, now, let's finish the examination," says the doctor.

"Did you warn him?" asks Eric. "Yes, don't worry," says the doctor. Eric lifts up his T-shirt to reveal that his back is completely lacerated. There are some 100 or so lash marks across the skin, which have scabbed over into one large mass. Up in one corner of his back, barely visible under the scabs, is a tattoo. "Now, what is this for?" asks Dr. Scott Smith, with the tone that he might use to ask a nephew about a new stamp in his collection. "That's a pride tattoo for the S&M group that I belong to," says Eric. Dr. Scott Smith hands Oscar his stethoscope and asks Eric to take some deep breaths. Oscar listens to Eric's lungs, from both the back and the front, and also to his heartbeat. "The heartbeat is fast because Eric's a little nervous," says Dr. Scott Smith, patting Eric on the shoulder. "Nothing to worry about."

Dr. Scott Smith ends the visit by asking Eric to make a follow-up appointment and encouraging him to read the stack of materials he's gotten. Back in his office, he talks to Oscar frankly about his concerns. "The thing with AIDS drugs is that it can actually be worse if you go on them and stop than if you don't go on them at all. So I want to be sure that this patient is ready to commit to the treatment before I give him anything.

"It's hard. You saw a bit about his lifestyle. It's not the type of thing you're used to seeing in Mexico, I'd guess. Maybe you're wondering what drives people into that.... I think we all need love. That's what everybody is looking for. In my practice, I see that that's why people get into trouble, use drugs—usually because they don't feel any love in their homes and they go out onto the streets to look for it."

The final patient that Oscar and Dr. Scott Smith see together is an elderly man who has come in for a checkup. He has a heart murmur that was caused by an infection he got when he was a child. "Aha!" says Dr. Scott Smith. "That murmur was caused by the same bacteria as the flesh-eating bacteria. Our cases have come full circle this morning."

When the examination is over, Oscar removes his white coat, and the doctor walks him to the door of the hospital. Dr. Scott Smith is full of encouraging words, gives Oscar his card and invites him to stay in touch and come back to the hospital if he'd like to. Oscar thanks him profusely. With a final farewell, the doctor heads back inside to see his next patient, and Oscar heads to an afternoon of working in the anesthesia department at the Palo Alto VA Hospital.

erik
cabral

"A man must bend to become straight."
— Tao Te Ching

Erik Cabral was 13 when he joined a gang—a young teenager flirting with rebellion on the streets of San Jose. The induction happened at a party on a Friday night: he was "jumped" by the gang's 20 or so members, knocked to the ground and beaten. When the violence was over, he was hugged and congratulated on being in. He felt excited, welcomed, more powerful. Suddenly, he was cruising the city in the back of a BMW. There were girls around, graffiti raids, and trips to the beach and the water park.

Before long, things started to get, in Erik's words, "too deep." Excursions became battle skirmishes, for all over the city there were other gangs looking for fights. He began carrying a knife. Walking through downtown San Jose one day, alone and on his way home from school, Erik was attacked and hit—hard—on the back of the head. But he was lucky: another gang member caught "slippin'" (out on the streets alone) was shot and killed. Another fell victim to the bad aim of a drive-by shooter. By the time the next death came along, it was too much for Erik, even though this killing was self-inflicted: a gang member committed suicide after first killing his girlfriend.

Erik was a high school freshman, dealing with murders at an age when many kids are sneaking their first cigarette. Toward the end of the year, he pulled away from the gang and spent many hours in a city park, alone, a 13-year-old boy sitting on a bench, thinking about his future. He was smart enough to see what road he was on, but then he had always been smart; it was his hallmark. He'd won the city of San Jose's spelling bee when he was in the second grade. His teachers were always pushing to advance him a grade or two, and at home his relatives were always exclaiming, "Wow! How does he know that?"

But while school was easy growing up, things at home were not. Erik's parents had both come from Mexico; their relationship was stormy and short-lived, and the two separated when Erik was 4. Erik's father moved out. His mother—struggling with the impact of the relationship and with her family's condemnation of the split—suffered from depression. She had two more children—a son, Roger Joel, and a daughter, Tinna Marie—and she cared for all three as a single parent. She worked two jobs: in the morning, she cleaned houses, and from 5 p.m. to midnight every night, she worked on the assembly line at an IBM processing plant. Erik worried about her constantly. Every night, he waited up for her to make sure she made it home; when he heard her car, he'd run into bed and pretend to be asleep. He took care of his younger brother and sister, warming up food his mother had prepared, or making Kool-Aid and sandwiches and supervising their homework. None of them were allowed to play outside, since the streets were dangerous. Walking home from school every day, Erik passed the local park, the epicenter of the neighborhood drug traffic. Even at home, they weren't entirely safe: their apartment was broken into and one of Erik's few possessions—his prized bicycle—was stolen.

When Erik was 9, his family received a government housing subsidy, which helped them move to the "quasi-suburbs," as Erik calls them. There, he and his siblings had a patch of lawn and were allowed to play outside—heaven for all three. The move to a new school was not so great. In his last school, Erik had been constantly supported, and the power of his intellect had been well-recognized. He had been placed in special computer classes, had been active in sports, and was a member of the young astronauts club. In his new school, he was still inundated with accolades, but he missed his buddies and his old teachers, who had been good friends and mentors.

Slowly, Erik started to make new friends from suburban families, friends who had fathers who went off to work and mothers who stayed home, friends who were out riding their bikes after school, not staying home to take care of younger brothers and sisters. Erik wanted their kind of life, a life where he didn't have to worry all the time. But it was nowhere in sight. Even with the government housing money, the family was barely making ends meet. When Erik was 11, he got a job selling candy door to door. You were supposed to be 13, but Erik was big for his age and a friend vouched for him. With peanut brittle, chocolate mints and honey-roasted peanuts in hand, he was a top seller and made $15 to $20 a night. He gave the money he made during the week to his mother; she told him to keep what he made on the weekends for himself. He saved it, but it still wasn't enough to get him into the one place he really wanted to be: Little League.

Erik loved sports, and during recess and lunch periods, he played everything: football, baseball, soccer. He was always part of the athletic crowd, and school friends were always pestering him with questions he didn't want to answer, like "Hey, why aren't you on the football team?" or "Why aren't you on the soccer team?" The reasons were simple: the uniform, the equipment, the registration fee, the travel fee—being in Little League cost a lot more than Erik could afford. He was tired of shouldering his family's burden and at an age where his resentment easily fed his rebellion. By the time he entered a new school for junior high, he was spending less time on academics, and for the first time in his life, his report card didn't hold a string of only A's. He invested a lot of his energy in hanging out, being cool, and by the end of the year, he'd been expelled from school. He spent eighth grade in another junior high, goofing off and talking back. By the time Erik entered high school, he was in bad shape. His classes meant almost nothing to him. He started hanging around with older guys, dressing a certain way, doing graffiti. Suddenly, he was the young one, the novice. He had never really had a father, never had an older brother, but now he was surrounded by older men— men who had nice cars, men who could intimidate people if they wanted to. They invited him to join their gang, and Erik readily accepted.

But it wasn't all good times. Fed up with his new ways, Erik's mother was threatening to kick him out of the house. He flunked two classes, his first F's. The gang he had joined suffered terrible violence. And on one awful night, he was put in jail. He was caught writing graffiti on a train at midnight and taken to San Jose's juvenile hall. The experience hit him hard. Years later, he found a description of the emotions he felt that night when he read Malcolm X's autobiography. "Malcolm X talks about how traumatic it is to lose your freedom, how you don't feel like a person anymore," Erik recalls. "You can't leave, and it's claustrophobic. I felt all of that—and I was in jail only one night."

Erik's dad went to the jail and picked him up. Erik paid a fine and did community service. He dropped out of the gang. And he sat in the park, thinking.

By the end of the summer, he knew what to do. He said good-bye to his mother and moved to Santa Clara to live with his father. He started at yet another high school, this one with a largely white student body and a small population of Latinos who lived in the tiny neighboring community of Alviso. Erik got serious about school, though he had a lot of catching up to do. He was a loner who hung out by himself and studied. Gone were the friends, the clothes, the gang.

99

Erik Cabral

One day in honors chemistry class, the teacher, Ms. Schmidt, made an announcement about the Stanford Medical Youth Science Program. Erik picked up an application off her desk as he was walking out of class. From the description, he saw that the program was looking for bright, creative students from low-income families who were interested in going to college. Most importantly, he saw that the program was free if you were accepted. "And I thought, 'Man, I'm sold!'" he says today. "I'd always thought that I didn't have the money, or that I wouldn't get selected. But this said, 'If you have this and this and this,' and they were things that I *did* have. I'd always been interested in science. And it said you didn't have to be the very best in school. And along with that, I wanted to do better. I didn't want to be involved with things I'd been involved with before. So I

a. Erik at the age of 2 with his mom. b. Erik at 4 with his sister. "Mr. Mom doing the dishes," he says. c. Erik at 5, wearing what he calls a "dorky" hat.

filled out the application. I remember going into school at 6 in the morning and asking the custodian if I could use the typewriter to fill it out. I thought, 'They'll never accept me if I write it by hand.' I was fixated on typing it."

Erik was asked to come to Stanford for an interview. His mother came with him, and when she saw the university's famed church, *she* was sold. Erik was nervous. Other candidates had come in suits, but he was in his beat-up blue jeans. He heard some of the students talking about their 4.0 grade point averages and thought about the two F's on his transcript from freshman year. He finally relaxed a bit when lunch was served to the candidates and their families: the staff had bought watermelons, and Erik and his mother made expert work of cutting them up.

Erik was chosen for SMYSP. He'd worked summers before: between eighth and ninth grade, he'd worked as a janitorial assistant, and between ninth and 10th grade, he'd been an office clerk. Things at SMYSP were very different. Erik was assigned to work in radiology at the Veterans Administration Hospital in Palo Alto. He worked alongside a petite nurse and helped her lift veterans into X-ray machines: he would adjust the patients' bodies and their wheelchairs, prop them up and cover their chests with lead vests. When the nurse and the patients thanked him, he felt rewarded and grateful and proud to be useful. He felt a kinship with the veterans, he says, because like them, he had lost friends to violence. At the nurse's urging, he talked to the radiologists. "If you want to do medicine, you need to talk to the doctors," she told him. The doctors weren't as nice as the nurse—Erik felt they were aloof—but he loved to watch them work and was impressed by how much intellectual and scientific understanding it took to do what they did. "The doctor would say 'This is a 30 degree angle of the right humoral axis, and the bone splint is here,' and I thought, 'Wow! They really know how to help this guy.'

"I saw an angioplasty. The radiologist was doing the radiograms, and I thought it

a. Erik in Washington D.C.; he was in the city as a participant in the National Hispanic Youth Initiative. b. Erik graduating from high school with (left to right) his mom, his second cousin, Christina, and his cousin, Elena, Christina's mother. "I was so happy to finish high school and head to college after so much trouble during my high school years," he remembers of the day.

was so amazing. They explained, 'This is the way your heart works, like a plumbing system. If one of the pipes gets clogged, we inflate this little balloon and open it back up, to allow everything to work again.' And we were watching it happen on the screen as they explained! It was gratifying to connect the intellectual side of medicine—watching the doctors work—with the emotional side—helping the nurse and the patients. And I got positive feedback from the staff, so I was in heaven."

In the SMYSP house, Erik found himself opening up and forming bonds with others. He worked up the nerve to talk to the students who'd managed to maintain a 4.0 average, to approach them and ask, "How'd you do that?" He took notes and mastered the nuts and bolts of taking the SATs and writing college applications. He talked about being on welfare and accepting food boxes from the church: "That, for me, was the hardest thing to do, but opening up that side of myself took a weight off my chest. I really felt cleansed and comforted. I talked about my past with the gang, and how I was trying to get out of that. And everyone said, 'You're going to make it.' I never had heard those words. I never had met a professional. I'd been to the doctor maybe once or twice in my life. At SMYSP, I had this amazing sense that I was valued."

101

When Erik left SMYSP, he was on fire. "I took off," he says. "The first thing I did was go back down to the park that used to scare me when I was a kid, the park where all the dealers were. The staff had told us, 'Go back to your community, do what you can to help and share what you've learned.' I volunteered to be a mentor and a tutor for younger students hanging around the park. The Parks and Rec guy there really liked me, so he referred me to a program through the mayor's office, and I became a youth leader."

Erik also moved back to his mother's home. It meant taking three buses to get to school every morning, but he was happy to be there. "My mom trusted me by that time," he remembers. "She saw me change. But my dad was still suspicious. He would check in all the time. It started to interfere with what I was trying to do. I would spend hours at the library, studying, but he didn't trust me when I told him I was there. I guess it was because he was the one who had to get me at juvenile hall."

But Erik didn't waver. "I did exactly what everyone at SMYSP told me to do. When we left, they gave us each a binder with information on getting into college. I kept it and followed it religiously. I still have it! I went back to school and fought with teachers to get into their classes. I wanted to take advanced placement chemistry, English and history. My history teacher, Mr. Elwell, said, 'Erik, how are you going to take this class? You got C's and D's last year.' I said, 'I want to take this class because it's a college class, and I want to go to college.' So he said, 'Okay, let's see how you do.' He ended up writing me a letter of recommendation for college because I scored in the top 5 percent of students who take the national exam."

Erik heard about a program called "Step to College" at San Jose State; if you were accepted, you could take college classes for free. He got in, and by the second semester of his junior year in high school, he was taking a college biology course. He scored one of the highest grades in the class. More important, he loved it. In the summer, on scholarship from a program called the Academic Talent and Development Program, he took more college classes at UC Berkeley: one in genetics and one in math analysis and trigonometry. He also took astronomy at Mission College in Santa Clara. By his senior year, all of his classes were college-level classes, and he was also taking general chemistry and psychology at San Jose State. It was a fast-paced time, full of work. Erik didn't belong to any clubs; he missed the prom. He spent his time with his teachers, talking politics and science. By the time he graduated, he'd won nearly every award the school offered: the Bank of America Award for Language, English and History. The Scholastic Federation Award. The American Chemical Society Award. The Physics Bowl. The American Legion Award. The awards included enough money to cover virtually all of the tuition for his freshman year of college. And Erik was definitely going.

In his senior year, he was accepted to both Stanford and Yale. He decided to go to Stanford so he could stay in California to work against Proposition 187, a ballot measure designed to cut services to non-legal immigrants. Erik had staged a rally against the measure at his high school and also worked at a local clinic to distribute information about its potential effects on immigrants. He was increasingly interested in politics. "I felt I had the capacity for leadership," he recalls. "I worked with the city in my junior year. I went to Washington, D.C., for two weeks for a National Hispanic Youth Initiative conference. I was very political. I would hang out with Mr. Elwell and my AP government teacher, Mr. Volta, and we would talk politics. I read *The New York Times* every day." Erik began to wonder if maybe he was better suited to a career in law and policy. "I was thinking things like, 'As a doctor, I'll see a thousand people and I might cure half of them. If I write a law, maybe thousands of people would have access to medical care.'"

In the summer after he graduated from high school, Erik took a job working in the Washington office of Congressman Solomon Ortiz. Ortiz's district in Texas sits along the Mexican border and is one of the poorest in the nation. It was a rude awakening to the real state of politics in America. "It was such a bureaucracy, and there was so much back-scratching going on," Erik says. "I didn't want to believe it, all this great stuff that I had just learned in AP civics just didn't apply. I felt like there was no respect for the voter, for the people, that the Washington bureaucracy was like a bubble, and only certain people were inside. I became very disillusioned. I decided I would never be a politician. So that's when I really got back into saying, 'What do I really find meaningful? Where can I really make a difference in someone's life?' And that reinforced wanting to do science."

Erik started at Stanford. He lived on campus in a dorm, a requirement for all incoming freshman. After his industrious existence in high school, his natural sociability reasserted itself, and he spent time making new friends and going out. He got a job doing survey research with a psychiatry professor. "We were looking at the ability of families to cope with having an infant in the neonatal intensive care unit. The literature had found that many of these families end up in divorce and in very difficult situations. The ultimate goal of the study was to convince hospitals to have support services for families. Many of the infants were coming from East Palo Alto, and it was hard knowing that their conditions could have been prevented with nutrition and prenatal care. The thing that got me was that we only conducted the survey in English, and the majority of the patients were Latino. I felt the investigator who was going to publish this study would not be representing the most needy segment of the public, in terms of demographics. I wanted to help those families, but all I could offer was moral support, hospital directions and a glass of water."

In the summer between his freshman and sophomore years of college, Erik took another big step toward his goal of becoming a doctor. He had heard about a program through the National Institutes for Health that paid $20,000 in scholarship tuition to students who came to the NIH to do summer science internships. "I said to myself, 'I'm going to apply because it will allow me to learn cutting-edge science and find out how research is done, so that I can be an investigator one day and represent diverse study populations,'" he remembers. He applied and was awarded an internship. Once again, he was back in D.C. for the summer. "I spent 13 weeks looking at how to control the replication of a virus in the brain," he says. "It was an intellectually invigorating experience."

When Erik returned to Stanford after his summer at the NIH, he was on top of the world. In fact, he says, he got so carried away that he got, as he puts it, "cocky" and signed up to take 21 credits. He was still working on the neonatal research project, and he was going home every three days or so to care for his mother, who was again suffering from depression. All his life, Erik had been trying to help his mother with her illness. When she was put on medication, he would remind her, "It's the red pill today, Mom,

103

and the blue pill on Friday." He felt like a watchdog. And, ironically, now that he was away studying to become a doctor, he was less able to take care of her, and she was in trouble. Erik didn't know whether to drop out and move home for a while, or to try to help from afar and keep everything at school together, too.

"When we were growing up, nobody said, 'Your mom has a serious problem,'" he recalls. "We did notice that sometimes she would be very sad and not want to go places. The family would always say, 'That's just your mom.' It was very tough during sophomore year. I felt like I had empowered myself so much with my learning and my training, but this was my own mother, and if I couldn't help her, it was meaningless." Eventually, things got better. With her son's help, Erik's mother changed doctors and found a good treatment plan. Erik made it through his 21-credit quarter—though he wound up with C's for the first time in college, a blow to his blossoming ego.

In his second summer of college, he went to Mexico, to a city called Cuernavaca, for two months, his first time ever living in the land where his parents were born. He volunteered at a local government hospital there and shadowed a doctor in an infectious diseases ward. It was a different world. Medicine was simpler, with a focus on public health issues—like making sure that people understood that pools of brackish water attract disease-carrying mosquitoes and encouraging mothers to breast-feed rather than use baby formula.

During his junior year, Erik started doing patient advocacy at a local clinic near Stanford, a job that he loved. He worked alongside the clinic's only Hispanic doctor, Christopher Soliz, an affable, compassionate, dedicated man who quickly became a role model for Erik. He also spent a quarter at Oxford University in England, where he took a class on the history of health care in London and studied issues in socialized medicine. Every other weekend, he traveled, heading to Scotland, Ireland, France, Spain. He went nightclubbing in Barcelona and hit the pubs in Dublin. Sitting in a pub with a pint of Guinness in hand, surrounded by new Irish friends, he thought how far he'd brought himself from his anguished days on the park bench seven years earlier.

Erik's senior year at Stanford was filled with classes, his senior honors thesis and days at the clinic. He also came full circle with SMYSP and spent his last summer of college as a counselor for the program. He organized labs, counseled students, washed dishes, led soccer games and became a big brother and cheerleader for the participants, as his counselors had been for him. "It was so meaningful to me to get to know these students," he says of the experience. "I loved getting to hear their stories, where they came from and where they wanted to go. It hits you hard when you see them on graduation day, and they've learned so much. And you remember the first time you read their application, the first time you shook their hand. All those late nights organizing the program didn't matter when I saw in their eyes that they knew how to go forward. And in the back of my mind, I was saying, 'I helped. I was here.' I didn't get emotional at my own SMYSP graduation, but that day I was so emotional.

"Without SMYSP, I don't know if I would have gotten where I am today. It's like, what if a guitarist never saw a guitar? I think I would have tried, but I don't think I would have had the confidence and the nuts-and-bolts knowledge to make it to Stanford. I probably would have made it to San Jose State. SMYSP let me see medicine happening, so I was able to say, 'This is what I want to do.' When I finished Stanford, I didn't want a big graduation party. I was proud, but I felt it was just a stop on the way to my true goal, which is to finish medical school and begin to help people with their health issues. But we did have a graduation celebration in the Latino way—with music, food and dancing. The whole family was there, and everyone gave a little speech. I addressed my speech to the younger members of my family, telling them, 'Even though challenges may come, never tire in your quest for knowledge, in books or in life experience. All the while, remain humbly true to your roots, so you will continually grow in your capacity to do for others.'"

Erik Cabral

game show night:
name that neuron!

By Friday night, everyone at the SMYSP house is beat. The week has been a non-stop whirlwind of lectures, hospital jobs, research projects and college workshops, all capped off by Friday afternoon's four-hour, hands-on anatomy lab. By the end of the day, students just want to wash the formaldehyde fumes off their bodies, eat something and relax.

They don't get their wish. Friday night is game show night at SMYSP, when the students review the scientific and educational material they've learned all week. They get their tests dressed up in the familiar guises of American game shows: *Hollywood Squares* becomes Stanford Squares; *Jeopardy!* becomes SMYSPardy!; *The $10,000 Pyramid* becomes The Stanford Pyramid, and somehow, the experience of taking a test is transformed into a night of festivity. Students find themselves faced with questions like, "Now, for the X, name five physiological symptoms of stress," or "For $400, when you swallow, you use this."

Tonight the game is SMYSPardy! After a dinner of tacos and salad, the students congregate in the living room. Some are clad in hospital scrubs—all students are issued these to wear at work, and a few get such a kick out of the clothing that they wear it whenever possible. Gathered together, the students have the ease of friends who've known each other for years. Jerome has his feet in big, bushy slippers that say "Tasmanian Devil" along the side; Kamille is wearing a moisturizing mask on her face that has dried to look like white plaster.

Erik, one of the counselors in charge of game shows, has been surfing around music sites on the Internet, and he's managed to find several versions of the *Jeopardy!* theme tune. He plays a techno version on his laptop computer; the theme, so familiar, is infectious. The students count off to form two teams. One side, with no shortage of hubris, names itself WGW, short for We're Gonna Win. The other team names itself Jubilee. Everyone gets ready to play.

The categories for the first round of SMYSPardy! are neuroanatomy, anatomy, organic chemistry, college and potpourri. Each category has five questions ranging in value from $100 to $500. The object of the game is to wind up with the most money, though contestants have to be careful—they get docked for wrong answers, and negative balances are not uncommon. Ivan and Vivian start the game, and Ivan, representing WGW, steps up and confidently chooses anatomy for $500. Kahea, the other counselor who runs the game shows, reads off the question in her best Alex Trebek imitation: "This results from swelling caused by a leakage of fluid from the lymph system." Ivan has 20 seconds to answer. He's stumped. He contorts his face as Erik plays the *Jeopardy!* theme in the background, and wails when the buzzer goes off.

"Hey, no negativity," Kahea says. "And the answer is—she pauses for effect— "elephantiasis."

Vivian, playing for Jubilee, picks anatomy for $100. "Name the lobes on the right lung respectively and then on the left lung," Kahea says.

"On the right lung, superior, middle and inferior," Vivian says confidently. "On the left, superior and inferior." Her teammates cheer.

Lee is up for WGW. He chooses college for $100. "Name two examples of assets," he is asked. Lee thinks hard, but he's lost. Lee, a Hmong immigrant, is completely bilingual and has a GPA of 4.08, but no one has ever taught him the story of wealth in America. The buzzer sounds and he looks chagrined. "Bank accounts and property," says Kahea, as she gives him a sympathetic, better-luck-next-time look.

"Where's the love?" whispers Corinne to Dy'Esha as she watches Lee sit back down. "There *is* no love," says Dy'Esha with a muffled giggle.

Oscar is up for Jubilee. He chooses neuroanatomy for $400. "True or false," Kahea asks, "a hemotoma is a medical term for bleeding in the brain." Oscar looks like he knows the answer, and he's got a 50-50 chance of getting it right even if he doesn't. "True," he says. The team cheers again.

Elizabeth is up for WGW, which now has a score of minus $900 to Jubilee's $500. She chooses college for $200 and gets the question, "What is the profile?" She's baffled, too. "Something you write about yourself?" she guesses. "Nope," comes the reply, "it's the name of the financial aid form you fill out to get aid from private universities."

LaTasha is up next. She's playing for Jubilee and, like Oscar, she has a calm confidence about her. "Anatomy for $200," she says. "Name the thinnest blood vessels responsible for blood-gas exchange," she's asked. She doesn't skip a beat. "The capillaries," she replies, gaining her team another $200.

Corinne, playing for WGW, selects potpourri for $100. "What are two types of connective tissue?" Kahea asks her. She stammers aloud as the music plays in the background. "I know this... I should study more!..." Just as the buzzer sounds, she says "I don't know this." Kahea says, "There are four: bone, tendons, ligaments and cartilage."

The rest of the round is played out. By the end of it, everyone has had a chance to try a question: Ivan nails anatomy for $500 when he identifies the carotid artery as one of the two main systems that carry blood to the brain. Anthony gets $500 on an organic chemistry question when he identifies analgesic as the only non-20th-century invention in the following list: Viagra, penicillin, flight, plastic and analgesic. Jerome takes college for $400 when he identifies scholarships and loans as the two main sources of financial aid that universities provide. By the end of the first round of SMYSPardy!, WGW has redeemed itself somewhat, and the score stands at minus $200 for We're Gonna Win and $200 for Jubilee.

In the 15-minute break before Double SMYSPardy! starts, students microwave hot chocolate, line up by the phone to make short calls home and sit and make jokes with each other. When the second half of the game is about to begin, Erik plays the theme music at full volume to call everyone back. Once the students are settled in, he flips the board over to reveal the Double SMYSPardy! categories. They're the same as the first round: neuroanatomy, anatomy, organic chemistry, college and potpourri, though this time the five questions in each category are worth $200 to $1,000. Lee gets his question this time (organic chemistry for $200) when he correctly identifies carbon as the most abundant atom on earth. Oscar takes organic chemistry for $600 when he draws the intricate structure of methane on the board correctly. Corinne takes anatomy for $200 when she identifies the aorta as the largest artery in the heart. LaTasha gets anatomy for $400 when she identifies the septum as the structure that divides the heart into the left and right ventricles.

There are strike-outs, too. Dy'Esha tries college for $1,000 and is asked, "What source should you consult to reveal problems about a school you're interested in?" She guesses the Internet, but the counselors are looking for "student newspaper" as the answer. Enrique tries neuroanatomy for $200 and is asked for the basic unit of the nervous system. He guesses the brain, but the answer is the neuron. Michelle tries neuroanatomy for $600 and gets a true-or-false question, "Cerebral hemispheres as well as basal ganglia help to refine and control body movements." She thinks that's false, but the answer is true.

By the end of Double SMYSPardy!, the tables have turned. WGW, with a score of $2,600, now looks like it might actually live up to its name; Jubilee is at zero. Everybody gets ready for the final SMYSPardy! question, which they all know will be a challenge.

"Okay, everybody come up to the board," Erik calls out. "WGW, you write on this side of the board. Jubilee, you're on this side." The students cluster around and get ready. "Okay, you've got two minutes," says Erik. "Diagram the body and trace the blood flow through all of the major organs."

The music starts up. Everyone is frantic to get the diagram down. Marcus has the felt marker and is drawing for WGW; Michelle is drawing for Jubilee. Cries like "No, no, through the liver next!" and "It's the right ventricle first!" resound throughout the room. Chantha, out on the edge of his group, is tech dancing to the *Jeopardy!* theme. Every second is used, but when the buzzer sounds, both teams have done it: as Erik and Kahea confirm, each side of the board contains a comprehensive and correct diagram of the way that blood moves through the human body.

Ivan holds his arms over his head triumphantly. "WGW!" he exults. Since they had $2,600 coming in, they are, in fact, the winners. Erik hands the team a bag of candy, and everyone offers congratulations and high fives. But the party breaks up quickly: it's 9:45 p.m., and the students have 15 minutes to get ready for bed and be in their rooms. Their SAT tutoring starts at 8 a.m. the next morning.

patricia reynoso jauregui

"Resourcefulness accomplishes more than brute strength."
— Mexican proverb

Patricia Reynoso Jauregui's interest in medicine was sparked in the seventh grade, but even before that—in the sixth grade—the principal of her school in Mexico had noticed Patricia's good grades and tireless work habits and suggested she become a doctor. "I said, 'I don't think so,'" recalls Dr. Jauregui today with a laugh. "I grew up thinking that doctors were men and that blood was disgusting, not feminine at all. I had many ideas of what I wanted to be: a hairdresser, a cashier at a grocery store, or a teacher." At the time, Patricia was attending a government-run school in Moyahua, a tiny town in Zacatecas, Mexico where her family had lived for generations. Sixth grade was the last year that education was free there; after that, students walked three miles to another school on the outskirts of town and paid to attend. The combination of distance and cost assured that few women continued their schooling. "Some of my friends in elementary school were very smart, but couldn't continue," recalls Patricia now, "either for financial reasons or because their parents couldn't see the point. Most girls in the town grew up to be housewives."

Patricia's parents valued education and wanted their daughter in school. And when she enrolled in a seventh-grade class in animal care, her thoughts of becoming a hairdresser or a cashier vanished. But she almost didn't make it into the class. Told that she could take bee keeping, meat processing, agriculture or animal care, Patricia had opted for animal care. It was an unconventional choice: girls, it was generally understood, learned to keep bees or process foods; boys learned to grow crops or take care of animals. To make matters more complex, Patricia was the only girl interested in animal care. The teacher decided to give Patricia a test, which he hoped would prove that the class was no place for her. He was the first of many teachers to discover that Patricia was not someone to underestimate. "I scored equally high in all subjects," she remembers, "so I was able to enroll. And really, that's where I started picking up an interest in medicine. We were vaccinating and castrating pigs and doing minor surgeries like hernia repairs. We worked with pigs, chickens and goats. I was injecting three-day-old pigs with vitamins A, D and E. Every procedure was an exciting challenge."

As Patricia neared the end of the eighth grade, she and her family grew increasingly uncertain about what to do next. Patricia was becoming more and more interested in training to become a doctor, but her school in the region stopped after the ninth grade. To continue her education after that, Patricia would have to move to the nearest city, a move that was both unthinkable and unaffordable for a family that by then numbered seven. Patricia's mother Emma decided it was time to take her family to the United States, where all of her children could attend high school.

Emma was a bold woman. When she was pregnant with Patricia—her first child—she decided that Patricia would be born in the United States. Emma's husband, Abel, had been crossing the border since he was a teenager; every summer, he, like most of the men in Moyahua, traveled north to California's Central Valley to harvest crops. "It's like a ghost town in the summer when people are in the United States, working," says Patricia of Moyahua. "The elderly, women and children are the only ones left."

Emma received the entry permit she needed to cross the border, and she and Abel agreed that when he took his next trip north, she would be with him. "It was a really big thing," says Patricia of her mother's decision. "My mom was warned by family

114

members and friends that California was a place for men. My dad bought the plane tickets, and they left secretly." Patricia was born in Los Banos, California, on January 7, 1973.

When Patricia was 2 months old, the family returned to the family homestead in Moyahua. Over the next two years, Emma had two sons, Alberto and Pedro. When Patricia was 3, the family left for the United States together. Soon Patricia's life and education took on the cadence of the crops: every April she left for the States; every December she returned to Mexico. "I remember it was fun," she says. "I looked forward to the three-day trips over the border, when we got to sleep in hotels and eat in many different restaurants. Looking back, it must have been challenging to have different sets of friends and to adjust to different schools, but at that time, it was just part of life. Even though we moved so much, I remember having a sense of confidence and security. My parents kept stability within the family. We always had enough, especially love.

"I was an energetic and happy kid, and because I was the oldest, I was very much the leader. I grew up thinking that I could just do anything. I was really creative. I had a tough time answering 'What's your favorite subject?' at school because I liked everything. I got good grades in the United States and in Mexico."

When Patricia reached the sixth grade, her parents decided to move back to Mexico permanently, hoping to provide more stability for their family. Patricia's mother had two more daughters, Maricela and Lilia Corina. Patricia's dad opened a grocery store, but to make ends meet, again returned to the United States seasonally to pick crops.

When Patricia finished the eighth grade, Emma and the children visited Abel in California. This time, Emma had made up her mind that the family would stay north of the border. "My brothers and I were a little hesitant," Patricia says, "because we didn't think we could speak English again and because my little sisters didn't speak English at all."

The family settled in Union City, where Patricia's Uncle Samuel lived. After spending a few months in Samuel's house, the family crowded into a one-bedroom apartment. But luck was with them. "Soon after," remembers Patricia, "we were driving around and we saw a house that was for sale. My dad said, 'Let's look at it,' but the rest of us stayed inside the car, convinced that we couldn't afford it. My dad went inside. He got the telephone number, called, asked my uncle for a loan and made it happen. It was a three-bedroom house with a big yard. The neighborhood was a little run-down, but it was quite safe."

Patricia prepared to start the ninth grade at James Logan High School and spent the summer taking writing and reading classes. "I wanted to be ready," she remembers. By the time high school started, she was.

"Once school started, everything was really simple, too simple," Patricia says. "So I went to see my counselor, Mrs. Hope, and told her that I wanted more challenging classes. I was taking Algebra I. She placed me in Algebra II/Trigonometry, and I got C's on quizzes. So I had to go back and tell her that Algebra I was fine." But Patricia's request sparked Hope's interest, and the counselor began to ask about her career plans. "I told her that I wanted to go to college, but realistically, I couldn't afford it," Patricia says. "She said, 'Don't worry. Just do well in your classes and the money will come.' She helped me pick classes and find scholarships. She was wonderful. Most of my teachers were great mentors. I think teachers like students who have an eagerness to learn, and I was like that."

115

When she started at James Logan High, Patricia was one of 3,000 students, taking classes taught exclusively in English; in Mexico, she had been one of 20, learning exclusively in Spanish. She found herself developing two sets of friends at Logan: teens she'd met on the first day of school, mainly Mexican immigrants who were bilingual or spoke only Spanish, and teens from many backgrounds whom she'd met in her college prep classes. She worked throughout high school, first answering phones at Pizza Hut, then as a cashier at McDonald's, then at a video store and finally, at the local library—her favorite job— with a program designed to improve library services for the Latino community.

"In high school, I thought that I could change the world, that I had absolute power to do anything," Patricia remembers. "The summer after my sophomore year, I went to a

a. Patricia at 6 months. b. Patricia at 3, with her brothers Alberto and Pedro. c. Patricia at 19, in Union City with her family.

program at Berkeley. My dad didn't want to give me permission to go, but I knew that it was important for my future. He was worried about my daily commute on the train." The Berkeley program focused on bio-medical science and introduced participants to scientific research. While she was there, Patricia heard about SMYSP from another participant. When she returned to Logan, she asked the vice principal—who she knew was a Stanford graduate—to look into the program for her. Soon after, she had an application.

Patricia hadn't lost the passion she'd developed working with animals in the seventh grade. She was still drawn to medicine and thought the SMYSP program would help her to decide if she truly wanted to become a doctor. She applied and was accepted. But it was not easy to convince her parents to allow her to leave home for five weeks. "I always had to struggle to get them to let me go away," she remembers. "Finally, they agreed, and dropped me off on the first day. My mom was in tears, and Union City is only 30 minutes away!"

116   Patricia worked in the heart and lung transplant unit at Stanford Hospital and, occasionally, in the ER. "I missed my first ER shift because I was scared," she says. "Finally, I had to go, and it was a very insightful experience. Each ER patient was a

special gift to me. The first patient was a man who had been shot and had an open-heart surgery, which I observed. Unfortunately, the man died during the surgery. When the doctor informed the family, they blamed him for their loss. I immediately became aware of the degree of responsibility that a doctor has. Another patient was a pregnant Spanish-speaking woman who came in with vaginal bleeding. She was afraid she was having a miscarriage. I was holding her hand. When the fetal heartbeat was audible, the doctor asked me to translate, but there was no need. She squeezed my hand very tight, signaling that she knew what I was going to say. These experiences showed me that there is a lot that a doctor can do for a patient. I experienced both the disappointment of not being able to save a life and the excitement of helping a person."

a. Patricia on her honeymoon with her husband, Alvino Jauregui. b. Patricia with her daughter Leilani and SMYSP's founder, Marilyn Winkleby.

It was her time at SMYSP, Patricia says, that really convinced her that she could become a doctor. Her experiences at the program also helped to win over her parents and to influence her younger brothers and sisters. "I was the first one to go to college both in my immediate and extended family," she says. "It made a career choice more tangible for everyone else. My brother Alberto graduated from Universal Technical Institute in Arizona. Pedro obtained his BS at Cal Poly San Luis Obispo and his master's in communications and library science at San Jose State. Maricela is currently attending San Diego State University, and Corina is a straight-A student at James Logan."

Patricia herself applied to Stanford and was accepted. "I was so happy when I came back," she says. "I couldn't believe it." She threw herself into college with the same enthusiasm with which she'd embraced high school. But she had to work harder.

"I wasn't used to studying very much," she says. "Most students were studying on weekends, while I was going out. I had to learn to go to the library and concentrate. When I was a sophomore, I really doubted that medicine was the right choice for me. Pre-med courses were difficult, and I had little personal time. My mother didn't want me to become a doctor. She thought that it required too much sacrifice. I started to think so, too." Alternate career choices again filled Patricia's head. This time, she thought

117

about becoming a Spanish teacher or a social worker, "something that would require less discipline on my part," she says. But in the end, she stayed with medicine. "I didn't want to give up," she says. "I'd been given this opportunity to be at Stanford, and I thought I owed it to myself to wind up with a job that I would really like. I volunteered at a local clinic, and the patient contact reminded me why I was interested in medicine. During the summer, I worked at Tiburcio Vasquez Community Clinic in Union City. It was wonderful to care and translate for people I knew."

Patricia also found that her Stanford classes became easier as she persevered. Organic chemistry—which she'd initially perceived as "an awful foreign language"—was gradually demystified. A turning point came when she got the highest grade in the class on a mid-term she'd been dreading: "I thought, 'Me, little me, I got the highest grade in an organic chemistry class at Stanford!' It was the boost I needed. It showed me that if I really tried, I could do it."

Patricia was president of the Chicano Latino Medical Student Association at Stanford in her junior year and organized a conference for minority, low-income high school students who were interested in medicine. It featured a talk by famed Stanford anatomy lecturer John Dolph, who she had first heard speak at SMYSP. Dolph handed out 3-D glasses to all of the students and led them on a fantastic voyage through the human body. Next came the real thing, when students were given a chance to participate in an anatomy lab. "We held the event on Dia de los Muertos (Day of the Dead) to honor the people who volunteer their bodies for medical science," says Patricia. "We had a great turnout, about 120 students. We had financial aid and college workshops. The whole event grew out of my experience with SMYSP."

After she graduated from Stanford, Patricia took a year's break from school to work for a biomedical company and to plan her wedding to her high school sweetheart, Alvino Jauregui. "He has been my biggest supporter throughout my journey in becoming a doctor," Patricia says. "He is a wonderful man who comes from a single-parent home. He worked very hard to finance his studies. He majored in business administration at San Jose State University." The two were married at Saint Joseph's Cathedral in San Jose in the spring of 1996, with staff and classmates from SMYSP in attendance.

A few months after her wedding, Patricia drove south with her husband to begin medical school. She'd been accepted at the University of California, Los Angeles and at the University of Southern California, and had decided on USC. "When I started medical school, I was very excited, very happy to be there," she remembers, "but it was over-whelming, trying to balance everything. We had been married for three months, and my husband was unemployed in a new city. On the first day, a panel of students told us that divorces commonly occurred throughout medical school. I knew that I would have to be the best medical student and the best wife that I could, to end up with both a career in family practice and a family of my own."

Medical school improved over time. "In the first year, it was all book work," Patricia recalls, "and we only saw patients once a week—and even they were 'standardized' patients played by actors. It was so intense. By the second year, the material got more interesting, and we were working with real patients. The third year was great. I worked in the hospital ward. It was more hours, but I was finally doing what I wanted to be

118

doing. By then, I knew that I'd made the right decision. In the fourth year, I focused on electives that I found interesting, like neurology, nephrology and dermatology."

Patricia graduated in 2000 and was accepted to the three-year San Jose Medical Center Family Practice Residency Program. Six months after she began her residency, she gave birth to her daughter, Leilani (Hawaiian for "heavenly flower"). As a family practice resident, she has now delivered many babies herself, though she takes care of everyone from newborns to the elderly.

As she begins her career as a doctor, Patricia notes the difference SMYSP has made in her life's evolution. "The program gave me confidence and solidified my interest in medicine. It taught me that there were people who really did care about my future, even though they didn't know me personally," she says. "That made me realize that there are different ways of helping and supporting people in their day-to-day lives as well as in their long-term goals."

NICOTIN

ine)

Nose Candy...

ystem (CNS)

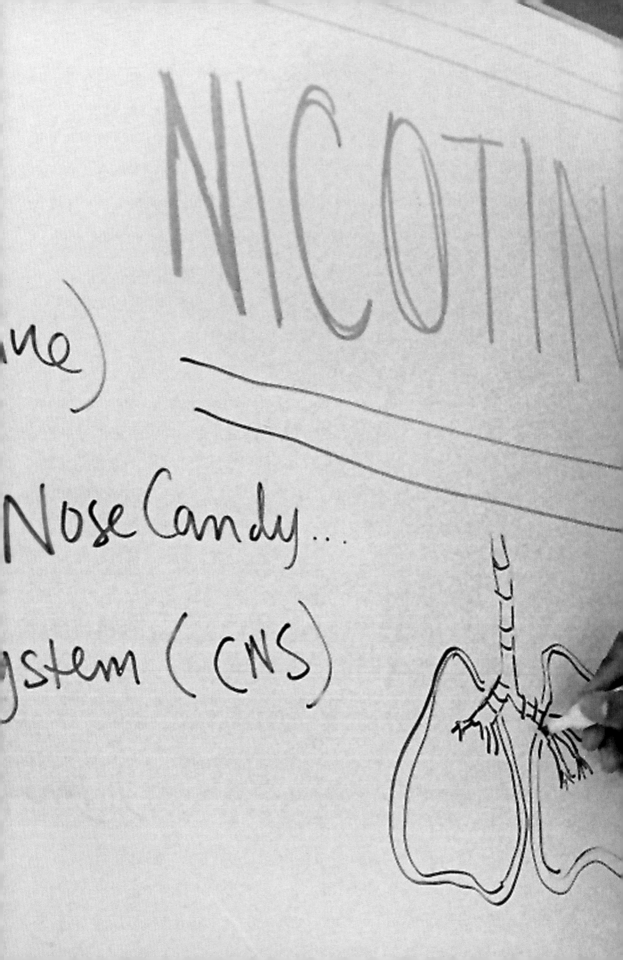

addiction:
the science of abuse

Today's lecture subject is familiar to the SMYSP students—and to people across the nation. The topic is addiction, and the students are hearing from "addictionologist" Dr. Barry Rosen. Rosen is tall and bearded, and he speaks with an oddly matched intensity and serenity: he is passionate, but his fervor seems to rest on a base of calm. He is an internist who spent nine years working as an ER doctor, but after hundreds of nights of witnessing, firsthand, the medical havoc that drug abuse can wreak, he gave up the ER and now devotes his practice exclusively to treating addiction. He is now the medical director of the Sequoia Alcohol & Drug Recovery Center in Redwood City, an innovative clinic known for its "bio-psycho-social-spiritual" approach to addiction. Dr. Rosen has come to talk to the SMYSP students about what addiction is, why it happens and what can be done about it.

He starts with some sobering statistics. "Eighty to 90 percent of people in this country can use alcohol and drugs without getting into trouble," he begins, "but 10 to 20 percent of users do get into trouble, and it's a big problem for them, their families and the country. Five percent of deaths in America are due to alcohol, and alcoholics increase their risk of post-operative complications 50 to 100 times. Twenty-eight percent of kids in schools today come from addicted family systems."

The issues around substance abuse are, Dr. Rosen says, ubiquitous. And yet few social systems are sensitive to the problem. "The whole approach to addiction medicine is primitive," he tells the students. "Addiction looks like a choice, looks like misconduct. But we now have enough science to know that addiction is a brain disease, and to know that telling an alcoholic to drink normally is like telling someone with inflammatory diarrhea to control their stool.

"I look at this problem through four different lenses, four different dimensions of life: biological, psychological, social and spiritual. People drink and use drugs to feel good, to relieve stress, to socialize, to escape, to manage life. No one consciously wants to get into trouble or create chaos in their lives. In our culture, there is a strong message that if you want to feel better, you take something. The question then is, 'What is okay to take?' Culture has a lot to do with what behaviors are considered normal. With alcohol, for example: drinking is more acceptable in the Irish culture than it is in the Jewish culture. Cultural biases are going to determine how people feel about acknowledging that they drink alcohol."

But how does someone become an alcoholic? At what point does a simple drink become a toxic bullet? Rosen plots out a line on the blackboard: at one end, he writes "use," on the other end, "dependency." Above "use," he writes "pleasure and fun."

"That is how it starts," he says, "but then, as one moves in the direction of abuse and dependency, it begins to shift." Across the line, he plots out "party," "pleasure/problem," "family issues," and finally, "big problem."

"By the time you see the disease, it's frequently already in its later stages," he says. "Addicts take a long time to go to the doctor because they never think it's the drug that's the problem: it's the wife, the children, the job, et cetera. Also, some people don't call for help because there's a bias against addicts, a belief that they are doing this to themselves because they're weak and morally depraved. I want to help remove that bias."

Dr. Rosen details the first component of addiction, biology. "Substance dependency is sustained by compelling biological and physiological demands," he says. "You've heard of a concept called homeostasis?" The students nod; they covered homeostasis in their neuroanatomy lab. "Okay," he says, "so you know that the body has a mechanism to balance itself, to sustain a point of normalcy. Now, with all disease, including addiction, there is a new set point called allostasis, which is the homeostasis of the disease state. The body feels more natural in this state, and the disease has its own capacity to sustain itself. Both genetic predisposition and protracted drug use cause changes to the central nervous system in addicts. This alters the regulation of the neuro-receptor mechanisms, rendering the addict more tolerant of the drug."

One of the students puts up a hand. "Could you explain how methadone works?" she asks.

"Methadone is what's called an opiate agonist," Rosen says. "An agonist is something that behaves like the drug inside your body at the proper receptor site—in this case, at the opiate receptor."

"Does it work?" the student asks. She hesitates, then adds, "The reason I'm asking is that my mom is trying to get off heroin, and she has started taking it."

"Yes, methadone works biologically," says Rosen. "Many people are significantly helped by methadone. They can return to normal life free of heroin because methadone satisfies the central nervous system's need for the opiate effect. But society may still have a problem with it." He casts the student a sympathetic look. "This is not a critical statement, it's a factual statement," he tells her. Then he looks to the entire class. "At times, there can be an odd relationship between what works clinically and what society sanctions.

"The world is run by money and power," he says. "Today, illicit drugs represent 10 percent of the world's GNP. Huge resources sustain the acquisition and allocation of illicit substances, and we can't casually dispose of that reality. Recreational drugs will be accessible to adolescents, and adolescents will be able to choose whether to use them. And, in a number of cases, people who do decide to use drugs will get addicted. Until the culture and the society are truly on board, it will be very difficult to dismantle the drug trade. And our adolescent culture is a using culture. The majority of kids smoke marijuana, and by 12th grade, 50 to 75 percent of kids are drinking."

123

"In my town, people drink a lot," says Marcus, "for fun. At all the parties, it's nothing but drinking."

"At my school," says Kamille, "you can get all kinds of drugs: pot, ecstasy, alcohol, LSD. Plenty of students are high within 30 minutes of getting to school."

Natalie mentions a friend who likes to go to raves. "They all take ecstasy," she says. "My friend went and dropped. I told her she shouldn't have, but she said, 'How can something so wonderful be so harmful?' I don't understand how they can be so into it."

"Well," says Dr. Rosen, "it's like a hike. You don't know: a hike can be potentially wonderful or awful. Ecstasy can be, too. But there is a biological difference between adolescents who take drugs and adults who do. When you're an adolescent, your liver and your central nervous system are not fully developed. Damage to these systems in adolescence can lead to anxiety and other disorders later in life."

There is a psychic cost, too. "If every time you come up against struggles, you use drugs, then you don't develop fortitude," says Rosen. "The body and the mind both need to work and engage the struggle of life. When you stay in bed for one week, you lose 30 percent of your bone mass..." The implication hangs in the air: what happens to the mind when it is not challenged? It is a perfect segue into the second of Dr. Rosen's four lenses for studying addiction: the psychology of the disease.

"At the psychological level, addiction is driven by denial, shame and by the hunger for love," Rosen says. "Gradually, using the drug changes one's personality, the sense of self. Cocaine can make you feel you're the king of the world for seven and a half minutes. It can catapult you over struggles with self-esteem. Eventually, as addiction takes over, the relationship with the drug becomes an essential coping device, and life isn't considered worth living without it. The user can't see how damaging the drug truly is, and that denial system ensures ongoing use even when there are bad consequences."

The students seem to feel comfortable with Dr. Rosen. He is not judgmental, just factual. He is not a hard-liner from the 'Just say no' school. "Drugs and alcohol are not bad, when used properly with the right intention," he said at the beginning of his talk. "It's when they're used improperly that they cause enormous problems." Now that Rosen has mentioned adolescent drug use, the student who earlier asked about methadone raises her hand again to volunteer her own story. "I took acid at school with my friends," she says.

"And what happened?" Rosen asks her.

"I got very paranoid. I couldn't stop crying. To get away from everyone, I slept in a closet at school. I felt suicidal."

"What stopped you from calling for help?" asks Rosen.

124

"We were afraid of what would happen to us," she replies. "We were afraid our families would know."

Another student says, "I did acid two times. Both times it was a very bad experience. But I didn't need help in those particular cases. I don't believe in addiction."

"Well," asks Rosen, "what does it mean when somebody does lose control?"

Again, the conversation has segued into one of the mechanisms Dr. Rosen uses to explain the disease: his third lens focuses on the social side of addiction. "In America, there is a multibillion dollar industry—legal and illegal—that makes it socially normative to drink or use something to feel better. Our medical establishment is not tuned to sorting out normal use from abnormal use, unless the users are underage or the drugs are illegal. And family systems tend to shift with the gradual onset of addictive disorder and become an integral part of the disease. Shame and denial are common in families—it's the refusal to see the elephant in the living room."

Gradually, Rosen says, the drugs become the organizing principle of the social set and settings. A person watching their own life falter can constantly downshift the definition of normal to reflect the lives of other addicts and find excuses to explain problems away: "It's common for all people to evolve a social set that reflects what they most like to do. People who are addicts find themselves going only to places where people are using; they avoid places where drug use isn't the norm."

Finally, there is the fourth lens: spirituality. "There is compelling need to find meaning and purpose in life," says Dr. Rosen. "If you don't feel like you're *in* your life, a drug can become your god. For the addict, drugs become the sustaining, driving force of existence. The fundamental nature of addiction is that drugs become the organizing factors of your life. Whatever you hold dear, whatever you come to know about the sacred and life itself, is commandeered by the addiction."

125

khalil
abdullah

"Throw him into the river, and he will come up with a fish in his mouth."
— Arabic proverb

Khalil Abdullah is barely out of his teens, but already he has an easy assurance and self-confidence that he carries gracefully. His body has an athlete's fluidity, his mind a sharpness honed on Sacramento city streets and in the classroom. He is now finishing an electrical engineering degree at the University of Pennsylvania. When he's done, he will be the first in his family to graduate from college. "In high school, I would put my report cards on the refrigerator—not to brag, but to just show what was going on," he remembers. "People would walk into the house and say, 'Oh man, look at your grades. You should go to college.' I said, 'Okay,' but I didn't know where or what I would study."

There weren't a lot of traditional role models around. Like so many of the families that SMYSP students come out of, Khalil's was strong but fractured: his parents divorced when he was 9 months old and by the time he was 12, Khalil had seen two stepfathers come and go as well. "After that, my mom just said, 'Forget it, I don't want to be married anymore,'" he remembers. Khalil, his mom and his older sister moved in with his grandmother. It was a house full of people coming and going, some stable, some not, some working, some not.

"It gets hard," says Khalil, looking back. "It seemed to me that some of my uncles had given up. They were young in '85 or '86, when crack swept through the neighborhood; that had a lot to do with it. Because, without knowing what they were doing, some of my relatives and a lot of their friends started using crack. I don't know who I can blame for that, but I can't really blame them. I think that created times in their lives when they just didn't want to do much of anything. It's like when it's time to start being responsible, you either answer the call, or fall victim. If you aren't ready to answer—get a job or do something—you get left behind."

Khalil was born in October 1980 in Sacramento, though his parents were both from the South: his mom from Jackson, Mississippi; his dad from Shreveport, Louisiana. His mother was a Baptist Christian; his father a Muslim and the one who gave Khalil his Islamic name, which means "close friend."

Looking back on his early years, Khalil describes himself as a child who was "worse than mischievous, but not wild." He taught himself to read by watching *Sesame Street* and the scrolling letters on infomercials. At home, he played games with his mom's second husband, who , he recalls, was "like an older brother." In the neighborhood, he hung out with the kids who lived on his street: Afghan immigrants, Mexican Americans and African Americans.

When school started, Khalil went to Peter Burnett Elementary, a public school in south Sacramento. His intellect ensured that he did well in his classes, but when it came to his classmates, he struggled. "My biggest problem was getting along with people. If there was ever a fight, I would be mixed up in it," he remembers of those first school years. "I had a bad temper and I didn't like losing." But there were bright spots. Khalil's second-grade teacher, Marilyn Ferris-Steed, took him roller-skating on Saturdays. "I think she saw that I had a problem and maybe this would help," he says. It did. From that point on, Khalil never gave her any problems in class.

Khalil loved to hang out with his Uncle Eric, one of the most important men in his early life. Eric was the outcast of the family—he was unemployed and struggling to find his place in the world—but to Khalil, Eric was a good friend and steady companion. "I

128

didn't understand that he was always around because he wasn't working," says Khalil. "I just knew he was able to play with me all the time, and he took time to listen to me and encourage me."

Sports were big events, in school and out: tetherball, kickball, basketball, baseball and team Frisbee. At home, Khalil was an avid *Cosby Show* fan, and he and his second stepfather would watch sports together. "He was older, not like my other stepfather," he remembers. "He had a trucking business: he had a big rig, and my mom managed his business." Khalil and his mother had their share of run-ins. She was tough, and he was the kind of child who never accepted things at face value, who always wanted an explanation. "I couldn't listen for the sake of listening," he remembers. "I always had to see *why* I should listen.

"I can remember a time when I was disciplined three times a day for 10 days. But let me preface this story by saying that my mother's disciplinary acts were warranted. I'd been stealing. I was about 7 when I got caught, but I had been getting away with it before that. I was taking stuff: my mom's jewelry and other things. She knew it was me and I finally gave up after the 10 days. She would say, 'Lying leads to stealing and stealing leads to killing,' and 'When you lie, you're giving way to a dishonest lifestyle.' It finally registered with me, and when I was about 9, I stopped doing it.

"Looking at the bigger picture, I have to commend her for the way she managed all the things you have to think about and care about when you're raising kids. She always had to look out for us. She always did her best to make me a man and to show me how to do better."

Khalil's mother taught him to manage money and her savvy about it ensured that there was enough of it. "We always had food in the house," he says. "We had everything we needed, but not fancy, brand-name things. That's where I learned that it didn't really matter how your stuff looked as opposed to how it functioned." But when Khalil's mother tired of her third husband's drinking, she decided to leave him, and the financial picture changed. Khalil, his mom and older sister moved in with his grandmother and applied for government assistance. "The money was definitely tighter at that point," Khalil says. His grandmother was working two part-time jobs: at the post office and at a classified advertising newspaper. His mom worked as a data entry clerk at a bank. Khalil's grandmother, a Baptist, was so strict she wouldn't let the kids play cards in her house, or say "darn" or "liar."

Khalil had been in California's Gifted and Talented Education (GATE) program for gifted students since the second grade, but it was when he got to the seventh grade that school really began to kick in. "I had this English teacher, Ms. Alice Krumenacher. She was strict from the beginning. We learned 20 words a week, words like 'bucolic.' And we were reading so many books in her class. We read a book called *Carlotta* about a Spanish girl on a ranch in early California. We read *Richard III* and *Hamlet*."

Khalil was happy. His rebellious streak had died out, and he found himself content, "just doing what I was supposed to do, which was basically doing right by my mother, having friends and fun, and doing well in school. I can't remember anyone telling me about the future. Maybe my grandmother. But I didn't worry. I could already tell at that point that I was different from a lot of people. I knew right from wrong. That had to have been my mother's influence. So I thought I would turn out all right, but I didn't know what the turn out would be."

Khalil enrolled in Sacramento's Grant Union High School. High school was easier academically than junior high for Khalil, and his social life bloomed: "I would chase after all these older girls. But I kept up with my work; I was ranked in the top 20 or 30 and I didn't slip much." But a near miss in the 10th grade proved to Khalil that he couldn't afford to be too cavalier: "I met my best friend, Cornelius Maurice Turner, in this 10th-grade, college prep English class. He asked for my telephone number so we could play basketball together, but I didn't give it to him. Finally, we started talking on the phone and hanging out. And it was just great. I never had a friend like that. So we

Khalil in a portrait for his 10th-grade yearbook at Sacramento's Grant Union High School.

would talk about the girls in the class and how much we hated the teacher and all this other stuff, and before I knew it, we weren't doing anything in class. I had an A in the first quarter, and in the second quarter I got an F. We realized we couldn't go on like that. We stayed good friends. I would always spend nights over at Maurice's house and eat up all the food in the kitchen. I love Maurice's dad, Rovan, very much because he never complained about me being in his house."

Maurice, says Khalil, "seemed like he never really wanted to go on to college." Khalil's mom and sister never talked about the idea of college. And Khalil himself wasn't thinking much about what he wanted to do after high school. College was just a vague notion, only mentioned when the report cards went up on the refrigerator. But then, when Khalil was in the 11th grade, his physics teacher, Getu Hammid, gave him an application to SMYSP. "He was always trying to throw extra opportunities at us. So he asked me if I'd like to go to Stanford for the summer. And I was like, 'Why wouldn't I?' I'd heard of Stanford from watching its sports teams on TV. He gave me an application, and I got it in by the deadline.

"I wasn't sure that I wanted to be a doctor. But I also wasn't sure that I *didn't* want to be a doctor. That's why I applied. I had my first interview over the phone, with a counselor named Jason Stephenson. Then they told me to come down to Stanford for another interview. I had to be there by 9 a.m., so we left real early in the morning. My Uncle Nate and his friend Pat took me. I had pressed my clothes, but I didn't want to wear them because we had to sit in the car for three hours for the drive. Uncle Nate wouldn't go over any bridges or take any roads where you had to pay tolls. He was nervous about the bridges and stingy for the tolls. But he was cool; he started helping me out all the time.

"When we got to Stanford, I took my pressed clothes and got dressed in the bathroom and then came out for the interview. Our interview group was given an ethics question. We had to say what we would do if there was a treatment that cured cancer but to create it, you had to wipe out two acres of trees for each dose—which would lead to massive pollution. I tried to always have something pertinent to say. That was my strategy."

It worked. Khalil was accepted into SMYSP in 1998. It was, he says, "one of the

130

best experiences I had ever had, just as far as being totally focused. I was listening in the classes and asking questions. I worked at the morgue at the Palo Alto VA Hospital. Dr. Ahmed was running the morgue. I liked him a lot. At first, he seemed real strict, but after a while, I saw he had to be strict to maintain safety in the morgue. Some of the bodies would be infected with hepatitis, and he did what he had to do to keep the interns safe. I wore three pairs of gloves. It was so interesting helping with the autopsies that I even got past the smell. We would peel the skin away and then saw open the rib cage and identify all the body parts. Sam would show us things and explain them, like an enlarged liver in an alcoholic, or lungs that were black and terrible-looking. So I don't smoke after seeing that.

"My SMYSP research project topic was on multiple personality disorder. We went to see a psychiatrist at the Stanford Hospital, and he gave us books about the disorder. And he let us watch videos of his patients who suffered from the disorder, which showed how they'd become like a baby at one point and how a woman would talk like she was a man. We learned so much stuff and wrote a 10-page paper about it. In school, when I was writing research papers, I would go to the encyclopedia, and that was pretty much it. Never would I have been able to go to a doctor and ask about it. So the resources were just tremendous."

Khalil also met one of his best friends at SMYSP: Jason Stephenson, the person who'd interviewed him on the phone and who was one of the program's student directors. "Meeting him was special for me because I hadn't known anyone who was black who had graduated from college," says Khalil. "He would tell me all kinds of stuff, like times when he messed up and times when he succeeded, and the way he told stories was funny as hell. I thought that we would lose touch with each other over time, but when I got back to high school for my senior year, we kept communicating via e-mail. And when I got to college, we would hang out together when he was visiting. He became more like an older brother. We could be more candid with each other because he wasn't an authority figure anymore.

"Jason's just finished his first year of medical school at Washington University Medical School. Recently, I told him about this position I got with the Society of Black Engineers: I'd been on the chapter board for two years, and I decided to step up to the plate and run for the regional board. I was telling Jason what my strategy was—which all came from stuff that I'd learned from him. And I ended up getting elected! After he heard that story, he decided to run for president of his medical school class. And he ended up getting elected by a landslide. A week and a half ago, I got fitted for my tuxedo for his wedding; he's getting married next month. It's programs like SMYSP that make way for relationships like that to be formed. They even put together a directory for all the participants from years past to keep in touch. I love it."

It was Jason, and the program's co-director that year, DeLise Cousins, who convinced Khalil that he had a shot at college and even an Ivy League school if he wanted. "They're the ones who got me thinking about schools like Stanford and Harvard," says Khalil. "But, in different ways, everyone at SMYSP helped me to see that I had more opportunities than I thought." DeLise told him about the University of Pennsylvania, that it was a member of the Ivy League, that it had a beautiful campus.

131

"When I left the program, I hit the ground running," says Khalil. "Pretty soon after I got back, I had all the applications. I applied to schools like MIT, Stanford, Penn, Princeton and UC Davis. I think I applied to seven in all. I got into Davis and Penn." Khalil headed to Penn.

"When I got there, there was pain," he says. "Pleasure and pain. That's when the academics hit me. I was pretty sure I wanted to be an engineer. I came in as a computer science student, but I switched to electrical engineering. But it was difficult. I wasn't used to having to be so academically disciplined. I wasn't really ready and I was in a new place. I almost came home. My mom talked me into finishing the first semester, and after that, I decided to stay. I saw that I'd made it. Also, they had a minority student support office, and there was a lady in there who would listen to everything I had to say. She knew I was from far away. Her name was Donna Hampton. She and I got really close. She didn't know at first how rough it was for me, but after she found out, she would look out for me. She would buy me birthday cards and hug me and encourage me. Without her, I can't say that I'd still be there."

Khalil is a senior at Penn now. With each passing year, he grows more hopeful, more sure of who he is and the work he wants to do. He credits an array of people for their compassion and their time, for convincing him of his worth and his abilities: "The principal of my high school, Mr. Larry Brown, saw that I was helping myself, and he helped me in so many ways. I thought he was the wisest guy on the planet. Maurice's dad helped me a lot, too: he would buy me stuff at the grocery store and he bought my tuxedo for the prom. And my Uncle Eric, the one that walks around, he brought me something different. When I look at him, I see what I could have been. But I still love and respect him because he's seen things other people haven't seen, and he'll warn me about things and he always encourages me. Because he didn't have a job to go to, he had more time to listen to my issues, and I needed that. And a lot of people were examples for me. Jason was an example of a college student, and Mr. Brown was an example of a guy who everybody loves who does good things for his people. Dr. Ahmed at the morgue showed me that all the help I needed I would get. And they all did this independently of one another. One time my Spanish teacher, Mr. James Hoover, sent me five bucks at a time when I was really hungry, and I went straight to McDonald's. He and I had become friends because I paid attention in class and noticed the patterns in conjugating verbs. I always go to see him when I'm home. I go to see all my old teachers who helped me: Mrs. Carter, Ms. Shoemaker, Mrs. Roberts, Mr. Celis, Mr. Hammid, my counselor Mr. Fields—the list goes on and on."

Though he is majoring in engineering, "eventually," Khalil says, "I want to end up in education. I'd like to be a high school principal. I figure by the time I get to be 40 or so, I will have quite a lot to share. I worry most now about how can I effect change and move forward. I want to help the people around me to develop themselves. Just recently, I helped my friends in Sacramento put their resumes together. I went home and they didn't have resumes, so we sat down and I showed them what I knew."

Of himself, Khalil says, "The path I've followed to this point has shown me that nothing is really guaranteed. I'm also thinking that life is a marathon and there are still a bunch of other things I have to do. Who knows what's coming? I'm only 20. For all the stuff that I've done up to this point, I'm still not there; I haven't arrived. I've accepted that I have to keep striving for what's next, and that's exciting. It helps me keep things in perspective.

"I know that any success I've experienced is not an accident. Each time I planned to do well, I did. The times I didn't have a plan, I didn't do well. I try to remind myself of that as often as I can. I might be able to skate by in some cases, like I did in high school, but it hit me in the face when I got to college. I've had to deal with the lesson that my success will not be an accident."

Khalil Abdullah

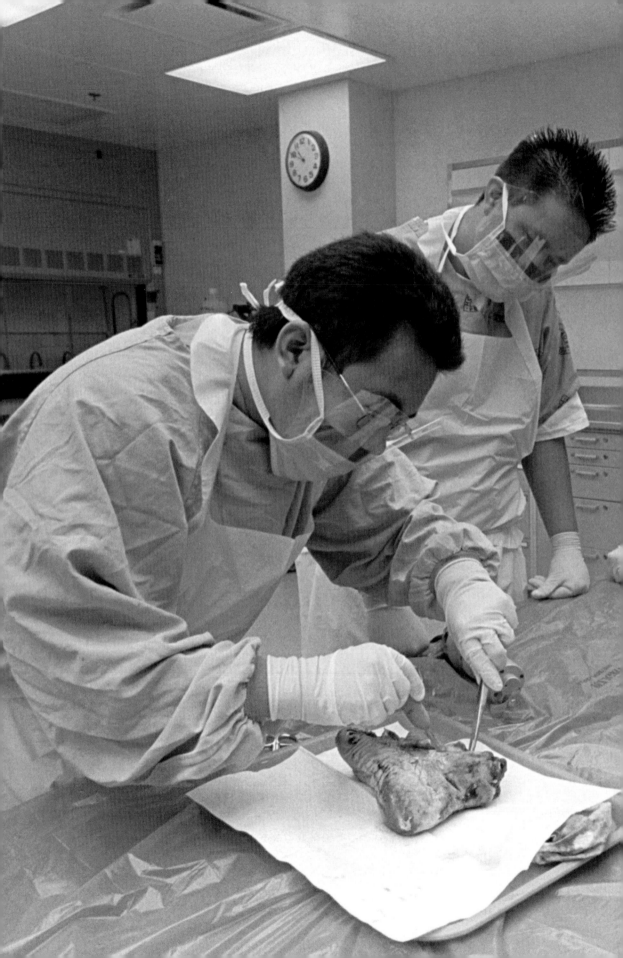

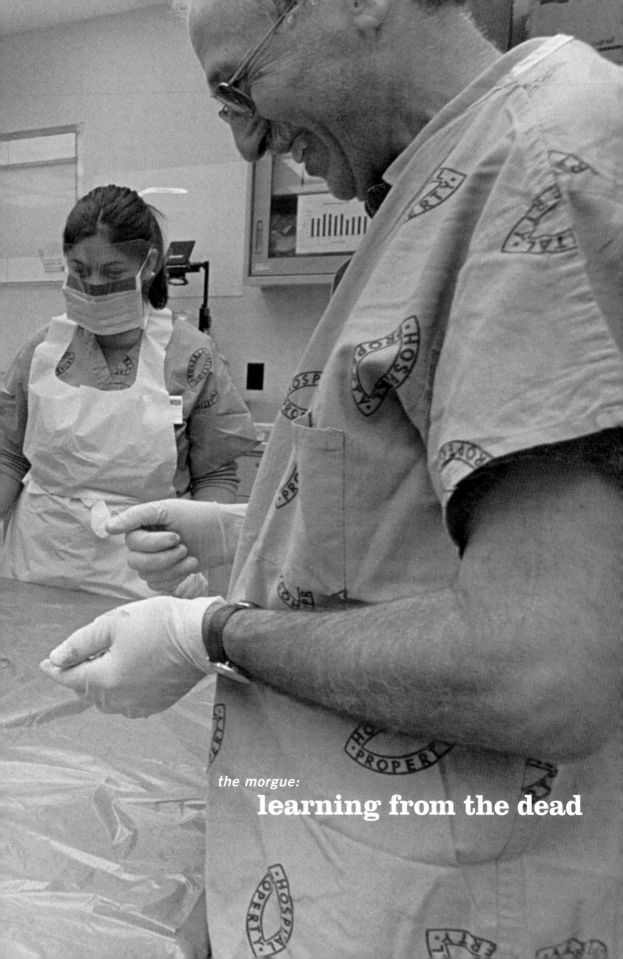

the morgue:
learning from the dead

The morgue at the Palo Alto VA Hospital is on the building's top floor, down a corridor, not readily in sight—which no doubt is how people in a hospital like it. Inside, it looks industrial: big, well lit, with lots of sinks and flat, steel surfaces. Doors along one wall lead to body storage lockers; tools in evidence range from soap dispensers to saws.

"People think we are just a place where they bring dead bodies," says Dr. Salah Ahmed, who has worked in the morgue for the last 20 years and who oversees the lab. "People don't realize how much knowledge is here. But when the students come, they see it."

His point is neatly proved by what's going on in the morgue at that very moment. Two pathologists are leading doctors and students through a post-mortem; they have just finished two autopsies, and the organs they've removed are laid out on stainless steel tables.

The pathologists, Dr. Fajardo and Dr. Kosek, both appear to be in their late 60s or early 70s, and they look like they have seen it all—many times. They handle each organ expertly, with a mixture of professional detachment and still-avid curiosity. Some 15 doctors from departments throughout the hospital have come to see these organs and to hear the pathologists' deconstructions of their patients' deaths. The three SMYSP interns assigned to the morgue—Tom, Thu and Ivan—bustle about with an air of authority, cleaning and organizing the room and stopping to listen whenever a particularly interesting or gruesome fact is shared. Two other SMYSP interns, Anthony and Thu's twin sister, Quynh, have come up from other departments to watch the post-mortems, too.

The first case the doctors discuss involves a man in his early 60s who suffered from alcoholism, portal hypertension and increasing weakness. Someone flips the light off, and the pathologists show a CT scan taken a year earlier. "The portal hypertension was caused by alcohol; you can see the damage," they point out. The pathologists also show an eco-cardiogram and point out that the right ventricle of the heart was enlarged. Then the lights come back on and they turn to the tissues.

"There are two interesting things here," says Dr. Fajardo, a stocky man with a pronounced European accent. "In the heart," he says, as he picks up the heart and holds it forth, "there are two very enlarged veins, which create a secondary chamber right below the pulmonary artery. I did a literature search and found that there is a rare condition in which the body has a double-chambered right ventricle." The doctors all lean in for a close look at the chambers.

"Now, here is another interesting component of this case," continues Dr. Fajarado. "This patient had very severe cirrhosis and an enlarged spleen. So this patient had two major problems, his heart and his liver." The pathologists have other viscera laid out: pieces of the patient's spine ("look at how much darker than normal the bone marrow is," they note, pointing to the dark, dense matter embedded in the vertebrae), the kidneys ("you'll note that these are small and wrinkled; he had evidence of renal failure") and the gastrointestinal tract ("note the ulcers here").

136

One of the program's counselors, Grace, has come to visit the morgue today. She is watching the doctors' faces as they listen to the pathologists. "It's wild," she says at one point. "All of these doctors… one day they're sitting with a person in their office and that's the patient, and then suddenly this"—she waves her hand across the organs arrayed on the table—"is the patient."

Certainly, the doctors seem detached, imperturbable, ultra-professional. They listen passively as Dr. Kosek, a wiry, athletic-looking man, details the second case. "This was a 68-year-old man with many severe physical and psychological symptoms," he begins. He mentions a number of the difficulties the patient suffered, including hyperthyroidism, diabetes and renal failure. The patient had had three coronary bypasses and carried a pacemaker. "The heart is enlarged and the spleen is huge," Dr. Kosek notes. He has cut a cross-section of the organ and laid it out; it is massive, nearly a foot long (in contrast to a cross-section of a healthy spleen, which is approximately 8 inches long). Tom cannot get over it. "I mean, look at this!" he whispers, pointing it out to Dr. Ahmed's teenage daughter Laleh, who is standing next to Tom by the soap dispensers. "It's *huge.*"

Laleh has a great enthusiasm for the morgue. She observed her first autopsy here when she was 9 years old and now spends all of her free time here. She has become fast friends with this year's three SMYSP morgue interns, and as Dr. Fajardo and Dr. Kosek discuss the cases, she talks with Tom about their future plans. Laleh intends to become a general surgeon or perhaps a cardiac surgeon. Tom plans to be a researcher, but, watching the pathologists, he says maybe he'd like to do what they do. "You could never mess up," he says to Laleh. "Right," she replies. "A slip-up wouldn't matter a bit."

When the pathologists' presentations are over, the doctors file out, back to their patients who are still alive and in one piece. Just after they leave, a SMYSP intern named Vivian shows up. She's on a short break from the oncology department and decided to head up to the morgue—it's a popular destination for the students, who know they will be welcomed by Dr. Ahmed and are sure to learn something new every time they visit. "Oh, everybody's here," she says with a smile as she surveys the room and sees SMYSPers scattered about.

"Hi Vivian," says Grace. She invites her over to look at the organs, and the two examine them together. Grace explains what the pathologists have just said. "Feel this,"she says, handing Vivian one of the organs. "You feel the calcification there?" Vivian nods as she runs her fingers over the surface.

Thu comes over to join them. When she first arrived and learned that she'd been assigned to work in the morgue, she was unnerved. She'd had a fear of ghosts and the dead for a long time, she explained to the other students at Todos Time, and she was uneasy at the idea of spending so much time around death. "I know that I'll be scared for the next five weeks," she'd said. "It's so creepy seeing brains in tubs and facing so much death." The counselors offered to have her transferred to a different department,

137

but Thu decided she should try to get over her qualms—and now, three weeks later, she seems relaxed and comfortable in the morgue.

"This is the trachea," Grace says to both girls as she points at something else on the table. "It's made out of cartilage. That's what keeps it open. Look, right here, this is where the vocal cords are."

She picks up another organ, which is lying in pieces and isn't readily identifiable. "Hey, Tom," she calls. "What's this?"

"Oh, the stomach," he says. After three weeks at the morgue, he has acquired the confidence of a pro. "We just dissected it so we could really examine it."

Tom comes over to join the girls, and the four look at the aorta of the first patient, which is dark and full of yellowed globules. "That's *scary*," says Grace. Dr. Ahmed looks up from what he's doing. "That's what McDonald's does to you," he says dryly. "Don't say that!" chorus the students in unison. They are laughing as they say it, but this is a serious point since fast food is *the* food of America, and obesity and diabetes have now reached epidemic levels in the country.

"These kids… we all know they come from underprivileged families," says Dr. Ahmed, sitting in his office while the students clean up the remains of the post-mortem outside. "With many of them, I wonder how they have managed to survive. But when they come here, it's as if they have forgotten all their hardships, and for those five weeks they are really focused on everything here. That's really amazing."

Dr. Ahmed is no stranger to struggle; 20 years earlier, he left everything behind when he moved from Iran to America in the wake of the Ayatollah Khomeni's rise to power. Every summer, he works at the morgue with the SMYSP interns. He has them begin by observing two or three autopsies, then he allows them to participate (though they are never allowed to work on infectious disease cases). He also gives each student a written assignment: they must choose an organ and write a paper on it. This year, Ivan has chosen to write on the heart, Thu on the lungs, and Tom on the spleen (hence his excitement over the post-mortem specimen).

"This program is too little," says Dr. Ahmed. "I personally wish it could last all summer and that it could take more students. But still…" he says, and his voice trails off. Then he smiles. "I love these kids, really," he says. "I wish I was in a good financial situation myself to help these kids, because they really deserve it. They just need someone to give them some help."

138   Dr. Ahmed gets up from his chair and wanders out to see how his pupils are progressing. Evidence of the recent post-mortem has disappeared, and Anthony, Quyhn and Vivian have returned to their departments. It is quiet again in the morgue. Tom asks if they

may start dissecting an amputated leg they have planned to work on that afternoon. Dr. Ahmed nods yes, it's okay to begin. They take up their tools and get to work.

the basel brothers

"Heaven is dark and yet out of it streams clear water."
— Afghan proverb

Masud and Sayed Basel are twins, hip dressers in black leather and brown corduroy who look right at home in the cosmopolitan confines of UC Berkeley, where they have just finished their undergraduate degrees. The brothers are convergence points on the globe, their identities a blend of East and West, North and South. They speak Farsi and English flawlessly; grew up in a small house in Kabul, praying toward Mecca five times a day; and can now be found debating American health policies in a California pizza parlor. After awhile, you start to see the differences between them: Masud is lighter, more forthcoming; Sayed is more intense, more cerebral. In conversation, they riff off each other constantly.

The Basel brothers were born in Afghanistan in 1977, two years before the country was invaded by its neighbor to the north, and the Soviet tanks rolled into town. The family lived in the capital city of Kabul, which in the mid-'70s was a cosmopolitan center with a healthy economy and basic but operative city services. The boys' father Naim was a fireman—in Afghanistan, a professional job that placed you squarely in the middle class as a government employee. He was not, though, a member of the Communist Party, a problem after the Soviets arrived. "The Secret Service knew he wasn't a spy, but they wanted him to join the party. They intimidated him," remembers Sayed of those days. One night, when the boys were 7, the Secret Service showed up, surrounded the house, cut the electric lines and forced their way in. Naim managed to escape and get to a neighbor's telephone to call his colleagues at the fire department—who got there fast, lights flashing and sirens blaring. The Secret Service backed off and left, claiming a case of mistaken identity, but the damage was done. The family moved to a different house and began making plans to leave the country altogether. "That experience was traumatic, and after it happened, we did believe we were in danger," says Masud. "It wasn't uncommon for families to just disappear. There was also the issue of shelling. The mujahadeen [the Afghan forces fighting the Soviet-installed government] would routinely shell Kabul. Every month, we would hear that someone's house had been hit."

It was complicated to leave. In 1979 and '80, when the Soviets had just entered Afghanistan, the American embassy in Kabul granted thousands of visas to political refugees. But by the time Masud and Sayed's family sought to leave, in the mid-'80s, leaving Afghanistan to travel to a non-communist country had been banned. And even if applicants were lucky enough to get a foreign visa and leave, any remaining relatives in Afghanistan would, at a minimum, be scrutinized by the Secret Service. The most common strategy for getting out was to cross the harsh, mountainous terrain to Pakistan and from there apply for political asylum in the West.

"Going out through Pakistan usually involved making night trips, riding on donkeys through war fields, where you would hire the services of a smuggler who would take you across the border," remembers Sayed. "We'd heard so many stories of botched escape attempts. You would be ripped off and left stranded by the smuggler. There was the risk of getting into a battle between the mujahadeen and the Russian forces, the risk of land mines. There was bad weather, lots of ice and snow. There were bandits who would attack and steal from escapees. And some people just got lost trying to make the trip."

Desperate to leave the country but unwilling to risk a flight to Pakistan, the boys' father devised an audacious plan of escape: he would take the family to Moscow. From

142

there, they would travel to the Soviet satellite states of Czechoslovakia and Yugoslavia, where Naim would try to get officials at the Indian Embassy to give him a visa for his family. He believed escaping through the Soviet Union was the safest way out of Afghanistan: his 20 years as a firefighter allowed him the right to travel there for medical care, and there was no precedent of people getting out through Moscow. He used false medical records to secure a visa, and, to deflect any suspicion, the family told no one of their real plans. Instead, until the day they left, they announced an impending operation and family vacation in Russia. They left virtually all of their belongings in Afghanistan.

The family traveled for a month or more—to Moscow, on to Prague and finally to Belgrade, where they hoped to exit from behind the Iron Curtain once and for all. Thanks to Wrigley's chewing gum and Wranglers blue jeans used to sway an official at the Indian Embassy, the family got a 72-hour visa for India, and they flew to New Delhi. As soon as they got off the plane, the Basels cleared customs and made their way to the United Nations field office. There, they requested political asylum as war refugees. The U.N. granted their request, and they were allowed to stay in India beyond their 72-hour deadline—but they couldn't stay permanently. Naim had family in Australia, and his wife Monisa had family in the United States. The Basels decided to try to get to the United States and applied for visas. Then they waited. Rent and food were cheap. The boys and their only other sibling, an older sister named Nelofar, enrolled in school and learned to speak Hindi. The twins spent their afternoons playing cricket with the neighbors.

After 14 months, the visas arrived from the U.S. Embassy. "I remember the day we got the letter," says Sayed. "I came home from school, and my mom told us we were going to the United States. The first thing I did was rip off the school uniform I was wearing. I was so excited, so happy. Shedding that uniform was about freedom, a way to celebrate a successful escape."

"It was a big deal, like winning the lottery," adds Masud. "And, in a way, it was winning the lottery. America was the most sought-after country for political refugees. It helped us out a lot that our aunt and uncle already lived here." The boys' aunt and uncle had left Afghanistan in 1979, the year after the invasion. "Our uncle was an English instructor. He was the son of the Afghan poet and writer Saljukhe, and he was considered an intellectual, so he was quickly accepted by the United States," explains Masud. "I think in most countries, when there's a revolution, the dominant force tries to crush any opposition, and often the intellectuals become prime targets because they're the first to speak against it."

The Basel family settled first in Virginia for a year and then moved on to Union City, California, after Naim heard that there were greater opportunities for new immigrants in the Golden State. By this time he was in his 40s, suffering from back problems and too old to work as a firefighter. In Virginia, he'd taken a job as a carpet cleaner.

Union City sits on the east side of San Francisco Bay. "They call it the gateway to Silicon Valley now," says Masud. "At the time we came, it was a working-class neighborhood. Our neighbors were mechanics, secretaries." The area was full of gladiola farms and immigrants. But the Basels had entered a community that was about to change rapidly. Soon after they arrived, Union City witnessed an economic boom. In celebration

143

of its new-found affluence, the city passed a bond measure to raise $35 million to upgrade all of the classrooms at the high school. By the time the Basels graduated, the school had a closed-circuit television system, at least three or four computers in every room, and modern laboratory facilities.

The boys started middle school, their sister started high school. All three struggled with their English and tried to fit in. "The neighborhood did have its share of gangs, and we even had a taste of that in junior high in a desperate attempt to fit in," remembers Sayed. "We went through this initiation where you got beat up by a bunch of guys so you'd be one of the clique." But the appeal of gang life quickly wore off. The boys had joined the group to gain a sense of collective identity, but most of the gang members in

a. Sayed (left) and Masud at 2 in their mother's home province of Herat in Afghanistan. b. Masud (with the ball) and Sayed at 7, in Kabul with (left to right) their father, sister, mother and a family friend. c. The twins at 9, a year after they'd arrived in the United States.

Union City were Filipino, from a culture foreign to the boys. They dropped out and reverted to their social isolationism. "I was kind of overweight, so I used to wear my dad's old shirts and slacks to school," says Sayed. "All the kids would have their Nike T-shirts and brand names. Our school was sometimes so much about having the coolest jacket or the newest brand of shoes. We knew we couldn't afford that. I remember thinking that shopping at Macy's was such an extravagant thing."

"Target was extravagant!" says Masud, laughing.

Ultimately, the boys found their place in the school when they discovered their intellects. Feelings of loneliness and depression dissipated in the classroom, the one place in their lives where the boys felt they had control. If they worked hard and performed well, they knew that they would be rewarded. Their success at school fueled their beliefs that they could fulfill their dream of becoming doctors. "Ever since I can remember, I've always wanted to be a doctor," says Masud as Sayed nods his agreement. "This was true even when I was 5 and my father was a fireman. It made sense for me to want to be a fireman, go on that truck and go up the big ladder. But even then, it was just medicine." In his application to SMYSP, Masud wrote of an incident he witnessed in a

144

Kabul hospital: "I was very young. I was in a hospital with my mother when I saw a man crying with joy, kissing the hands of a doctor and thanking him with all his feelings. The doctor had just saved the man's wife in an operation. To be able to heal someone and save a precious human life is like being able to perform a miracle. The satisfaction that I felt watching that doctor was just immeasurable."

These days, Masud and Sayed each seem possessed by an unshakable confidence and buoyant enthusiasm, and it's hard to escape the impression that they are both primed to go out into the world and succeed, whatever the terms. Watching them together and witnessing their closeness, it's evident that a good deal of their self-assuredness must come from the fact that they are twins and know they can count on each other for anything.

a. The twins celebrating their 13th birthday with friends in Union City. b. Sayed (second from left) and Masud with their parents, the week they graduated from UC Berkeley.

They also credit their parents for lavishing them with love and teaching them to be honest and comfortable with themselves. "There wasn't any of this thing at home about Dad doesn't kiss the son," remembers Sayed. "He always used to sit us on his lap and hug and kiss us. He still does. Family was extremely important."

While the boys' parents were loving, they weren't lenient. Despite the fact that there was very little money around and the family lived in government housing, they refused to let the boys work during high school. They also nixed sports, insisting on a focus on academics. But by and large, they were removed from their sons' intellectual lives. "We respected our parents for being very aware, for having their set views on what we could do and what our culture was," says Masud. "But they weren't associated with anything we did once we left home in the morning. They didn't go to open house or join the PTA because of the language barrier, the cultural barrier. Our intellectual awakening had nothing to do—practically speaking—with our parents. We had no hero or role model who came from our own Afghan background. To us, the realm of academia was a world that belonged to white America. For the longest time, I believed that only blond, blue-eyed people were true Americans."

145

It was in high school that the two found the greatest influences in their academic lives. For Sayed, it was his AP history teacher in junior year, Walter Cozine. "He was a tall academic guy with glasses and blond hair. He would talk from the minute the bell rang until the bell rang again to let us out. We would actually have cramped hands at the end of his class from writing so much! When you listened to one of his lectures, history became dynamic, salty; it had a flavor. He introduced us to the intellectual delights of truth. Through and through, I think I owe whatever intellectual interest I have in philosophy, history and politics to what Mr. Cozine planted. He was the first teacher who really cared."

Masud's greatest influence was his sophomore year world history teacher, Sharilyn Scharf. "She made me feel that there's a lot of worth in me, that I can achieve whatever it is that I want," he recalls. "Sayed and I applied to about 14 colleges. After I got accepted by some, Ms. Scharf told me, 'You need to visit these schools before you pick one.' And I said, 'That would be great, but I don't have the money.' A week later, she said, 'Narrow it down to three or four schools, and I'll pay for it.' I remember coming home and telling my parents, 'Guess what? There's a teacher who's willing to pay for me to visit schools to see which one is right for me.' It gave me an incredible sense of self-worth. You think: 'Look! People think I can do it, so of course I can.'"

In the middle of their sophomore year in high school, the boys organized a field trip to visit Stanford Hospital with their science club. "On the trip, there was a tour guide, and we asked her so many questions," remembers Masud. "Toward the end of the tour, she said, 'Hey! There's a program for students just like you who are interested in medicine. Here's the phone number.' We got the number and we were on it. And that summer, we got into the program."

The boys entered the SMYSP program in the summer of 1993. "SMYSP moved us much closer to the goal of going into medicine by taking the idea that we could become doctors and making it real," says Sayed. "I worked in the morgue, helping with autopsies. We were involved in all elements of what was going on, the academic as well as the rudimentary. You rolled up your sleeves—actually, you rolled down your sleeves—and did everything. After that summer, it was no longer an extravagant, fanciful thought to say, 'I want to go into medicine.' And you meet incredible people through the program. One of the distinguished professors who came and talked to us told us his father worked in a coal mine. He told us how his father would come home and stick his finger up his nose to clear his nostril and his finger would come out entirely black, and his father did this day-in and day-out for decades. And it became normal to think, 'I can reach for this type of position even if I came from this type of background.'"

"I did romanticize the whole experience I had in SMYSP," says Masud. "I was putting on scrubs, I was living out a dream. Once I went into an operating room and saw a surgeon doing breast reconstructive surgery. She was listening to Yanni. I love Yanni's music! The idea that surgeons listen to music while they operate never occurred to me; I thought it was so wonderful. To see the nuances of medicine, the little tiny details; those were very pleasant surprises for me."

146

The twins were both accepted at the University of California, Berkeley, where they spent five years. Sayed majored in philosophy and biology, Masud in biology. They lived in one small room on the fourth floor of an aging hotel on Telegraph Avenue, just above the town's most famous pizza parlor, Blondie's. They shared the 12-by-12-foot space with one other man, which, Masud says gleefully, kept their rent below $300 a month. Though the two had been forbidden to work during high school, they were employed throughout college as tutors and as assistants in a small medical research laboratory near the Berkeley campus.

The lab job provided an excellent place for the twins to practice their surgical skills, since most of the work involved dissecting mice and other small animals to gain tissue samples. As a result, the Basels have both become very precise and deft in their work. The training that started six years earlier in the SMYSP operating room was evident— though the soundtrack in the lab was National Public Radio, not Yanni.

"I remember the first surgery I did at the lab," Sayed says. "I had to do a femoral exposure on a hamster. I was told by the instructor that he'd only once seen a student not lose the animal on the first try. My surgery took about seven hours. If you're proficient, it shouldn't take more than 15 minutes! I did everything very slowly and methodically, and I remember throughout the entire procedure saying, 'I'm not going to lose you, you're not going to die.' I went to the instructor and said, 'I'm going to be the second guy who got this right.' I checked on my hamster every day, and sure enough, he got back to normal. These experiences gave us a sense of the awesome responsibility of holding a life in your hands."

Throughout college, the brothers tutored students who were part of the MESA (Math, Engineering and Science Achievements) program. "It's an outreach program that targets low-income students," says Sayed. "Working at MESA helped us develop sensibilities for those subtle, unique needs of communities that are not so commonly voiced. MESA helped us become closer to people by appreciating who they are as people."

"When you're a doctor, obviously, you want to know your sciences and your biology really well, but you have to also be a healer," adds Masud. "And to be a healer, you have to know about a lot more than just the physical symptoms, you have to know about the person as a whole."

The Basels, newly graduated from Berkeley, are now busy taking their MCATs and preparing to apply to medical school. They have also returned to Union City and begun work at Tiburcio Vasquez Health Center, a clinic that serves the city's low-income population.

"The clinic serves patients who are 200 percent or more below the poverty line, so we are predominantly helping the very low-income working poor," says Sayed. "There are about 26,000 patient encounters annually."

"We were initially hired as graduate interns," explains Masud. "Our positions didn't exist before we got there. The CEO brought us on with the hope of recruiting us once we get out of medical school. He's very interested in nurturing a relationship with physicians who want to work in under-served communities."

The twins have now both been hired full-time at the clinic: Masud as a communications associate, and Sayed as an information technology coordinator. "It's been a blessing," says Sayed. "We're really starting our medical education. For example, every week, we sit in on a meeting with the doctors, the social workers and the administrators. They talk about the patients, and we watch them figure out how to solve people's problems. It's great to see it on ground-zero level.

"Our work at the clinic is not all that different from SMYSP. At SMYSP, we were given this license to see what the doctors were doing. At this clinic, we are free to observe. This truly has been the legacy of SMYSP: we view ourselves as *entitled* to prepare for this ultimate goal of becoming doctors."

When they finish medical school, the twins intend to work closely with California's Afghan community; they are well aware that as Farsi-fluent primary-care physicians, they will be among a small and significant group. "Currently, there are fewer than 10 practicing Afghan physicians in the Bay Area, and there are 65,000 Afghans living here," says Sayed. "Like every ethnic group, this group has its own unique needs and certain idiosyncrasies about how its members live their lives. Most times, patients don't articulate their medical needs—it's something far more subtle that they wouldn't think of telling their doctors about. For instance, in Afghan parties, it is incredibly disrespectful if the food you serve is not very rich. That contributes to high cholesterol, which is extremely prevalent. Every Afghan family I know has a member with some kind of cardiovascular problem. So how do you inform an old lady whose cholesterol and blood pressure are off the roof that she needs to make lifestyle adjustments? How do you do that with a sensibility to her customs? What's needed is the perspective of someone who brings that culture inside the system so it can permeate out into the services for the community."

"I want to caution against the message that we're only doing medicine to serve Afghans," Masud adds. "Medicine is universal; the human body is universal. It's good to have helping the Afghan community as a general goal, but there are things the Afghan community experiences that many other minority communities experience, too. So I see my utility in a more universal way. That's the beauty of it. You can go anywhere in the world and practice medicine."

While Masud and Sayed are driven to help Afghan immigrants, they have also acculturated and abandoned some components of their culture.

"I'm not religious at all now," says Masud. "It's hard for our parents, but they're hopeful that we will one day become wiser and appreciate religion. I think they know that our hearts are clean. My mom has told me that, meaning you abide by the commandments of Islam with the exception of technicalities like praying five times a day or fasting."

"We're just as much a product of this society as my parents were of theirs," says Sayed, "and this is a very secular society. The majority here subscribe to science. That's the emerging religion of the world.

"The main thing I feel sad about now is how lonely my parents are. It was very hard for them. They raised three children not knowing anything about the culture or education system here. My mom has suffered from depression. When she was in Kabul, she had to go to the morgue and identify the body of her brother. He'd been run over by a Russian tank. That was about two years before we left. It was called an accident. None of us are immune to the psychological effects of all those things that happen in life.

"The adjustment to a new lifestyle, living in poverty, struggling with the language: it took its toll. You still feel it. The transition to a new country affects you in just about every way conceivable. And you thank the powers that be that you survived. You just go on, focus on the good. But there are so many reasons to say, 'Oh, the hell with it! It's too hard!'"

One night at a popular Berkeley restaurant, Masud and Sayed sit in the back, around a large wooden table on an open-air patio, drinking lemonade and eating hamburgers. Their talk is lighter, about the arts, how they fill their free time.

"You already know my favorite music," says Masud. "I love Yanni. *Pulp Fiction* is my favorite movie. I just want to be entertained. I like doing fun things. I think you do well at things you enjoy, and I like to think about surgery like that."

"It's a long time since I've seen a good movie," says Sayed. "I'd say *The English Patient* is a good movie. I like a story line that's not insulting to one's intelligence, dialogue that's engaging, a plot that's complex. I hate optimistic propaganda, TV shows that put a sugar glaze over life's incredible complexity."

"You like *The English Patient* because it's the opposite of pop culture?" asks Masud skeptically.

"The life the media portrays is so outside the realm of reality experienced by 90 percent of the world," says Sayed. "Life is hard. You have to struggle to make ends meet, to keep your sanity, to not be taken advantage of. In India, a laborer spends his whole day's earnings to watch one of these fanciful stories that portray these unrealistic worlds because that's the relief from the everyday misery of barely making ends meet."

"What do you suggest?" counters Masud. "That people concentrate on the misery in their lives and not escape for that small moment? I think you need a good balance of optimism in life to survive."

"No," says Sayed. "You need courageous pessimism. The whole point of life is the struggle to make sense of the uncertainty, to know that in the storm, you're this little boat floating in the sea, and there's little to no point in this chaos except the struggle."

There is a silence and a rare tension between the two.

"I like instrumental music," says Sayed, after a pause. "My boss makes fun of me because I listen to instrumental music with the sounds of the rain forest or tropical animal and bird noises. I like romantic ballads because sometimes you just want to lose yourself in the illusion."

"Like the Indian peasant," shoots back Masud.

"Right," says Sayed. "Absolutely. I think life is a wonderful thing, and everyone has every reason to make the best of it. But you have to be open to the other realities that people experience. You can't forget that the wrong end of a bayonet-mounted rifle could have been the other way around."

public health:
the big picture

Every summer, SMYSP's founder, Dr. Marilyn Winkleby, lectures at the program on her specialty, public health. By the time her talk rolls around, Marilyn knows each of the students—not just their names, but where they come from and what they hope to do with their lives. She is friendly and encouraging with the SMYSPers, and they are relaxed and comfortable with her. Her lecture is one of the summer's most popular: she is passionate about public health and has taught it for 20 years. For most of the students, her talk provides their first exposure to the field, and on some, it makes a profound impression. Over the years, a number of SMYSP graduates have opted for careers in public health over doctoring.

"Public health and medical care are two very different things," Marilyn begins her lecture as the students settle into their seats. "Public health focuses on promoting health and preventing disease in the population as a whole. It considers the social environment of health; it recognizes that social, economic and political forces influence health behaviors and disease. Do you remember the story that Dr. Schoolnik told you about eradicating smallpox? That program used a public health model. It involved collective social action. Scientists partnered with local experts and health workers to find out where the last cases of disease were occurring and addressed misconceptions about vaccines. Fundamentally, public health is a better long-term approach to controlling disease than just treating illness after it appears.

"Epidemiology is a branch of public health, and it's what I do. Epidemiologists study the occurrence of disease. Hippocrates, the Greek physician who is considered the father of modern medicine, was one of the first to use epidemiologic observations—he proposed that air, water and land could actually cause disease. In the 1700s, when epidemics were killing hundreds of thousands of people, there was a huge controversy about how they really occur. There were two competing theories. The first was the miasma theory, the idea that breathing bad air makes you sick. The second was the germ theory, the idea that micro-organisms make you sick. We now know the germ theory was correct, but at the time, it was discredited by people who didn't believe that microbes could make people ill.

"Epidemiology is possible because disease is not randomly allocated; it clusters. To study it, we look to three characteristics: person, place and time. Can you think of some characteristics of people that might relate to their health?"

Marilyn turns to the classroom's blackboard, ready to write, as the students call out ideas. They suggest that age, gender, ethnicity, culture and income may play a role in how disease varies. "Very good," says Marilyn, writing down their answers. "Now how about place? How might characteristics of places relate to health?"

152

The students guess that disease may vary across countries, within regions and maybe even by migration patterns. Marilyn smiles with each suggestion as she writes it on the board. "Great," she says. "Those are all important factors that epidemiologists consider.

The third characteristic we study is time. Diseases ebb and flow. For example, heart disease increased after World War II, during the postwar boom. Soldiers had been given free cigarettes during the war, and then they came home and convinced their wives to smoke, too. Everyone was eating a lot of steak and butter, watching more TV and exercising less. By 1970, heart disease was an epidemic. Then, as people learned about the dangers of smoking, poor diets, sedentary lifestyles, obesity and high blood pressure, behavior changed and rates of heart disease declined dramatically.

"There are two major types of disease: chronic and infectious. Infectious diseases, like colds, tuberculosis and AIDS, are caused by an agent like a virus or bacteria that is transmitted from person to person. Illnesses are often short-term. The patient either gets well quickly or dies. Chronic diseases, like heart disease, cancer and diabetes, are more long-lasting. They're not infectious and are often linked to lifestyle. Very early on, people acquire behaviors that are linked to health problems that occur later in their lives. The majority of people who become long-term, addicted smokers start smoking in adolescence. Food choices are influenced by marketing at an even younger age. Who can tell me about chronic diseases they've seen?"

Again, the students call out responses: an aunt with diabetes, a grandfather who had a stroke, an uncle with arthritis, a neighbor with lung cancer. "Today, most people in the United States die from chronic disease," says Marilyn. "In developing countries, there are still a lot of infectious diseases—malaria, hepatitis—but as people in developing countries live longer, they are suffering from chronic diseases, too. The health care systems in these countries now face the double burden of trying to prevent and treat both types of disease.

"Great achievements have been accomplished by public health in the last century," Marilyn says. "Let's think about some broad societal achievements. Ideas?"

"Immunizations," Oscar calls out.

"You are all so smart!" she says, smiling as she writes "immunizations" on the board.

"Pasteurization of milk," comes another suggestion.

"Exactly," says Marilyn as she writes "safer and healthier food."

Other suggestions are made and written down: safer automobiles and workplaces, improved medical care for mothers and babies, fluoridation of drinking water, and knowledge about the dangers of smoking. Marilyn tells a story from the 1980s when her husband, a doctor at Kaiser, tried to get smoking banned in the hospital where he worked. "No one would support it," remembers Marilyn. "Even some of the patients and surgeons were smoking in the hospital! Now, you are not even allowed to smoke on the hospital grounds. This is another example of how public health policies can create safer environments for everyone."

153

Statistics and data are a large part of the public health world; they are the tools researchers use to dissect and track disease. Marilyn next shows a number of charts that illustrate the ways in which illness is quantified and questioned. She shows a graph that focuses on ethnicity, education and infant mortality which illustrates that the lower the mother's education, the higher the infant mortality rates. African-American women have an infant mortality rate that is twice as high as the average. "Why might that be?" asks Marilyn.

The students call out ideas. "Poor food availability," says Elizabeth. "Lack of resources to get food," says Kamille. "No health insurance," ventures Corinne.

"Exactly," says Marilyn. "That's the way to be thinking. But none of those factors are mentioned in this graph. It focuses on ethnicity and education, but infant mortality is not determined by these factors per se; rather, they are proxies for underlying causes."

Marilyn shows other statistics. A startling series of slides from the Centers for Disease Control tracks the recent explosion of obesity in America. The first slide, from 1990, shows no state where more than 15 percent of the population is overweight. As the slides advance year by year, the number of overweight Americans grows dramatically. By 1992, six states show more than 15 percent of the population overweight; by 1997, a whopping 36 states show more than 15 percent of the population overweight. The students gasp and whisper to each other as they watch the slides and the story unfolding.

"We are seeing annual shifts in obesity rates that we would typically see over a 50-year span," Marilyn says. "There has been an explosion of fast food in this country. Portion sizes are getting larger, too. There are eight to 10 teaspoons of sugar in a regular can of cola, so imagine how many there are in a super-sized drink."

"KFC is now selling buckets of soda with a handle on the side," says Jose. The students laugh at the absurdity of it.

When Marilyn asks for questions, Michelle raises a hand to ask, "How do you feel about gathering data on race?"

"That's a good question," says Marilyn. "There are ongoing discussions among epidemiologists about protecting confidentiality versus gathering data to understand populations with high disease rates. Personally, I feel that we need to know about the three characteristics we discussed—person, place and time—to understand patterns of disease and to identify populations that may be missed by public health programs and medical services. We need information to create strategies to enhance health."

Marilyn ends her lecture, as one might expect, on an inspirational note. "There is a huge need for diversity in public health," she says. "As you move forward in your careers, remember: we need people who understand different cultures to enter our field. Public health is wide open for people with ideas and questions."

myisha
patterson

"Smile... heaven is watching!"
— African proverb

Even at 20, Myisha Patterson has the warmth of an earth mother, the fire of a crusader, the enthusiasm of a campaigner. She radiates energy. Asked for three words to describe herself, she has five at hand immediately: "Independent. Strong-willed. Fun-loving. Dedicated. Committed." She ticks them off on her fingers as she speaks, her crimson nails flashing.

These days, she is an undergraduate at Stanford University. She wears a fur-lined leather jacket that lends her a Pam Grier-ish chic, takes classes in molecular biology and organic chemistry, and organizes programming to celebrate Dr. Martin Luther King, Jr. Day and Black Liberation Month. In her downtime, she relaxes with stories of lives: she has just finished *Long Walk to Freedom*, Nelson Mandela's autobiography. Her own story—the tale of a journey from Stockton to Stanford, replete with a voyage to South Africa—may not be as momentous as Mandela's, but it is a story of triumph nonetheless, a story of music and faith, hard work and hope, and love's charity.

Myisha was born in Stockton, the daughter of a bank teller and a baker. Her mother, a good student, had finished high school a year early and started college. But she left school at 20 when she married, and three years later, Myisha was born. Myisha's dad was working at the Rainbow Bakery, her mom as a teller at the Union Safe Deposit Bank. Their marriage was rocky; when drugs entered the picture, it got rockier still. Myisha was taken in and cradled by her mother's large, warm family.

"My grandmother is a really loving person. She isn't always tactful," says Myisha of the family matriarch, "but everything she does is out of love. Every time I see her, she gives me a present. She worries a lot. She worries about me driving on the freeway! My grandfather is very loving, too, and he's funny. He's down-to-earth, very old-fashioned and set in his ways."

Myisha's grandfather has been a minister for more than 50 years, since he moved to California from Arkansas to start a church. He's been the pastor at the First Missionary Baptist Church in Stockton for 30 years, and Myisha grew up there, singing *Jesus Loves Me* to the congregation, wearing dresses covered with ruffles. (A decade later would find her halfway around the world, clad in vibrant African fabrics and singing Swahili folk songs in Cape Town.)

Myisha was a gregarious child, and her whole world revolved around her grandfather's church. Tuesday night was choir rehearsal, Wednesday night was Bible study, Thursday and Friday nights were usually spent visiting other churches, and all day Sunday was devoted to church. "We're a really close family and we're all in the church," she says. "Of my five uncles, two are ministers. The membership in First Missionary Baptist Church is over 200, and all the people are either related to me or they seem like they are because I've known them forever."

Through the church, Myisha became a missionary. From a young age, she worked in soup kitchens, cooking and serving food to those in need. She read to children in the day-care center and fried bacon and eggs for the annual Martin Luther King, Jr. prayer breakfast. She saw firsthand how people need each other to survive and what a difference support can make to a person in crisis. She saw that lesson reflected in her own life, living in the calm glow of her grandparents' love while her mother struggled with her addiction. Then one day, her mother came to Myisha's grandparents, to tell them that she had

158

prayed and was going to change her life. She had just given birth to Myisha's baby brother Myron, and he was living with Myisha's aunt. Myisha's mother entered a drug rehabilitation program, and when she had completed it, she got her children back. Myisha's father, though, was no longer in the picture.

Through it all, Myisha made friends, enjoyed school and delighted in having fun whenever she could. Even as a child, she says, she was confident in herself, in who she was and what she was going to do with her life. She adored reading and "used to live in the library." She liked all of her school subjects—except history. "I wanted to know why we weren't learning about Africa," she says. "I remember being really interested in African-American history, and I made it my personal goal to know a lot about it. I had my own agenda about what I wanted to learn. And my teachers were willing to accommodate that. Every report or project that I had to do, I related it to Africa or African-American history in some way. In the sixth grade, I read *Roots*."

While Myisha was busy reading history, her mom was working an extra job at the election polls. There she met a sweet older woman who told her she had a nephew she thought Myisha's mom might like, an electrician.

"So she introduced them and they dated for a while, and they fell in love and got married," says Myisha. She loved her stepfather. "He was awesome: he took care of us and he was a father to me and my brothers. He always pushed me to do my best." The family moved to the better side of town and settled down. A harmony came into the house. Myisha's mother was happy, and with her new husband she had a son, Nicholas, and a daughter, Brea. And then, six months after Brea was born, Myisha lost her second father when he died suddenly of a heart attack at the age of 42.

"It has really left a lasting impression," she says now, six years later. "I often think about him, and I'm still grieving. I considered him my father, but I never told him that and that bothered me a lot. Now, I always tell my friends and family that I love them—I don't take things for granted so much anymore."

At the time, eager to banish her grief, Myisha threw herself into school. When the family moved across town, the schools changed and Myisha found herself in a different environment. "There weren't many black people or minorities, and I used to get teased," she recalls. "Once, another student called me a nigger. I couldn't believe he said it. I told the teacher and the student apologized. But I remember being very aware that there were hardly any other black people around. At my middle school, Brookside, I was the only black girl in the class. There were two black guys, and one got expelled. That really upset me because I felt we had to be role models."

Myisha made it her goal to enlighten her classmates about African and African-American history. Soon, one of her middle school teachers asked her to give a class presentation on the subject. "It was an honor," Myisha says. "I talked about Africa and I went in depth about slavery. I talked about *Roots*. The kids asked a lot of questions. I remember people talking to me afterwards and telling me how interested they were."

Myisha longed to know about her own family's heritage of slavery. She says she wishes that family histories were more commonly passed on in America, and, in her own family, she wishes that her grandfather would talk to her more about his early life in Arkansas. "A lot of these people were in marches, confronting racism. Now it's

159

buried. I wish more of the older people would talk about that with us. That would mean a lot more than reading about it in the library. You know, we're African kings and queens. We really are. They brought kings and queens from Africa to be slaves. I know that my roots are in Africa. I take pride in that."

In her freshman year of high school, Myisha joined a group called Images for Black Women and she stayed with them to the end of her senior year. "They were all about helping black women get on the right track for a career," she says. "We did a lot just on self-esteem and confidence. We performed poems that boost black women's confidence, like *Phenomenal Woman* by Maya Angelou, and had talks on a variety of issues. On our meeting days, we had to dress up, look good; we were not allowed to wear jeans or

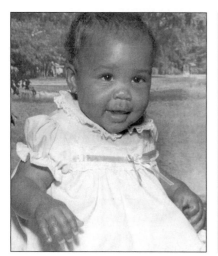

a. Myisha as an infant, in Stockton. b. Myisha with her grandparents, just outside the doors to her grandfather's church.

tennis shoes. A lot of my habits were influenced by Images. It has a lot to do with why I'm very confident. We learned to carry ourselves," she says.

In her sophomore year, Myisha became very active with the National Association for the Advancement of Colored People, or NAACP. She was treasurer, then vice president, then president of her high school chapter. A close family friend and her husband convinced Myisha to enter a program called ACT-SO, or Afro-Academic, Cultural, Technological, Scientific Olympics. Myisha was chosen to go to the program's nationals in Pittsburgh, Pennsylvania.

The ACT-SO convention was timed to coincide with the NAACP's national convention, "so I had to choose whether I wanted to go to Pittsburgh to compete or to go there as an officer. I chose to be an officer. It was awesome," she recalls. "There were over 10,000 black people. There were people in the forefront of the civil rights movement. Incredible speakers. Bill Clinton was there. I met him, Coretta Scott King and Jesse Jackson. I got to network with youth from all over the country. It inspired me to do more. I remember one thing that really affected me was that at some point during the convention, the Klu Klux Klan threatened to come. And I thought, 'Will it ever end?' They ended up not coming, but I was scared."

160

Myisha tutored younger students in math and reading. She volunteered as a conflict manager. And she began singing in school drama productions. In her junior year, she was featured in *Sweet Charity*, and as a senior, she was in *Guys and Dolls*—playing a guy rather than a doll—and she brought down the house with her rendition of *Sit Down, You're Rocking the Boat*. Her intellect was applauded, too. She had supportive teachers and singles out her math teacher, Ms. Green, as a particular light: "I'll never forget her—she was the best math teacher ever. Math was my hardest subject. All my other subjects I breezed through, but I had to work hard at math. She spent time with me and she was very encouraging. She had so much pride in her class. She and my counselor, Ms. Burhoe, never doubted me. It's great to know that they're still there and doing the same thing for other students."

One day, Myisha was in class when someone passed her a call slip from one of the deans, Ms. Marseille. "She called me into her office and said, 'I've got these applications for a program called the Stanford Medical Youth Science Program, and maybe you'll be interested,'" Myisha recalls. "I had done well in the sciences. But at that time, I was set on law—I'd wanted to be a lawyer since I was little. And then I saw the dates of the program, and it conflicted with the next NAACP national convention. But I went and talked to my science teacher about it. I talked to my counselor, too, and she said it sounded like a great program, so I thought I should do it.

"I got the phone interview and then the campus interview. I came with my mother. I was excited and I prayed about it, but I wasn't really nervous. When I got the call, I was sick at home and in bed. My mom came in and said there was a phone call for me, and I found out I got in. Then I started getting really excited."

Myisha entered SMYSP between her junior and senior years. She had never been away from her family for more than a week at a time, and the hardest part of the program was leaving Stockton—some 50 miles away from Stanford—for five weeks. "My mom was out of town the weekend I arrived at the program, so I traveled to Oakland, to my aunt's, and she drove me to Stanford. I was late because we got lost, and I felt a little reluctant to let my aunt go. I remember thinking, 'I don't know any of these people!' But toward the end of the program, we were so close."

When the first anatomy lab rolled around, Myisha reacted the way most SMYSP students do: she was nervous. "I was familiar with dissecting, because in biology we'd done frogs," she says. Still, she wasn't sure she'd be able to make the transition to human beings. But in the end, she relished the labs. "I remember smelling the formaldehyde when they brought out the cadavers the first time. Some people had to leave the room, but I found I was able to detach myself." At Stanford Hospital, Myisha worked in the operating room, assisting an anesthesiology technician. "I loved it," she says. "I got to see a lot of surgeries. The most interesting surgery was probably the removal of a brain tumor. The technology they were using was really cool. The doctor was doing it all by watching the screen.

"When I was there, I saw a trauma I still think of: some guy who'd been injecting heroin had run out of veins, and he had been injecting his back. The skin had gotten so rotted away, it was like he didn't have a back. The doctors couldn't do much; they just tried to stop the bleeding. I remember thanking the Lord that it hadn't happened to my

161

mom or my dad. I remember the doctors talking about how the guy didn't have insurance, and they still had to operate on him. The doctors kept telling us, 'This is why you shouldn't do drugs.'"

Myisha made friends, played practical jokes on the counselors, went to San Francisco to see *Phantom of the Opera* and went swimming in the Pacific Ocean for the first time. Irene Linetskaya, a SMYSP graduate who was a counselor for Myisha's class, taught her to say "I love you" in Russian. "She would come in at night to tuck us in," remembers Myisha. "It was such a bonding experience. The staff went out of their way to see that we were comfortable, and put a lot of effort into making sure we all realized that we were capable of going to a four-year university. I remember one of the girls in my class: at the beginning, she said she was just going to a community college, but by the end, she had changed her mind and decided to try for a four-year college. And I think she got into UC Berkeley. The program changed the way you thought about your ability to do things. It was a life-changing experience. It has everything to do with me being at Stanford right now."

When Myisha got back to Stockton, SMYSP was all she talked about. "My friends were like, 'Shut up! Stop talking about it already!'" she says, laughing at the memory. "I got recognition in my community for being accepted into such a prestigious program and I wanted to make sure that people in my high school knew about this opportunity. I tried to start a program at my school's career center, a workshop for preparing for college. I knew that my counselor had 400 or 500 students assigned to her. That was unreasonable, so you had to be doing things yourself: looking at schools and requirements, looking for scholarship money. I'm one of the first in my family to go to college, and I knew that if I didn't do well and get financial aid, my mom couldn't pay for me to go. So I tried to encourage my cousins and the people at my church, and I gave them information. I ended up doing the college workshops.

"I've always believed in giving back to the community. The summer after I graduated from high school, I took a job working in the Stockton ghetto. The kids there have a lot of problems, and it seemed important to tell them that someone cares about them. There was a lot of raw talent there. They were kids from 5 to 13. I challenged them and made them believe they could get out of the ghetto. I felt it was my job. I think that's a problem with the black community: some people who become successful forget about the people at the bottom. When I first came to Stanford, I saw such a disparity between here and the world outside. It's almost like apartheid, and there's so much work to do."

Myisha applied to Stanford and was accepted. Thanks to SMYSP, she felt comfortable at the university; she was familiar with the campus and knew her way around. During freshman orientation, she auditioned for one of Stanford's most respected a cappella singing groups, Talisman, and they asked her to join. "That shaped a lot of my freshman year experience," she says.

With Talisman, Myisha took the most significant trip of her life to date: to South Africa, on a two-week singing tour. "It was an emotionally overwhelming trip," she says. "I identified with a lot of the people, and I was encouraged and inspired by their stories. It seemed like all the time we were there, the clouds hung lower. We were in the townships where black people lived. In those shacks, there would be maybe three beds,

162

and each bed was for one family. There was no plumbing, no water, no electricity. People in the townships were the poorest of the poor. It was a harsh reality to be in a place with so much physical beauty and so much poverty. At every streetlight, we saw kids begging, asking for food. At the same time, there was an electricity in the air, a charge. It felt like the government was taking steps to improve things—more steps than the United States took after slavery ended. Still, the disparities are profound, ridiculous. There's a huge separation: you don't see any white people in the townships and you don't see any black people in the white neighborhoods, unless they are the help.

"In the townships, we would sing in the marketplace. I'm sure it must have been weird for the people watching us sing, because Talisman is very multicultural: in the group there are blacks, whites, Asians. And we were singing in languages that they know and we really don't know. I was just overwhelmed by that trip. I feel like I'll be called to go back to South Africa at some point in my life. I met Nelson Mandela's grandson at Stanford—he stayed in our dorm—and he said he would try to help me find a way to go back if he could."

At the end of her first year at Stanford, Myisha was given the Freshman of the Year award for service to the community. "I almost didn't go to the awards because we had a Talisman dinner that night," she says. "But I went, and I was feeling sad because so many parents were there and I wished my mom was there. Then suddenly she appeared at the door. She hadn't told me she was coming, because she wanted to surprise me. That was great. I admire my mom a lot. She's on her own and has five of us to take care of, and her health isn't that great. But I have never gone without. My mom always makes sure that I have what I need; she always makes sure that I have the necessities of life. I am blessed to have a mother like that who loves me and will support me in everything I do."

In her sophomore year, Myisha left Talisman to allow her more time to work in the university's black community. She took a job as the coordinator for community programming with the Black Community Service Center and spent her sophomore and junior years as president of Stanford's NAACP student chapter. "It's so good to network with a lot of successful black people," she says. "In the media, I don't hear about black success that much. It's more about black people murdering someone. You have to seek out the good news about black people, because that's not the story that sells. But the conferences I go to are full of successful, talented black people."

In her junior year, Myisha got sick: "I ended up in the hospital. The doctors couldn't figure out what was wrong with me. They did a colonoscopy, endoscopy, blood work, CAT scans. I think now that it was stress. I have a tendency to put commitments before my health sometimes. I went through a rough time and into a deep depression. But now that I'm over it, I know that it happened for a reason. The Lord brought it into my life to slow me down and see what I'm meant to do. In James 1:1, it says—I'm paraphrasing, but basically it says—'Consider it pure joy, my brother, when you go through trials, because the Lord brings about trials so you can grow and persevere.' Things caught up with me: the grief of my stepfather dying, the stress over my real father, the stress of being at Stanford. But I believe if the Lord brings you to it, he'll bring you through it. People in my family and my church prayed for me. The amount of support I receive from my family... I can't even describe it. I love being around them. Just recently, we

163

had a big get-together at the home of my uncle, who is a police chief in Stockton. We talked, played dominoes, cooked, ate. It was wonderful. My family has so much to do with who I am."

Now that she is well and preparing to graduate, Myisha plans to go on to graduate school to study both public health and law: public health because she has become so interested in the social context of illness and healing, law because she remains so committed to the need for social change. "I feel the two fields overlap so often that it's a very useful thing to do," she says. "I'm not sure exactly what my career will be like when I do them both, but I know I'll figure it out eventually. At the moment, I'm working on getting involved in eliminating disparities in health care. Minorities just don't receive the same standard of care as non-minorities. They get less invasive treatments, they get sent home from the hospital sooner. So I would be looking at access issues, quality of care, health insurance disparities, things like that.

"When I think about my career, I'm not worried. I know it will just unfold. My grandfather is so full of pride in me. He says, 'Baby, I can't wait to see you graduate.' It's very significant for my family. They understand everything I've overcome. Just being a black woman who's successful as a policy-maker and a lawyer... I just hope when I get to that point, I won't forget where I've come from.

"I feel that God has touched me in so many ways. I can feel His favor: time and again, doors have opened in my life. I feel this story is my testimony that anyone can make it. Look at me—I'm not rich, I come from the bad side of Stockton, my parents were on drugs, but I made it. I know it's all part of God's plan for me, and He doesn't intend me to fail. I'm His child. And I know that there are so many people like me but who haven't had the opportunities that I have been blessed with.... That's why I feel such a strong obligation to give back."

164

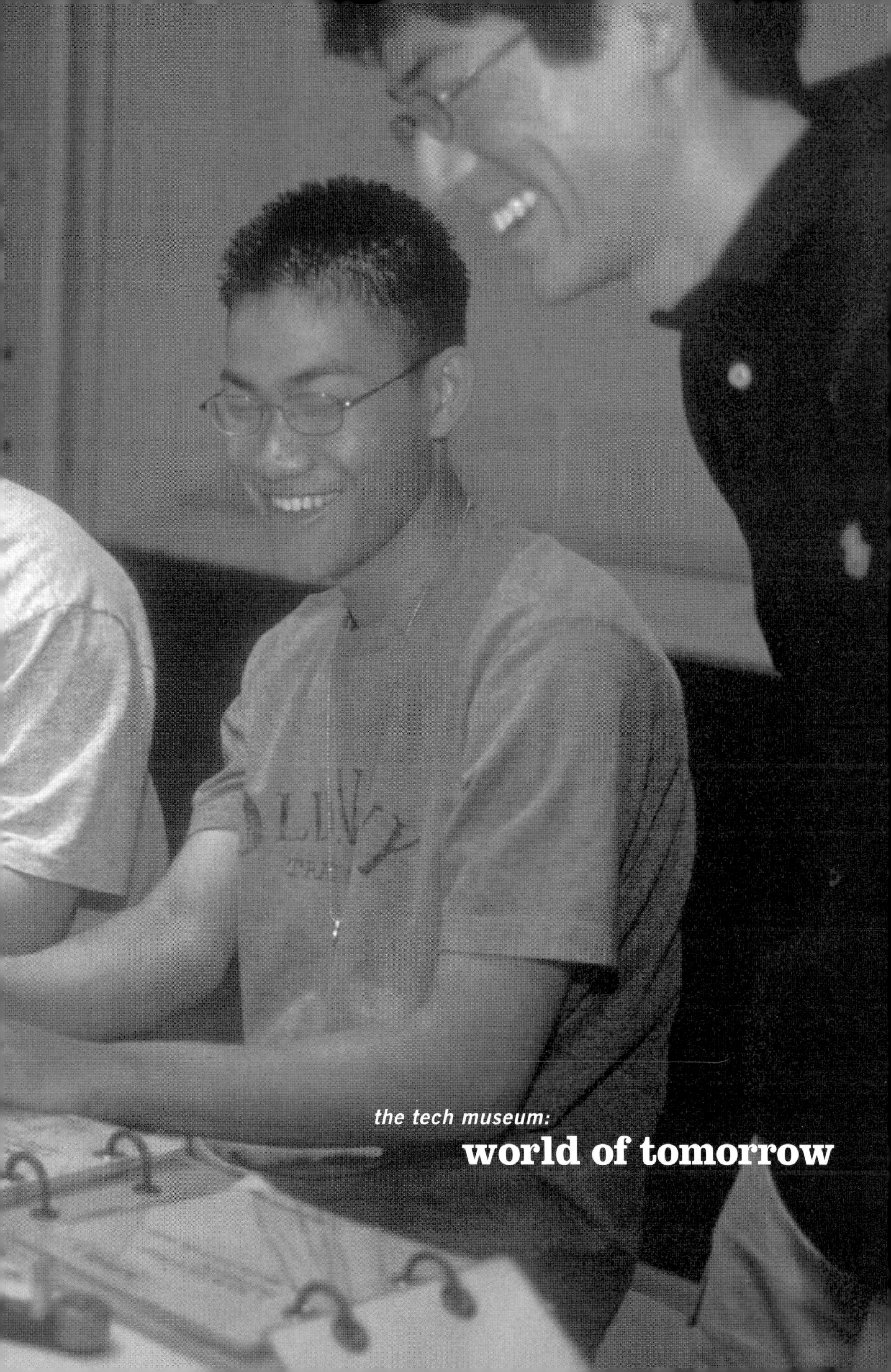

the tech museum:
world of tomorrow

San Jose's Tech Museum is Silicon Valley's monument to itself, a place that celebrates technology and the huge changes that have come with it. Its outside surfaces are covered with quotes from legendary innovators, everyone from Albert Einstein to Bill Hewlett of Hewlett-Packard fame. "Optimism is an essential ingredient for innovation," reads one quote near the entrance. "How else can the individual welcome change over security, adventure over staying in a safe place?" The sentiment is not lost on the SMYSP counselors, who work throughout the program to encourage optimism in their students and promote the value of welcoming change and adventure.

Today, Saturday, the counselors have brought the students to tour the museum. The outing is one of several the group will take over the summer: each year, students visit the beach on the Fourth of July to watch fireworks, see a show in San Francisco and tour the city's Yerba Buena Gardens, where they can ride the merry-go-round and read the sayings of another legendary innovator, Dr. Martin Luther King, Jr., whose words are inscribed on a granite fountain in the gardens. "Through our scientific genius, we have made this world a neighborhood," reads one of his quotes at Yerba Buena. "Now through our moral and spiritual development, we must make of it a brotherhood."

As the students filter into the Tech, they are greeted by its clean, futuristic design. The orange and purple color scheme is reminiscent of a science textbook, or George Jetson's living room; the finely finished pale wood floors echo the corporate offices of the Valley's many start-ups. "Inspiring the innovator in everyone!" read the banners slung along the walls. Everything in the Tech is man-made, and virtually everything has been invented in the last decade: the museum is the country's most comprehensive introduction to our emerging brave new world.

The students ride an escalator to reach the museum's exhibits; once they are at the top of the building, they find displays on everything from thermocameras to sonograms. They divide into small groups and fan out to explore the exhibits. Many of the displays are devoted to advances in knowledge about the human body—the students are surprised that even here, they are learning about medicine. A few students stop in front of a bank of TV monitors devoted to the human genome project. "Scientists are getting to know all about you," the introductory screen reads. "Click on any of the chromosomes to find out more about it." Clicking on one pair of chromosomes reveals that it is linked to Lou Gehrig's Disease; clicking on another reveals that it is linked to breast cancer. Nearby, a section on technology and medicine outlines the latest breakthroughs. "Technology is helping researchers understand ailments at the molecular level," it reads. "Researchers can then build drugs atom by atom that target disease precisely."

From the genetics section, one group of students heads to the electronics area, where teams of three can "ride" the virtual reality bobsled that athletes use to train for the Winter Olympics. After a few exhilarating minutes of simulated sledding, the students get off, looking woozy but eager to ride again. Another group tries out a wheelchair-racing device that allows two people to sit in fixed wheelchairs hooked up to a video monitor:

168

they race by pushing the wheels and watching their progress on the monitor. The students love it. "Go, go, go!" urge some, while others take turns racing. "It's hard!" Jessica exclaims, laughing and rubbing her sore wrists after her turn. "Yeah," Elizabeth says. "I've been pushing wheelchairs in the hospital for weeks, but it's different to be in one."

The students tour the genetic engineering displays, which feature redesigned plants and animals. They see tobacco plants that have had a gene inserted to make them glow, and obese mice that have been bred without the ability to create leptin, the chemical needed to tell the brain that the stomach is full. Around a corner, a series of exhibits focuses on advances in medical imaging. A display panel beside an MRI scanner explains how magnetic imaging works and invites viewers to climb inside the machine. Next door, an exhibit on sonograms details how doctors are able to use sound waves to see inside the body. The technologies used in CAT scans and X-rays are described, too, as well as an ambitious new project called "the visible human," which offers a virtual 3-D view of the human body that incorporates all systems: bone, muscle, sinew and skin.

In the middle of one of the exhibit halls stands the Tech's Curiosity Counter, its surfaces covered with a variety of new inventions. There is an electronic stethoscope and glasses that simulate what it feels like to drive drunk. There is a hand-held device that measures the fat content in the body; students take turns getting a reading and joke about the obesity stats from Marilyn's public health lecture. Most curious of all at the Curiosity Counter is a small purple pill, the size of the average drugstore capsule, that contains a miniscule camera. Doctors are beginning to use this very sci-fi device to get pictures of patients' intestines: the patient swallows the capsule, and the camera records its journey. "No way!" says Mark as he peers closer at the pill. "Can that be possible?"

The students explore the museum through the afternoon. They sit at the Inventor's Workbench, where they learn to build circuits, measure voltage and wire a circuit for sound. They send their voices out over a laser and giggle over their messages. They visit the Innovation Forum, a place for people to talk about technology—though they are more interested in videotaping each other than in recording their own thoughts.

At the end of the day, they file into the Tech's IMAX theater to watch a movie on the space station Mir. The movie details the hurdles scientists and engineers overcame to create and maintain the space station and it introduces viewers to the Russian and American crews living onboard Mir. As the movie unfolds, it becomes clear that the story of Mir is the story of people from different cultures living far from home—away from their families and their communities—in the name of discovery and changing the way lives are lived. "It's a whole new world up here," says one of the Russian astronauts at one point as the earth glides by below. "The old divisions mean nothing in this new environment." It's another sentiment not lost on the students, who are in their own new environment on a voyage of discovery. As they drift out of the theater after the movie, they walk by one final thought on the walls, this one from Madame Marie Curie: "You cannot hope to build a better world without improving the individuals."

leonard
marquez

"Every tree feels the force of the wind."
— African proverb

Leonard Marquez was born into a working-class family in a decaying steel town, to parents who finished high school and went straight on to blue-collar jobs. Twenty years later, he was at one of America's most blue-blooded universities, Princeton, putting the finishing touches on his senior thesis, an inquiry into the role that Dominican friars played in ushering democracy into medieval England. Today, he is a litigator at a top Oakland law firm. Those facts only begin to hint at who Leonard is: an uncommonly smart and gifted young man who has vaulted from Pittsburg to Princeton and beyond and emerged from the experience with an energy and ease that seem unshakable.

Leonard was raised in Pittsburg, California, an industrial town set on the banks of the Sacramento and San Joaquin rivers. Thanks to the waterways, in the 1920s and '30s, Pittsburg was a thriving industrial center anchored by a massive steel mill; the town was named after its counterpart in the East. But by the time Leonard was born in 1974, plant closures and a vanishing industrial base had mired Pittsburg in a recession.

Leonard's family saw the whole boom, the complete cycle of the town's highs and lows. All of Leonard's grandparents made their way to Pittsburg and worked there for decades: his father's father as a brick maker, his mother's father as a pipe fitter. His paternal grandfather, Henry Marquez, was originally from Mexico, grew up in Texas, and, with his brothers, moved to California when he was young, looking for work. He found it in the brickyard and stayed for 50 years. He took a break when World War II broke out, became a sergeant in the army and was sent to Europe. Henry fought in the Battle of the Bulge and was captured, though that story is more *Hogan's Heroes* than *Stalag 17*: separated from his unit, he came to a small town and snuck into a barn to find a place to relieve himself. Unfortunately, a German soldier with just the same idea was there, too, and Henry was captured and sent to a POW camp. He was fortunate that one of the German officers in the camp spoke Spanish and treated him well, and after he'd been there a few months, the Allies retook the area and he was freed. He returned to Pittsburg and married his sweetheart, a young Mexican-American woman named Ruth whose family had come north from the far south of Mexico to harvest crops in the San Joaquin Valley. They had five children, three girls and two boys, including Leonard's father.

Leonard's mother's family, Leonard says, "were totally different. Both my mom's mother and father, Verna and Howard Jennings, were from Oklahoma. They're European immigrants if you go way back, but they'd been in Oklahoma for generations. My grandfather was a rough old guy, always getting into fights. In Pittsburg, he was a pipe fitter. They're the guys who run the pipe through buildings: take the engineering plans, figure out how the pipe is going to be laid, direct the welders." The couple had three girls, including Leonard's mom.

When Leonard's parents grew up, things were changing in Pittsburg. The economy was stagnant, and there was ethnic unrest. "The Mexican Americans were fighting the African Americans and the Filipinos," says Leonard. "Who knows what sparked it. Part of it was linked to economics: the poorer it gets, the more violence there is. Then there were all the cultural tensions on top of that. I think it was just part of the times, the '60s and early '70s. My Aunt Anita was a member of the Brown Berets, a Mexican offshoot of the Black Panthers."

Leonard's parents met in junior high. His dad was two years older than his mom and known around school as a troublemaker, Leonard says. "He was banned from the junior high school that I ended up going to—he went to one too many dances and started one too many fights. When I was at that school, I was always in the honors classes. I remember my mom showing me my dad's old report card: it was straight F's with an A in physical education or shop. He used to joke about it every once in a while. I think that was part of the times, too. One thing about my family: even though some of them may have been irresponsible in high school, today they've all got families and jobs."

Leonard's parents married in 1972, right after his mother graduated. Leonard, their first child, was born two years later. The family lived near the railroad tracks that divide Pittsburg in half. Their house was near a city park, near aunts and uncles, and Leonard felt part of a loving family. His mother worked as a clerk at a grocery store for many years; she'd done well in high school, but didn't continue with her education. "My mom is smarter than she gives herself credit for," says Leonard. "She has a great sense of humor and she's very caring. She was always the one that the younger girls in the family would go to for advice."

When Leonard was born, his dad was working at the naval weapons station just over the hill in Concord, helping load ships with munitions for Vietnam. "But my father only worked at the naval station for a couple of years," Leonard says. "His main job when I was growing up was as a draftsman for engineering firms. He would take drawings and turn them into blueprints. It was one of those professions where you worked someplace and then you'd get laid off. He never had the luxury of going back to school to get an engineering degree. He was always telling me that I should be an engineer."

Leonard remembers himself as "a nerdy little kid." His early school experiences were positive, peaceful. In preschool, he met Cecilia Lafleur, who now, two decades later, is his girlfriend. He spent kindergarten through fifth grade at a school two blocks from his house and did well. "My family always encouraged me," he says. "I was the kid who didn't like to go out and play at recess, who liked to stay inside and read or do a project for extra credit."

Leonard's mom adored romance novels. Whenever she finished one, she and Leonard would head off to the bookstore to get another, and Leonard always got a book, too. By the time he was in the sixth grade, he was reading at the 12th-grade level. "One of my favorite books was this giant encyclopedia-dictionary that I had," he remembers. In it, he learned that Leonard was a Germanic name that meant "lionhearted."

It was fitting. Leonard may have thought of himself as a nerd, but he was no wimp. His great imagination was matched by his sense of adventure. He and his friends were always building something: forts, treehouses, rockets, explosives. "One time, my cousin and I tried to build a bomb in the front yard," he remembers. "We had the tall, skinny Coke bottles, and we took anything from the garage that would ignite. I think what we ended up making was a Molotov cocktail. We were trying to light it on the driveway, and my dad came out and saw us." There was an explosion, but it wasn't the intended one; it came from Leonard's dad. Still, says Leonard, "we just had a little bit of knowledge, and luckily, we never got in real trouble. We would have been terrors if we'd had the Internet as an information source back then."

173

School was another place for daring exploits. Leonard's fifth-grade teacher, Mr. Smertnik, had the entire class build hot-air balloons, which they flew clear across the football field behind the school. The balloons were nearly 5 feet high, made from multi-colored crepe paper, and looked great soaring over the field. Leonard was so inspired he joined Mr. Smertnik's more exclusive rocket club and spent the school year building a model rocket with a solid fuel propellant. He was so enthused that he and his cousin Jon wrote to NASA, asking for their formula for rocket fuel. They never got a reply.

In junior high, Leonard used the school's Macintosh to teach himself computer programming. By the time he reached the eighth grade, he was writing programs of his own. But while his grades stayed strong, his identity was changing, thanks in large part

a. Leonard's parents on their wedding day in Pittsburg in 1972. b. Leonard with his paternal grandparents on the day of his baptism. "They are standing in front of St. Peter Martyr, a historic little Catholic church in downtown Pittsburg, their long-time parish," he says.

to one of his aunts, who had taken Leonard aside at the start of junior high. "You're going to play football," she said.

"I hated sports, and I begged and pleaded not to do it," remembers Leonard. "I wasn't good at it, so I didn't want to do it. Then I started playing tackle football, and I found I liked it. I became Mr. Popular, the opposite of the little, insecure kid I'd been before. It's amazing—especially in junior high—how kids get into these cliques. There was a hierarchy of coolness depending on where you ate lunch."

At the start of high school, Leonard was assigned to honors courses. He was smart, good on the football field, and, he says, looking back, "probably a little cocky. As far as my personality: I was stubborn and headstrong. I had to be the best at whatever I did." That attitude took its toll in Leonard's junior year. In the ninth and 10th grade, he'd been a first-team inside linebacker and an offensive lineman, "one of the big guys that blocked while other guys were trying to run the ball." But by his junior year, Leonard was no longer all that big. Suddenly, he was, as he describes it, "getting the stuffing knocked out" of him. And one day, after he missed a block and was yelled at by the coach in front of everyone, he walked off the field and quit for the year. "Everything's traumatic when you're in high school," he says. "But looking back now, I think that was one of the worst things for me, the moment I walked off the field. I still don't know why I just gave up like that. It felt like utter defeat."

Off the field, Leonard's junior year brought him a happier experience: his American history class. "My teacher, David Littleton, was a teacher students loved. He ran the mock trial program at our high school and encouraged me to try that. I liked to spar with him. He had a Darth Vader doll on this little podium in the classroom, and he would challenge us to come up and match wits with the master. If we scored a couple of good points, he would make the Darth Vader noise, the breathing sound, and maybe break into the Darth Vader theme. I was always willing to get into those sparring matches."

a. Leonard (left) with his cousin Jon. b. Leonard as a football player, sophomore year at Pittsburg High.

Leonard decided to join the mock trial program. "There were 15 or 20 students on our team," he recalls. "You would take either the defense or the prosecution. You prepared both sides, and then you would be chosen randomly to do one or the other." Leonard's group of "lawyers" started going up against those from other schools. "Really, it was quite an experience," he says. "Pittsburg High has always been a powerhouse in football, but it's not known for academics. Our mock trial coach was a district attorney named Karen Zelis. She came in and got us all enthused. We went up against all these schools in our area, and, against all odds, ended up winning. We went on to the state competition and made it all the way to the semi-finals. By the end, I was certain I wanted to be a lawyer. To this day, Mr. Littleton is proud that I became a lawyer."

In the middle of his junior year, during Leonard's shift away from engineering and toward law, his chemistry teacher, Mr. Jang, handed him an application to SMYSP. "I don't know where he got it," says Leonard. "The school counselors didn't have time to do things like that. We had more than 2,000 students and maybe four or five counselors. They had way too much to do." Leonard decided to apply. Now that he was investigating law and it looked interesting, he thought perhaps he might find medicine even more appealing.

"When I got to SMYSP, I was a little apprehensive," he remembers. "I wasn't like all the other Hispanic students; I didn't speak Spanish, and my family had been in Pittsburg for two or three generations. I felt like an outsider. I think that was my own perception; after a while, I started to get to know people and make friends. I worked in the operating room at the VA Hospital, where I watched a number of surgeries, including an open-heart surgery that was amazing.

"I think the most important thing I got from SMYSP was the confidence," he says now. "Just getting into the program was a huge deal. And when it came round to the college applications, I was able to think, 'Okay, you can do this.' It was hard figuring out how to do it, but I knew that I *could* do it. The counselors at my high school were too busy to help me, and my parents didn't know what I needed to do and were in no position at that time to help me."

In Leonard's senior year, his parents' marriage began to dissolve. "The worst thing for me was that it was out of the blue," he says. "To this day, I still don't know what triggered the whole thing. The first thing I noticed when I came back from SMYSP was that my dad wasn't around very much. He'd be gone for days on end. Maybe he was having a mid-life crisis. Drugs weren't foreign to him. It was a commonplace thing at my house, but it was never a big problem. Then I suppose he started partying harder with some of his old buddies. By the time I was a senior, it was chaos. I remember going to visit my grandparents that fall or winter, probably at Christmas. My dad was supposed to pick us up, but I found out later that he was in a car chase with the police, smashed up the truck he was driving and ended up in jail. My dad lost his job, we couldn't pay the mortgage, and the house was being foreclosed. My mom had her job but she didn't have enough money to pay the mortgage. She ended up selling the house. I know my dad felt badly about what had happened, and when they got divorced, he gave anything that was left to my mom."

Through it all, Leonard kept himself on track. He knew it was important to go back to the only thing in his life he'd ever walked out on, so in his senior year he played football again for Pittsburg High. He was only a second-string player, but he was present at every game. He researched colleges and applied to the two places he thought he'd most like to attend. "If it hadn't been for SMYSP, I'm not sure I would have applied to Stanford and Princeton," he says. "I think it gave me a whole different mindset about the possibilities. Not a lot of students from Pittsburg High went to four-year colleges. Very few went to private schools.

"I ended up doing an early application to Princeton, and I heard from them in December that they'd accepted me. Stanford took me, too, and then I had to agonize over which one to attend. I think the main factor in my decision was that Princeton was on the East Coast and it was something completely different." The only other person from Pittsburg High to head to an Ivy League school was Cecilia, Leonard's friend from preschool, who was accepted at Harvard.

Leonard arrived at Princeton in the fall of 1992. He was a conscientious, industrious, working-class student suddenly going to school with the sons and daughters of government ministers, corporate CEOs and academic luminaries. It took a lot of personal resilience and self-confidence.

"I loved Princeton, but I was never happy there," he says. "I was always socially isolated. I majored in politics, and the program was awesome. I only really got to know one professor, a former Marxist from Cuba, Carlos Forment. I took a class from him in my junior year. I always wore a baseball cap turned around backwards, and as the semester wore on, I would get progressively worse about getting to class on time. And some days I would sleep in class. One day, Professor Forment fixed his gaze on me and said, 'Our friend with the backward hat is here, and awake, too.' It was embarrassing, but he meant it as a joke." After Professor Forment's ribbing, the two gradually became friends. Leonard, still a computer wiz, became Forment's personal computer advisor and repairman; Forment became Leonard's senior thesis adviser.

Among the students, Leonard's one social outlet came on the football field, though this time, he was there in a somewhat different capacity: "I had a cousin who was a junior at Princeton, and she was on the cheerleading squad. When I got to Princeton, she invited me to dinner, and these two guys came and sat down with us. They were the coach and the captain of the team. They were desperate to get guys to join the team. She convinced me to try out, and in the end, I spent four years on Princeton's cheerleading team. I'm lucky I did it, because it was the one way I got to meet and hang out with people." Whenever he got a longer break, he would travel to Boston to see Cecilia at Harvard.

Despite the disconnection he often felt, Leonard thinks back on his Princeton experience as a time of growth, a time when he was "becoming more worldly, seeing the East Coast and meeting new people, slowly getting a better idea of the world outside of Pittsburg." Convinced by his classes that law was the right profession, he applied to law school while still a senior in college.

"I went to UCLA law school," he says. "I loved it. There were some stressful periods, of course, but I was a much happier person. I was an editor at the *Chicano Law Review*. There were a lot of Hispanic students at UCLA. It was one of the most diverse schools in the nation."

When Leonard was in law school, he spent some time examining a subject he knew firsthand from life in Pittsburg: economic inequalities and how they manifest in education. He spent a summer working with a professor who was assessing the academic performance of schools in San Francisco against race and economics. "In the late '70s or early '80s, the NAACP had filed a lawsuit against the city," says Leonard. "As a result, there was a consent decree to remedy discrimination or disparate distribution of resources. Each day, we'd visit a different school and evaluate it."

Leonard completed law school and passed the California bar exam. He moved back to Northern California and took a job as an associate with Wendel, Rosen, Black & Dean in Oakland. Cecilia is back in the East Bay, too; she graduated from Harvard with a History of Science degree and is now teaching eighth grade science at a school in Castro Valley.

Leonard credits his parents as the single greatest source of support in his life. "Neither of my parents were model children," he says, "but they always motivated me with encouragement and recognition. They were really supportive. My dad was always willing to take a truckload of kids to football practice; my mom never missed an open house at school." Musing on the other mentors who've helped him, Leonard says,

"There has to be some sort of mechanism for transferring knowledge from the people who have it to those who don't. If that's not built into the system, you're dependent on people like my high school history teacher, Mr. Littleton, people who take it on themselves to be mentors and raise expectations.

"I think society should increase the rewards for people who mentor. It's great when people do it just for the sake of doing it, but to institutionalize it, you have to increase the rewards. One example is my cousin Jon, who ended up becoming a teacher. He went to Humboldt State because of Mr. Littleton. He taught in Los Angeles, in schools for kids that got into trouble, but he was being paid less than teachers in ordinary high schools. He's now teaching at Pittsburg High. He benefited from the efforts of teachers like Mr. Littleton; now he's gone back to help the next generation."

Leonard, too, tries to be a mentor. "I think my beliefs have given me a sense of duty to try to do those same things," he explains. He has judged the mock trial competition that he loved so much when he was student. He also volunteers in the Youth Court in Oakland. "It handles minor infractions by high school kids, and their peers handle the sentencing," he explains. "Kids can avoid the traditional juvenile justice system, and hopefully, the scrutiny of their own peers will make an impact."

Leonard's own goals are financial security, a nice home, opportunities for the children he plans to have. But as he thinks about his children's future, he is drawn to his past, and he finds himself torn between his fear of losing his heritage and his desire to better the lives of the next generation: "I've talked about this a lot with my Aunt Anita. In her parent's generation, everyone in the family spoke Spanish. In her and my father's generation, only the older siblings speak any Spanish. I still can't speak Spanish. That's a concrete example of loss from generation to generation. Yet, I benefited from family ties, from having my extended family living around me. The experience of being in a multicultural melting pot gave me a sense of family and community.

"Growing up in Pittsburg like we did gave us a certain perspective," he says. "It's all relative: we weren't super-poor inner-city kids, but we weren't squarely in the middle class, either. We were really on the verge of a middle-class existence. It took scrapping and work to get by. And that bred independence and resilience. If I get my big house and move up, my kids will be completely removed from the life I went through. Is that good or bad? At every stage of evolution, you wonder what you're gaining and what you're losing."

mentor right:
career guides

Dr. Raul Calderon is finishing his post-doctoral degree in epidemiology and public health at Stanford. He is tall, slim, in his late 30s and has a quiet patience about him that suggests a teacher. It's not a coincidence: Raul was a teacher, off and on, for 10 years before he decided to pursue a career in public health. He taught in schools and gyms in Mexico, Puerto Rico, Iowa and California and coached volleyball, basketball and track and field. Over the years, he has been an informal mentor to hundreds of kids in high schools and at the YMCA.

When Raul was offered the chance to be a mentor at SMYSP, he took it. He thought he would have something useful to share since he comes from a background not far removed from those of the SMYSP students: he grew up in Stockton, one of six children in a family with few resources. Raul remembers a childhood of just getting by and the importance of things in his early life that made him aware of the larger world. In his junior year in high school, Raul was among the first wave of students who were bused in the wake of desegregation rulings. He was sent to a high school across town where a science teacher named Mr. Anderson wrote a grant to take his new, less-affluent students on outdoor learning adventures that included cross-country skiing, snow camping, rock climbing and alpine skiing. Raul was an avid participant in all of it; everyone, he thought, should have similar opportunities to try new things.

Raul became a part of SMYSP's Mentor Night. The event is another pivotal part of the program: every summer, each student is teamed up with a medical or post-doctoral student. Mentors and their students meet every Thursday night over the course of the program. They get together at the house for dinner and then head out to talk, explore, go for a drive, go to a movie. The relationships are informal; the idea behind the night is to connect a more experienced but still youthful person in the medical field with a high school student in need of guidance. If the relationship works and the two develop a bond, the student will have a confidant and advisor in medicine for years to come.

Raul is mentoring a student named Jose, who is just about to enter his senior year at Los Altos High School. Like Raul, he is tall and slim, athletic. At school, he is a champion badminton player and at SMYSP, he uses the rare, short breaks in the program for quick games of basketball around the hoop out back. "My mother has always supported me in my education," Jose wrote in his introduction to the other students, "and she is the reason that I wish to excel in life. She has taught me the value of a good education."

Jose and Raul meet on the first Thursday of the program. There is an immediate affinity. Raul remembers, "Jose was very sincere, humble and had a genuine quality about him that immediately struck a chord." The two talk about family, sports, school and what they might do over the next five weeks. Raul, thinking back to the importance of his own high school outdoor adventures with Mr. Anderson, offers to teach Jose to paraglide.

182

Jose loves the idea, and the next week, the two set out for Stanford's "oval," a large patch of grass at the entrance to the university's main buildings. Raul helps Jose climb into the paraglider's harness. The yellow-and-fuchsia chute drags behind Jose as Raul straps him in. Then, with Raul's encouragement, he sets off running across the grass. The chute soars over his head. The air pulls at his feet, trying to lift him into the sky. In the remaining weeks of the program, Raul and Jose venture into the foothills surrounding the university. Jose runs through hills covered with high summer grasses. His confidence complete, he springs from the hillside and, for the first time, feels his feet lift off the ground and his body fly through the air.

Musing on what makes a mentor, Raul pulls a metaphor from his high-altitude past. "I would say a mentor is someone who is at a higher level up the mountain," he says. "They're someone who has had more life experience, someone who's already passed through the section of the forest that you are traveling through, someone you can look to for advice. They're not there to tell you exactly which way to go; they're there to orient you to the terrain, to say, 'Well, this path is a little steeper,' or 'This path is windier.' They give you information to help you make your own decisions."

Shaun Kunnavatana is also a mentor at SMYSP. A Stanford graduate who is now in Stanford Medical School, Shaun grew up in Los Angeles. From kindergarten on, he was placed in special programs for gifted students. "It's a funnel," he remembers. "The teachers pull what they consider talent and focus their research, learning and teaching on those kids. I realized during my interactions with the students who weren't in gifted programs that a lot of them were really smart, but they'd been overlooked. I realized that luck and chance had a lot to do with getting academic help. So I was drawn to SMYSP because it empowers students and gives them opportunities. As far as the mentoring night itself, it really offers students some space to breathe and relax, because being in the program is an intensive experience."

Shaun is mentoring David, the son of Vietnamese refugees. David is talkative, outgoing, full of questions. When Shaun picks him up for a night of Vietnamese food and golf, he asks about Shaun's work, study habits, medical inclinations, hobbies. In Shaun's car, a souped-up Acura, they talk about college, medical research, David's internship in the VA radiology department and Shaun's love of auto racing. At a restaurant in downtown Mountain View, the next town south of Palo Alto, they both order *bun tom thit nuong*, a bowl of charbroiled, marinated shrimp and pork served over vermicelli noodles. They talk about the schools David plans to apply to. "When you're deciding about schools, don't be too swayed by rankings," advises Shaun. "Get to know what you want if you can. The most important thing is to have fun with what you're doing. In college, you'll find a wealth of diversity and opportunity to gain exposure to all kinds of things."

After the meal, the two head for the Mountain View golf course and driving range. The light is waning and the temperature is dropping as they pick up clubs and a bucket of balls. A number of management types are already out on the driving range, slicing and dicing. Shaun and David join them, set up their balls and prepare to tee off. Shaun has tried this before; David has never hit a golf ball in his life. Shaun goes first: his ball is

183

wide and low, bouncing off to the side of the green. David's ball arcs high, powerful and straight.

"Wow!" says Shaun. "How'd you do that?"

David shrugs sheepishly. "Luck?" he says.

But as the two make their way through their bucket of balls, it's clear that David has a knack for the sport: his eyes and hands seem naturally attuned to the game. By the time the bucket is empty, it's dark, the temperature has sunk to 50 degrees, and David has discovered a new talent he didn't know he had. The two climb back into Shaun's car and drive back to the house, making plans for what they'll do next week.

destinee cooper

*"I have seen that in any great undertaking,
it is not enough for a man to depend simply on himself."*
— Sioux proverb

Destinee Cooper's words are measured and delivered with a quiet certitude.
"A lot of people tell me I'm blunt," she says, but there is nothing thoughtless or curt in her candor—she simply calls life as she sees it. And she has seen a lot of it. On the streets of her neighborhood, a drive-by shooting marked virtually every weekend. At home, drugs and alcohol mired her family in violence. But as she grew, Destinee began to discover the gifts that were going to provide her with a different kind of life: her strong intellect and unflagging determination.

Destinee had always been the sort of child in whom an answer sparked another question, a child whose mind leap-frogged constantly, finding meaning and connection everywhere. In the sixth grade at Chrysler Elementary School in Modesto, her intellectual awakening really took hold: on the first day of classes, in walked teacher Mary Elizabeth Hill, who, as Destinee remembers her, seemed just like Arnold Schwarzenegger in *The Terminator*. She made an impact on Destinee that resonates to this day.

"She told us, 'Kids, this is your chance. I can either be your best friend or your worst enemy,'" Destinee recalls. "She knew all about the drugs and alcohol and violence in our neighborhood, but she said, 'You can't use your neighborhood as an excuse in my classroom. There *are* no excuses here. You each have an A now, and you can keep it or lose it. It's up to you. Education is your key.' She really shocked us. She just came in and told us, 'This is the way it is.' She even put up a picture of Schwarzenegger on the wall as a reminder!" says Destinee, laughing.

Destinee took Hill at her word. A self-described "sickly child" who was often away from school with colds and the flu, Destinee had met a lot of doctors before she met Hill, and she had already decided that she wanted to be one. She even knew what kind: an emergency room doc. Every Thursday night, she made it a point to have her homework done early so she could watch her favorite TV show, *ER*. Ms. Hill's speech just proved the right incentive to push the 11-year-old forward. The moment Destinee heard the words, the equation registered in her head: dedication plus education equals Dr. Destinee Cooper. But the realization came at a cost. "When I made that decision, emotional barriers went up between me and my family," says Destinee. "I started getting straight A's, and I got more involved with my community. It was an escape."

It was an escape for a bright child in a maelstrom. Destinee and her sister, who is four years older, lived in a small apartment with thin walls. The girls were acutely aware of their parents' drug use.

"My father was an alcoholic; he would come home from work and drink and then go to bed," says Destinee of those days. "If he didn't go to bed by 8 o'clock, we always knew something bad was going to happen." Destinee calls her sister "the balancing act": in the face of violence, she was the one who tried to keep peace in the family by taking the brunt of the abuse directed at the girls. As she aged, Destinee, too, felt an obligation to defuse tension in the family. She tried to smooth things over at home, and to this day, she carries the air of an efficient organizer, always making sure that things are done right, that concerns are addressed.

Relief came during the time Destinee and her sister spent with their beloved grandparents, Beverly and Joe. "My grandmother was more like a mother because of the support she gave me," Destinee says of the woman who cared for her almost every weekend.

188

"Our grandparents stressed the importance of education. They read to us. They helped us with our lunch money."

Beverly had grown up in Billings, Montana. She never knew her father, and his identity remained a mystery for much of her life. But she and her brother Charlie had an intuitive sense of where he might be from. "The Crow Indian reservation was nearby," says Destinee. "The only time it was ever mentioned was when my grandmother's stepfather would say, 'I know that girl has native blood, because she knows too much' and comments like that. But her mother never talked about it. In those days, if you didn't have European blood, you didn't talk about it."

Six months before Beverly's and Charlie's father died, Charlie met him and discovered that he and Beverly were indeed descendents of the Crow. "Apparently, their father tried to leave them some land on the reservation," says Destinee, "but their mother stopped that. She didn't want to acknowledge any connection because they'd had a huge argument before they split up."

When Beverly was a young woman, she met and married Destinee's grandfather Joe, then a truck driver who had traveled to Montana from Minnesota. The two moved west and in the early 1960s settled in Modesto. Joe continued trucking; Beverly worked in a cannery, preserving tomatoes, peaches and applesauce. Destinee describes Modesto as a "small, industrialized town." Both Beverly and Joe were instrumental in unionizing their workplaces: Beverly successfully led the union movement at the cannery; Joe was a key person in Modesto's truck drivers union.

Destinee's mother grew up working in the cannery alongside her mother, graduated from high school and started classes at the local community college. When she was 20, she gave birth to Destinee's older sister. The baby's father left town, and Destinee's mother quit college.

"A little after that," says Destinee, "my mother met another man, my father, and they got married. He hadn't finished college, either. They traveled a lot with my father's parents, who were going around the country, looking for oil. My mother's parents were raising my sister." When Destinee's mother became pregnant with Destinee, she decided to leave the nomadic life. The family moved into a trailer; Destinee's sister, then 4, moved back to help raise Destinee.

Just before Destinee entered kindergarten, the family moved into an apartment in a bleak part of the city. "There were drive-by shootings, raids for drug dealers. You learned which places were off-limits. Still, I had friends everywhere: black, white, Hispanic." The neighborhood took its toll: many of Destinee's friends ended up in gangs or juvenile detention facilities. But when her friends started to run into trouble, Destinee pulled back. "I realized that I could get through life without drugs and alcohol," she says. "My grandparents had a stable home, and they showed me another way."

Though today she is the picture of health, Destinee was in and out of the hospital as a child. "The first time I remember going to the hospital was in the second grade, after someone hit me with a soccer ball. I fainted. I was all bloody, so my mother took me in. I had a concussion but I was okay. My father was always getting sick, too. He was an alcoholic and a hypochondriac. I became a hypochondriac, too. Every time we got sick, we went to the emergency room."

189

Destinee believes that the seeds of her interest in science were sown during those numerous trips to the hospital, though it wasn't until sixth grade that she really began to think seriously about how she would actually become a doctor. "Ms. Hill had us write about our goals," she remembers. "I don't remember how or why I knew that I wanted to be a doctor, but I did. Maybe because of all the drugs and alcohol, and my family going in and out of the hospital. And it provided a mental challenge for me."

She began volunteering at a convalescent home. She would play Go Fish and Crazy Eights with the home's elderly residents, sit and listen to stories, help people walk and make sure they took their medicine. "I've always loved hearing stories of the old times," says Destinee, "and people helped boost my self-esteem. They'd hold my hand, tell me I'd go far."

a. Destinee as a baby. "I was told that people didn't have to do anything to make me smile," she remembers. "I was naturally happy."
b. Destinee at 12 in her family's apartment. "My cousin did my hair and picked out my clothes. Then we took the picture," Destinee says.
c. Destinee at 18 in Colorado with her paternal grandparents and great-grandmother.

Though she was only 11, Destinee was beginning to get a sense of what it meant to be a medical caretaker, as she dealt with people losing their memories, people who were incontinent, people who were depressed. She also volunteered at the other end of the age spectrum, taking care of young children in her school's kindergarten. She threw herself into academics. "I remember when we started learning about the Egyptians and about the pyramids and mummies. I jumped up to a whole new reading level. Ms. Hill made us understand *why* we were doing things."

Destinee's successful negotiation of the challenges in her life did not go unnoticed. At the end of the sixth grade, she was given a number of awards, including one from the superintendent of the schools. "It was a good feeling, and it inspired me," she recalls. "There were a lot of connections between the teachers and the community in my junior high school. The teachers got the community involved and made sure that they got the support they needed. We were constantly having fundraisers, everything from car washes to candy sales." At the end of the eighth grade, Destinee graduated as class valedictorian.

Junior high summers are a memorable time for any child, a time for gaining perspective and independence, creating identity, making plans, taking chances. In Destinee's seventh grade summer, she took a trip to Montana for the first time. She was amazed. "When you live in California, you get used to gray horizons," she says. "But Montana is 'big sky country.' You can see forever. I went with my grandparents, and we stayed on the Crow reservation. I was in culture shock for a couple of days. Did you ever see the movie *Thunderheart*? The reservation is like that: a lot of open space with old wooden houses, abandoned houses. I love the open space there and the fact that they let everything return to its origin, earth. When I think about the community, I think of a dying group of traditionalists who are fighting to save their way but who will soon leave behind generations of assimilated children."

Once Destinee got used to "the rez," she adored it, and she has returned every summer since seventh grade. Each time, she gains a better understanding of and a greater appreciation for her heritage. During Christmas of her sophomore year in college, she was given her Crow name: Ikooscha Itchiish, which means "Comes Out Pretty." "It comes from some visions that my Uncle Brian had when I was in high school," she explains. "He lives on the reservation, and during my 10th grade summer, he went through the ceremony of the Sun Dance, which people do to solidify their relationship with God. You fast throughout it. And that's when he had the vision for my name."

But as Destinee finished junior high, things at home were in turmoil. "During eighth grade, I found out that an aunt I was close to had breast cancer. Then, during my freshman year in high school, my parents separated. My mother and I went to live with my grandparents. In December, my grandmother went to San Diego to help take care of my aunt. And when Christmas vacation came, my mother and dad got together again. My mom moved in with my dad, but she said I didn't have to move until the end of Christmas vacation. So I was all alone: my grandma was in San Diego, my grandpa was at work as a truck driver, my mom was with my dad, and my sister had graduated from high school and left for college. It was a sad time for me because I was by myself for the first time during the holidays. The day after Christmas, my grandmother called and said if we wanted to see my aunt again, we had to come. So we drove down to San Diego and saw my aunt in the hospital. I'd never seen anyone so sick.

"We came home on New Year's Eve. As soon as I got in, I turned on the TV, and the ball in Times Square was dropping. I felt so sad. It just didn't seem like there was anything to celebrate. And then, on January 5th, my aunt died.

"I moved back in with my parents the next day. At that point, I just didn't care anymore. I finished my freshman year and I did fine, still getting A's and B's, but it took me about a year and a half to get over my aunt's death. I went into a deep depression and I walked around mummified for a long time."

By her own description, Destinee started to question many aspects of her life. She confronted her father about his drug use. She turned further away from her family. She got more involved in outside activities. And she spent a lot of time with her friends, whom, she says, "really got me through that depression: they would listen to me and they were objective.

"Then, one day in May of 1997, my grandmother was waiting for me after school. She told me that my mom was moving out of the apartment we were living in with my dad. By this time, my mother had stopped drinking and doing drugs. The night before,

191

there had been a big fight and I'd called the police; I'd never done that before, and it scared my mom.

"My father came home. I was packing my stuff, and my parents started to argue, and the neighbors called the police again. My mother and grandmother were carrying loads of our belongings to my grandparents' house. And I was sitting outside on the grass with the last of my stuff, waiting for them to come back. My father came out and stared at me. He said, 'You called the cops? Why did you do that?' I said it was because he was scaring me. He said he would never hurt me, but I said it was about him hurting my mom, not me. He started to cry, and then finally, he just got on his bike and rode off. Then my mother picked me up and we went to my grandmother's house. We spent the rest of my sophomore year and all of my junior year there."

Through all of the tumult, Destinee kept up her near-perfect grades and her tireless volunteering: it was her escape and her reward. In the eighth grade, she began helping at Youth Court, an innovative system set up to allow peers to try first-time offenders guilty of minor violations such as shoplifting, breaking curfew or possessing small amounts of drugs. "Basically, this was their second chance," says Destinee. "Results didn't go on their records. The trials were all run by minors, and the decisions were binding." Over the course of the five years she worked at the court, Destinee took on the roles of clerk, bailiff and jury member. By the time she graduated from high school, she had a clear understanding of what a life in the law would be like—and a commitment to medicine that was stronger than ever.

In her freshman year of high school, she started volunteering at the local hospital as a candy striper. There, she did errands for the nurses: took specimens to the lab, transported patients in the hospital, helped take care of babies in the ICU and observed in the ER. She loved the people she worked with at the hospital—a big, healthy de facto family of people who all worked together and ate dinner together every night, with much laughter and joking. "Working at the hospital, I became even more enthusiastic and focused about being a doctor," she recalls.

Destinee heard about SMYSP from one of her biology teachers. She was busy—volunteering, keeping up her grades and working at McDonald's 20 hours a week. She quickly filled out the SMYSP application and sent it in. "I got through the phone interviews, which was a surprise," she recalls. "Then they called me for the campus interview, but I still thought, 'This is never going to happen.' My mother was shocked that I was going to Stanford for an interview. My grandparents drove me to Stanford. I had three interviews: one in a group, one with Marilyn and the executive director and one with the student directors. And then I got the acceptance letter in the mail and I was like, 'I'm going!' My mother was even more shocked. My grandfather drove me up again. I was the first one there."

Unlike many SMYSP students, Destinee already had years of experience volunteering in a hospital when she arrived at the program. Still, she found much that was new and fascinating. "We got to work on cadavers, which was awesome," she says. "At the hospital, I was in the physical therapy department. And at one point, I got to talk to an ER physician. And being there and talking to him, I thought, 'Yeah, this fits me.' I think if you work in an ER, you have to be positive and energetic.

"The most important part of SMYSP, for me, was getting to know everyone in the house. We had such a good time there: we had water fights, played practical jokes on each other. My group project was on all of the different medicines that have been found in the rain forest and the need to preserve the rain forest for future research. On the last day, when we did our presentations and graduated, I locked arms with two of my friends and cried. When my family drove me home, I cried the whole time. It was so fantastic, because being at SMYSP broke down a lot of the emotional barriers I'd put up in the sixth grade. I realized how many helpful, good people are out there for me. My mentor at SMYSP was Melissa Williamson, and I still keep in contact with her. She is a constant reminder to me of what I'm striving for."

When she returned from SMYSP, Destinee applied to and was accepted at UC Berkeley, UC Davis, UC Riverside and UC Irvine. She chose Davis, fearing that Berkeley would be "too chaotic." She graduated from high school with a raft of honors, including an award for performing more than 1,300 hours of community service during high school.

At UC Davis, Destinee remains a committed student and activist who is on the dean's list and involved with the Native American Student Union. Last year, her mother moved to the reservation in Montana; her grandparents, ever supportive, decided to stay in nearby Modesto so she can visit and live with them during school vacations. After finishing medical school, Destinee hopes to practice medicine on the reservation and live the rest of her life in Montana. "That's where my roots are," she says. "In this complicated world, the people on the rez remind me that leading a simple life is good."

193

Destinee Cooper

gynecological oncology:
on the cutting edge of cancer

It's the fourth week of SMYSP. The students spent the weekend around the house, working on their research projects and doing SAT prep. On Monday, it was back to the program's arduous 8 a.m. to 11 p.m. schedule—though the evening held a midsummer night's treat, an expedition to the local ice skating rink. Everyone loved their adventures on ice, even Oscar, who got a whole different take on physician shadowing when— after taking a spill on his skates—he wound up in the ER with a torn ligament. Now, two days later, with crutches by his side, he is sitting in a classroom in Stanford's main quad along with his 23 classmates, preparing for the day's first lecture.

Just before 9 a.m., a tall, confident woman walks into the room. She is Dr. Kate O'Hanlan, a gynecological oncologist, here to talk about women's health and cancer. She has the aura of healing that is carried by the most comforting doctors, and the room feels warmer with her in it. When she speaks, she is funny and engaging. Throughout her lecture, the students listen intently and laugh a lot.

O'Hanlan begins by telling the story of her own educational odyssey. It is clear, as she talks, that her aim in telling her story is to convince the students that their own academic dreams are viable. She was born in what she describes as "a small, hick country town in Virginia." In high school, all of her classmates planned to work at the local factory after graduation. O'Hanlan had other ideas. "I would go into Charlottesville when I was a girl, and seeing that wider world made me want to go to school and make good," she remembers.

O'Hanlan started on that road at Duke University, where she double-majored in zoology and psychology. As the end of college neared, she decided to take the medical school admissions test. She was a little intimidated. "I was a studious hippie," she remembers. "The pre-meds were nerdy, and I always thought they were smarter than me because they wore calculators on their belts."

O'Hanlan's results proved calculators on belts aren't the most reliable gauge of intelligence. She attended the Medical College of Virginia; when she found she liked delivering babies, she did a residency program in obstetrics and gynecology at Atlanta's Georgia Baptist Medical Center. There she honed her studies further. "During my residency, I saw a subset of women who were getting cancers of the female organs," she tells the students. "When they needed to be operated on, I found that was very challenging. It felt like arts and crafts, doing a lot of careful, expert work with the hands. So I applied to do two extra years of training in gynecologic oncology." O'Hanlan was 32 when she graduated with the training she needed for the career she wanted. Today, she is the associate director of gynecologic cancer surgery at Stanford, and she has several times been named one of the Bay Area's best doctors. Her enthusiasm for her work is obvious and infectious. Laughing, she amazes the students when she tells them she is in the *Guinness Book of World Records* for taking out the world's largest tumor, a benign ovarian mass that weighed 303 pounds by the time it was removed.

"As a doctor today, I care about what kills us and about what will make us live longer," O'Hanlan tells the students. "I ask all of the women who come to see me, 'Do you exercise?' Women need at least 30 minutes of exercise four times a week." O'Hanlan shows slides of arteries, both normal and clogged, and talks about the dangers of cardiovascular disease, the nation's leading cause of death. From there, she turns to her own specialty: cancer.

She hands out a two-page fact sheet detailing women's cancers, a document that lists items like risk factors, symptoms, treatment and survival rates. The students pore over it as she begins to talk about some of the cancers that plague women: breast, ovarian, cervical, endometrial.

"Breast cancer is the most common cancer that women get," O'Hanlan says, "although lung cancer is actually a bigger killer, and more women will die from it. With breast cancer, I always check for swollen glands under the arms, because cancer from the breast can invade the lymph nodes located in the surrounding tissue. If it's not caught, from there the cancer can get into the circulatory system and into the lungs." O'Hanlan asks Grace to stand up; deftly she examines her to demonstrate to the class how the check is performed. "Okay," says O'Hanlan, thanking Grace with a smile, "you're fine."

"The third biggest cancer killer, after lung cancer and breast cancer, is colorectal cancer. It starts as a little polyp. So everybody after 50 should have a colonoscopy"— O'Hanlan jokingly refers to it as a "lookupthebuttofme"—"and the doctors can remove any polyps that they see, thus preventing a cancer."

O'Hanlan outlines cancers of the reproductive organs. She projects a slide of a cancer-riddled cervix, and the students, now used to a dispassionate, scientific analysis of the human body, barely react. "Cervical cancer is another cancer that can easily spread to the lymph nodes, and often to treat it, we have to do a radical hysterectomy and take out the top half of the vagina," O'Hanlan says, indicating where surgical cuts might need to be made. "Cervical cancer is fairly common in the United States, and we know that the human papilloma virus that causes genital warts can cause cervical cancer.

"Ovarian cancer is another concern. With this form of cancer, there are very few known risk factors. One of them is not having many babies. But it's a difficult cancer to diagnose early, because the ovaries are so deep in the body." According to O'Hanlan's handout, the survival rate for ovarian cancer is 40 percent overall; it rises to 88 percent when detection is early. Another cancer O'Hanlan sees in her practice is endometrial cancer. "With this cancer, obesity is a big risk factor," she says. "Obesity causes extra estrogens to be secreted into the bloodstream, and those create all kinds of problems."

From the problems, O'Hanlan turns to the solutions. "We are really working on improving cancer control," she tells the students. "One of the things that we can do now is to identify a person's genetic predisposition to cancer. Some breast, colon and ovarian cancers are now known to have a genetic link. A very few women have up to an 80 percent chance of getting breast cancer! So one of the things we can do to help control cancer is to closely monitor those at risk.

"Another key thing that can be done to control cancer is to reduce exposure to environmental carcinogens. Smoking, air pollution—those contain carcinogens that, when inhaled, can cause cancer. Viruses are another thing to try to avoid. We've already talked about how the human papilloma virus can cause cervical cancer. Safe sex is that important.

"A third thing we can do to control cancer is to increase exposure to protective agents like antioxidants. The very best way to avoid cancer is to eat low on the food chain and stick to a diet predominantly made up of fresh vegetables, fruits, beans and legumes. Basically, I like to tell my patients that there is one cosmic list for staying healthy and avoiding cancer: don't smoke, don't drink excessively, make sure you exercise, eat healthy foods and avoid risky sex.

"When you're actually at the doctor's, though, another key thing is early diagnosis. Every woman should have a Pap smear each year regardless of how healthy she is. Other screening tests cover blood pressure, bone density and cholesterol levels. Women should get their first mammograms at age 35 and then yearly after they're 40, and a colonoscopy after 50.

"Finally, if cancer is present, the most important thing is effective intervention," says O'Hanlan—and that, of course, is where her surgical skills come in. "I went into cancer work for two reasons," she says. "The first is that it challenges me to be the best I can be; it makes me be smart and think on my feet. The second is that women need compassion. They need understanding. When you have cancer, what you don't need is a doctor who tells you, 'Don't you worry about it, that's my problem, little lady.' We need compassionate, humanist doctors, but there are still a lot of problems out there with patronizing, sexist doctors. As a woman doctor, I had to be twice as good to be half as recognized."

O'Hanlan has had to deal with more than just gender discrimination. She is also gay, she tells the students, and that has provided its own set of challenges. But in a style that seems true to her spirit, Dr. O'Hanlan has used her training to become a crusader for gay and lesbian health issues. A national authority on the subject, she is a former president of America's Gay & Lesbian Medical Association and is the author of the articles, "Homophobia as a Health Hazard" and "Lesbian Health and Homophobia."

Ultimately, O'Hanlan says what she loves most about being a doctor is her patients. "They are so nice to me," she tells the students. "They send me flowers and champagne to mark the anniversaries of their surgeries and to celebrate their continued lives with me."

198

xavier
livermon

"There are three friends in this world: courage, sense and insight."
— African proverb

Xavier Livermon has clear, lively eyes and high cheekbones that curve down to meet his broad smile. Incisive and keen, he is among the most philosophical of SMYSP's graduates and the most overtly political, too. He chose a life in academia over a life in medicine, though his path is still one of healing. The disease he studies is racism, and the healing needed is more sociological than medicinal, more psychological than physical. Xavier's adult life has been spent examining what it means to be African and American, questions that have taken him from Ghana to a Peace Corps assignment in Lesotho, to his current home at UC Berkeley, where he is working on a Ph.D. in studies of the African diaspora.

Xavier was born in Virginia, the same area where the first Africans were forced into slavery in North America almost 400 years earlier. He lived in Smithfield, where poverty was prevalent, education was mediocre and opportunities for African Americans were limited. The main employer in the town was a huge meat processing plant; if you were one of the lucky ones in Smithfield, you found work at the nearby shipyard, where the wages and working conditions were better. Xavier was born into this world in 1973, to an 18-year-old mother and 20-year-old father.

He spent the first two years of his life with his mother. His parents' relationship, tenuous from the start, had ended before Xavier was born, although Xavier's father spent time with him and contributed financially. The difference between his parents' families was evident. Xavier's mother was from a family "just barely out of poverty. There was a lot more instability. When I visited them later in life, I was struck by the lack of male figures," says Xavier—though he is quick to add, "But I don't want to sound like an advocate for those very conservative theories about black family structure. Poverty was just something that was much more obvious in my mother's family." His father's family, by contrast, "was a much more stable unit. People were able to get jobs and keep their families together. They worked in semi-skilled positions. My grandmother worked at the meat processing plant, and by the time I was born, she had one of the better jobs that a black woman could hold in Smithfield."

When Xavier was 2, his mother traveled to New York City in search of greater freedom and left Xavier in Virginia to be cared for by her mother. When Xavier's father, who had been in North Carolina attending computer school, came home, he decided it was time for Xavier to live with his family. Xavier was just beginning to adjust to his new home when his mother called from New York City to say that she was ready to have her son join her.

Xavier doesn't remember getting to New York or being in the city; his very first childhood memory is of the day he left New York: an image of being on a Greyhound bus with his aunt, looking out the window, heading back to Virginia. Years later, he learned that his mother had called his father's family after just a few weeks of caring for him to ask the family to take Xavier back. Xavier's aunt traveled north to claim him, and his departure on the bus marked the end of his relationship with his biological mother. But, says Xavier, "my father's family made sure that I continued to interact with her family, that I saw my maternal grandmother."

With Xavier's father's family, things were secure and stable. Xavier's father joined the Navy to provide financial support for his son, and Xavier lived with his paternal grandmother in her three-bedroom house. Of those days, he recalls, "I was spoiled. I remember everyone loving me. My grandfather, especially. He was very kind-hearted, always bringing me a toy or candy and taking me places. He would cook meals for me, and I got to the point where I would only eat granddaddy's food." Xavier's grandmother enrolled him in preschool. His older cousins all read to him. Everyone could see he was a very bright child.

When Xavier was 4, everything changed again. Xavier's father married, and he and his wife moved to Vallejo, California, and took Xavier with them. Soon after, the Navy transferred Xavier's dad, leaving Xavier with his new stepmother.

"Moving out to California and then having my father leave soon after... it left me with no point of reference," says Xavier. "I went from being extroverted to very introverted. My stepmother and I clashed. I was used to being the center of attention, and she was used to children who were seen and not heard. I think it must have been difficult for us both. My father was in and out because of his responsibilities with the Navy. He played a mediating role, but it seemed to have the unintended consequence of exacerbating tensions, because my mom and I were still not communicating."

Xavier and his new mother were able to agree on the value—and the joy—of education. She was a teacher, so the two kept the same schedule: out the door early and home by mid-afternoon with homework to do or papers to grade. She encouraged Xavier to read. "She was an educator, so she was good about things like that," he says. "She got me a library card and made sure there were reading materials around the house. I really liked Maurice Sendak."

Xavier started kindergarten at a school close to the apartment where they lived. The first day was a fashion adventure. "My mom dressed me in a suit to go to school," Xavier recalls. "This was in the '70s, so it was probably a powder-blue color. I remember feeling *very* uncomfortable. But my mom, who was used to Virginia, said, 'You wear a suit on the first day, and that's it.'"

Later, clothing became a uniter. "A couple of times a year, we would go to the mall for a whole day," Xavier says. "My mom would buy me Jordache jeans and Izod shirts. It was part of an effort to create certain types of middle-class values in me. My parents wanted to let me know that because I was a black male, people would be watching me, and, whether it was fair or not, appearance—particularly in the form of attire—was often the yardstick by which one might be judged in society." As he aged, Xavier grew closer to his stepmother; today he credits her as an important mentor and guide, one who has been unconditionally supportive of all of his endeavors.

Xavier liked school. Vallejo was a Navy town, with large African-American, white and Filipino populations. Classes were diverse, much more diverse than they'd been in Smithfield—though Xavier was still sent to speech class to lose his Southern accent.

In the second grade, he met a great teacher. "She was a black woman, and she encouraged me and identified me as a student who should be in a gifted program," Xavier recalls. "I think she was committed to promoting bright kids of color. She was the first person to put it into my mind that I was smart, that I was one of the top students. I remember a parent-teacher conference where she said things like that to my parents and I was present. At that point, I was getting straight A's. In the third grade, I remember

203

me and some of my friends being escorted out of the class one day and given a battery of tests; after that, they said I was gifted. I had to change schools again to go to a GATE school, a school with a program for gifted and talented students."

Students in the GATE program were segregated; it was, says Xavier, like "a cocoon." He missed his friends but gradually adjusted. When, in junior high, a few classes began to once again mix GATE and non-GATE students, he found he was shocked. "In GATE, the kids are all highly motivated and work hard. I had to adjust to being in a classroom with students who didn't care. The worst was physical education. It was awful, although for a short time in seventh grade, I was on the football team. Parts of it I liked: I liked hanging out with the other players and I liked the teamwork, but in the

a. Xavier (far left) at 11, visiting relatives in Virginia. b. Xavier with his sister, at home in Vallejo.

end I stopped playing because I thought it was overly competitive. To be successful, you had to humiliate your opponent.

"When I got to junior high, I began to feel socially left out, and I realized that I was in a whole different realm than a lot of my peers. You had to deal with a stigma if you were a good student, particularly as a black male. There was an iciness toward me, or snickers if I came into a room. I think there's more leeway for black women to do well in school. I began to realize how few black students there were in GATE programs, especially how few black men. The year I played football was probably the last year that I had interaction with other black men... except in high school, where there were two other black males in the honors program. So I became very conscious of race and the way it operates.

"My reality was very different from most of the black students. I knew that I wanted to do well in school and go to college. My parents expected me to succeed academically. Anything less was not even considered a possibility. By this time, my parents were a little better off financially—they'd been able to save and buy a house—and I think those expectations came with that rise in status. I thought the kids at my school didn't know what was important. In junior high, I felt very victimized and introverted. In high

204

school, I reacted more with superiority, like, 'One day you'll be washing my Mercedes Benz because that's the only job you'll know how to do.' In high school, I was all about money and the corporate American dream. I saw myself as a lawyer jet-setting to London, making deals. I wanted those suits. But in junior high, I was just trying to walk with my head down and get through it."

The classroom became a place of refuge. Xavier recalls having "fairly good teachers," though he did have "a couple of negative experiences. My ninth grade English teacher really didn't like me. There was nothing I could do or say that was right. He didn't recommend me for honors English or honors history. And I do believe it was all based on race, because at least one other person in the class—a young white woman—had the same grades as me, and the teacher deemed her capable of doing honors work."

When Xavier tried to get into honors English and history on his own initiative, he had to face a whole different kind of prejudice. "During 10th grade, my regular classes in English and history were way too easy," he recalls. "So I approached my counselor and asked to be placed in the honors classes for the 11th grade. My counselor was reluctant to do it. She was black, and she was concerned that I would lower my GPA by going into a more rigorous program. Later, I found out that midway through my 10th-grade year, both my English and history teachers approached my counselor and told her I was too bright for their classes and should be moved into the honors track in my second semester. Without consulting me, she just told them that I wasn't interested. Later, my mom told me that the counselor had come to her and asked my parents to keep me out of the honors program because she was concerned about my GPA. I don't think the counselor was being malicious. I honestly believe that she thought she was doing the best thing for me. I was one of the black 'stars,' one of the few 'UC eligible' black students at Vallejo, and she wanted to ensure my success."

The one honors class Xavier did take in the 10th grade was biology. "I really worked hard in that class," he remembers. "We had a lot of labs, wrote long reports, did presentations and completed major projects. The class was scheduled just before lunch because sometimes we needed to work during lunch. The coursework was overwhelming and intense, but it was great preparation for college, and it was stimulating and interesting. The teacher was Mr. Delgado. He was the one who suggested I apply to SMYSP."

Xavier applied, did the interviews and was accepted. "If I had any doubts about going, it was about how serious I was about a career in medicine, and whether I should be taking the place of someone who was more certain," he says. "At that time, I was still very young. I had just turned 16. But I really wanted to go. And I thought being at Stanford for a summer might make a difference in how easily I could get into college. I thought it would be good for my school. Plus, it was a great opportunity to do something productive with my summer. Otherwise, I would have gotten some menial job for $4.25 an hour."

The most daunting part of the program at first was the communalism. "You know, I'd never lived in a communal situation, I'd never lived in a home with more than four people," Xavier says. "But in the end, the social aspect was the best thing about the program. Having to encounter a group of strangers and make a community—so that you could all live together and respect one another's quirks—for me, that was *the* experience. As the years have gone by, I don't really remember the lectures or lecturers. I remember feeling a little ill from the smell of formaldehyde. I was not interested in cutting up bodies. In fact, the only thing I was adamant about was that I didn't want to work in the morgue. I was more interested in genetics and research. That's what I did my research project on: genetic engineering and ethics. I wrote that paper with a girl named Thuy; she was probably the person I was closest to in the program. She was one of the first people I opened up to in my life. At that time, I was still having a lot of issues around my mother and my stepmom. I recall her being a great listener. She wasn't very boisterous or vocal, but when she had something to say, it was important, and you needed to be quiet and listen to her."

Xavier took two key things from SMYSP: "Number one was the confidence I got from the program. The other kids were all extremely bright and focused, and knowing that I could do as well as any of those students, and sometimes better, really carried over into my next year in school—my junior year, which is the hardest year in high school. The program brought me to a point where I felt I could compete with anyone, and that's the kind of confidence you can only get with that type of experience. Equally as significant, I think, were the interpersonal relationships; it was like a dry run for college. I got to experience what it was like to do a research project and give a presentation, live in a college environment, use a big university library. All those things made a lasting impact on someone like me, who was introverted and not too confident about my abilities or interpersonal skills."

When Xavier returned to high school, it was to the honors classes he'd lobbied so hard to get into. "It was extremely rigorous coursework, but I felt better able to handle it because of SMYSP," he says. "I never doubted my ability, though English was definitely a struggle. I got a C-plus the first quarter. I knew the teacher, Ms. Cheney, had very high expectations. She would give people F's on their papers. But I really have to thank her because my writing improved so much that year, and that really helped me later in college. She was also very good about having us read books by women and people of color. We read *Native Son*. And in history, we read *The Autobiography of Malcolm X*."

But while Xavier may have been encountering African-American realities on the printed page, his isolation from the community itself continued. Socially, "there was still a lack of contact and affiliation with other black students," he says. "People still felt like they had to take pot shots at me, but there were so many students, you just went about your business, and it didn't feel as oppressive as junior high. The only black friends I had were other honors students; there were four of us in total, two boys, two girls. Looking at other black kids… I think I had the perception that people were wasting opportunities. Later on, in college, I got a better perspective about what is really going on as far as race and class. Before then, coming from a relatively privileged background for a black student, where higher education was encouraged and seen to be possible, I had this viewpoint that a lot of the black students were ignorant and throwing away opportunities. I looked down on those who weren't interested in their academic work."

Still seeing himself as a high-powered corporate mover and shaker in the making, Xavier applied to seven colleges, mostly small liberal arts schools. "Berkeley and Los Angeles' UC campuses seemed too large and overwhelming," he recalls. "I didn't apply to Berkeley because it was dirty and not serene enough. I didn't apply to UCLA because

I thought I might get shot in a drive-by. I went for suburban campuses. I got accepted everywhere." Xavier's first choice was Yale, but he couldn't afford it: "My parents made too much money for me to get a full scholarship, and we didn't have the tuition. The University of California, San Diego gave me a scholarship, and it was in a nice area with lots of trees. So I decided to go there."

College started to change a lot of Xavier's ideas. For one thing, his father lost his job at the beginning of Xavier's freshman year at UCSD. "A lot of people in Vallejo were losing jobs at that time, but black families were disproportionately affected," he says. "And it wasn't until after my senior year in college that my father had a steady new career. I can only imagine the stress those years placed on my family. He eventually became a security guard and then went into armed security, which is higher paying.

"That period of instability coincided with my time at UCSD. When I arrived, the one thing I was not prepared for was the amount of wealth that my fellow students had. The white students, especially, but some of the black students, too. I was feeling poor: my father losing his job reminded me very vividly that I was a black kid from rural Virginia and that my parents were not able to isolate themselves from the economic shocks that hit working-class black families in the early '90s. It made me more cognizant of race. There were so few black students at UCSD. I began to see racism and prejudice differently. Before, my concept of racism was based on the idea of someone hating someone else and acting on that prejudice. I began to realize a lot of people may not hate black people at all, they may actually like them. But still there's an institutional racism that goes beyond any individual feelings, an apparatus that makes it difficult for black people to succeed.

"For example, look at something as simple as using the SAT to decide who should be admitted to college. The marker for how students perform on the SAT is income: in general, the higher the family income, the higher the student's SAT scores. And income in the United States is not racially neutral. There were only 83 black male undergraduates at UCSD, out of a student population of 16,000 undergraduates."

Beyond race, Xavier realized, there was also an issue of culture. "In American society, there is also this whole notion of 'diversity without difference'—the idea that being black or Asian or Latino is okay; you just can't be *different*. At UCSD, they talked about wanting diversity, but they didn't really want to deal with cultural differences. It's something you see over and over again. I call it the Tommy Hilfiger approach to diversity.

"Black people themselves often imposed constraining definitions of blackness on each other, and those who failed to conform were ostracized. That can be difficult when there are only a total of 300 blacks on the campus and you're ostracized even from that small community. I think I did get a little caught up in that during my earlier years, trying to make sure that I did the right things to fit in with the 'right' definition of blackness. Because there was no alternative."

His political awareness growing, Xavier decided to major in political science, which he thought would be the best foundation for law school. He had decided his strengths lay in reading, writing and interpretation rather than in the sciences, so, despite SMYSP, he had returned to his original plan of law—though now he saw himself as a human rights lawyer rather than a big firm partner. "In my first two years at UCSD,

207

my professors were all fairly conservative," he recalls. "During my sophomore year, I was involved in all these things, including a group that was supposed to be an inter-cultural group dealing with racism. I was involved in a lot of committees. After a while, you had to be on every committee, and I got burned out.

"I decided to apply to go abroad. Initially, I wanted to go to Spain and improve my Spanish. My roommate that year, Dontraneil, was a guy from South Central L.A., and he wanted to go to Ghana. We had a Ghanaian professor, Edward Reynolds, who taught a course called, *The Making of the Modern World*, about how the Western world rose to dominance." Swayed by conversations with his roommate and his professor, Xavier decided to nix Spain for Africa. It was the right decision.

"Being in Ghana was the most profound experience of my life," he says of the year he spent in the country. "It gave me a sense of history and of belonging. I saw so many connections between African-American culture and Ghanaian culture. The beauty of the people, the beauty of the culture. It is a place where black really is beautiful, where it is more than just a phrase.

"All the stereotypes I had about Africa were turned upside down. I remember when the plane was coming in to land in Accra, the capital, I was surprised that there were so many lights. Accra was a city of contrasts: some areas were like shantytowns, and some were very elegant. Mostly, it's very lush and green, very humid and hot. Most people assumed I was Ghanaian. People welcomed me into their homes and shared their culture. I felt accepted."

Xavier traveled through Ghana, went to neighboring Togo and Benin and the Ivory Coast. He lived on-campus at the University of Ghana, rooming with a Ghanaian medical student. He would go out in the morning to buy eggs and bread and then cook breakfast. Lunches and dinners consisted of rice and stew and traditional foods from the cafeteria; clothing of African prints and dashikis.

"I came back to UCSD with a better notion of myself," he says, "confident not only about my academic abilities, but also about my blackness. I didn't have a lot of time or patience for people defining blackness in a very narrow way. That feeling that I wasn't black enough was something I'd been struggling with since I was 12 years old, and after Ghana, I was able to put it behind me.

"My final year in college was by far the best. I had two professors who were very instrumental in me being where I'm at now. One was a professor of sociology, Dr. Bennetta Jules-Rossette; the other was in ethnic studies, Dr. George Lipsitz. Dr. Jules-Rossette was the first to suggest that I should do academic work. My interest at that point was in human rights, public advocacy. She pointed out that being a professor could be as lucrative as being an attorney in some cases. She said she'd like me to consider that. It had never even occurred to me. But I've always liked school and been an intellectual."

Unsure of what to do next but sure that he wanted to return to Africa, Xavier applied to the Peace Corps and was sent to Lesotho to teach. He was happy to be back on the continent, though he found Lesotho colder, harsher and less vibrant than Ghana. Still, he was learning more about the region he was growing to love, and Lesotho's location in the southeast of Africa meant that South Africa was right across the border. Xavier visited as often as he could. "South Africa has a very liberal, post-apartheid constitution and a very vibrant gay life. There I was in a place that wasn't terribly homophobic." Before, Africa had helped Xavier to embrace his race; now it helped him to embrace his sexuality. By the time he returned to America, he was officially, he says, "out."

After two years in Lesotho, Xavier returned to the United States and worked for the Peace Corps in San Francisco while he applied to graduate schools. His feelings about the organization are mixed. "I think the Peace Corps is a valuable program for inter-cultural and development assistance exchange," he says, "but the help that the Peace Corps brings comes with a price: certain cultural values and assumptions. Because of this, I'm ambivalent about my role in the organization. But I would do it again and I wouldn't discourage anyone else from doing it. It was an amazing growth and learning experience. I might do something else in the Peace Corps once I finish my Ph.D."

Xavier was accepted into UC Berkeley's graduate program in African diaspora studies. No longer troubled by what he once perceived as the "dirtiness" of the campus, he decided to enter the program. He has just finished his master's degree and is now constructing his dissertation committee and deciding on his topic.

"I'm looking at black identities in post-apartheid South Africa, at music and fashion and what they say about identities in South Africa and the relationship with gender and sexuality," he says. "I'm very wary of ethnography. I think it can make people look different, you know, 'Let's study the natives.' If I can think of a way I can do an ethnography that doesn't fall into that trap, I feel like I can really give something back to the community, because they're sharing their culture with me."

Xavier is happy to be at Berkeley. His fellow graduate students have been supportive, and, he says, "It's been very helpful to be a graduate student in African-American studies, versus other departments where the work I'm interested in might be more marginalized. Also, since I'm older, I'm plugged into community networks. Being a graduate student is like training for the work force of academia."

Xavier is now in South Africa, doing research. While there, he is also working on the HIV/AIDS epidemic. In fact, his path may actually loop back to medicine and disease. "I could be just as happy working for AIDS relief efforts," he says. "I'm very open. I know that the path I have traveled has been influenced greatly by my experience in SMYSP. I feel that I always had the ability to be an assertive, confident person, but dealing with circumstances created by messages such as, 'Black men cannot be good in school' caused me to be in a shell. SMYSP, particularly the confident mentors and role models that I met there—some of whom were young black men, others who were just caring and compassionate people who believed in me—was very important in getting me to the point where I can fully enjoy my life as an intellectual and a social being. The fact that the program always checks on you is important as well, because I know I'm being watched by people who care about me and want me to be successful, and I don't want to let them or myself down. I think this is invaluable. It has been over 10 years, but I am *still* connected to the program."

Xavier Livermon

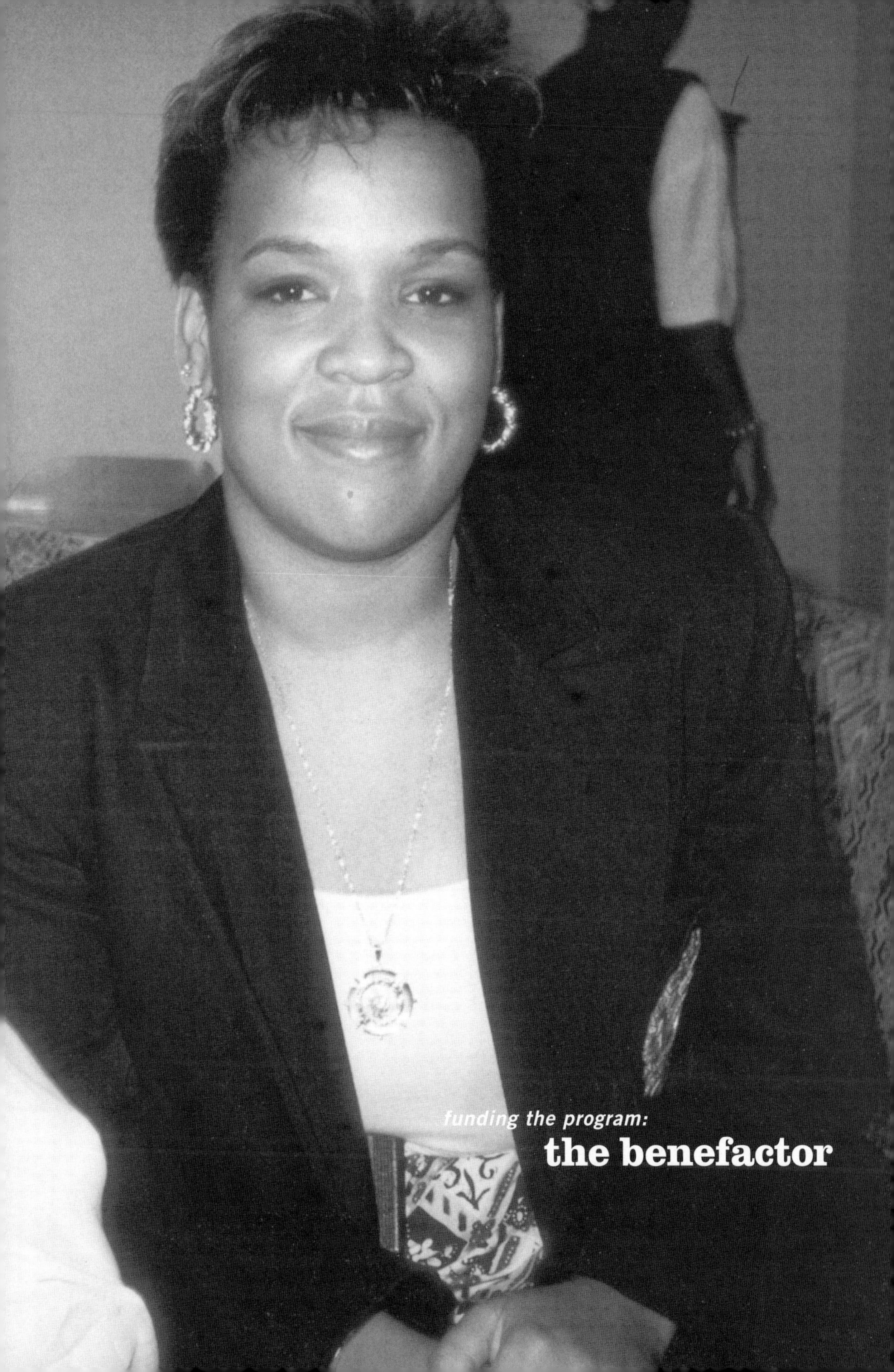

funding the program:

the benefactor

In September 1995, Leo Hindery Jr. lay dying in Stanford Hospital's surgery recovery room. He'd gone into the hospital for a routine operation, but a crisis had arisen when his liver mysteriously shut down after the surgery. The doctors could think of nothing to do. A priest was called and last rites were given. Leo said good-bye to his wife and only child. And then, as Leo remembers it, his savior appeared—Sonya Pettus, a young anesthesia resident. "She refused to let me die," he recalls now. "She ran to the library, did research, devised a drug cocktail that might save my liver. At night, she wouldn't leave me and sat by my bedside hour after hour.

"She kept me alive through the first night. And then through the next. And the one after that. In the end, this young woman—new, brilliant and willing to try anything—was the one who saved my life. And I realized that if no one had helped that remarkable young woman to become a doctor, I would not be alive."

Sonya wasn't a SMYSP graduate, but she could have been. She was an African-American woman from Fresno, an only child whose parents had moved to California from the South. Sonya's mother was a teacher; her father worked in the cotton industry. When Sonya was 14, her father was robbed and murdered as he was leaving a boxing match. "My mother was strong but she was dependent on my dad," says Sonya. "After he was killed, she decided to go back to school to get a master's in administration. I'd known since I was 5 that I wanted to be a doctor and she knew that there was no way that she could put me through medical school on a teacher's salary." Sonya's mother became an elementary school principal, and the money she made paid Sonya's way through college and the University of California, San Francisco medical school. "My mom really put an emphasis on education," Sonya says. "I went to an urban high school in Fresno, Roosevelt High, and half to two-thirds of the class never went to college. Only 6 to 7 percent finished an undergraduate degree. A lot of students wound up dead from gangs."

Leo hadn't had an easy time of it growing up, either. His family had little money, and he took his first job when he was 9 years old. He spent his teens and 20s working at farms and shipyards and sailing the seas as a merchant marine. But by the time he entered Stanford Hospital for surgery in 1995, he'd gotten a degree from the Stanford Graduate School of Business and become a tycoon in the telecommunications industry.

In a miraculous bit of serendipity, Leo was scheduled to meet Marilyn Winkleby for the first time soon after he was released from the hospital. Long before his surgery, Leo had been interested in helping at-risk youth; years earlier, he had established a scholarship at his alma mater, a Jesuit high school in Tacoma, Washington. One day, Marilyn saw a copy of the high school's newsletter; it mentioned Hindery and his interest in mentoring. She wrote him a letter, telling him about SMYSP.

212

Leo was intrigued. He and Marilyn set up an informational breakfast meeting, scheduled to take place after he got out of the hospital. For her part, Marilyn had no idea that she was about to meet a philanthropic-minded multimillionaire. She was just planning to ask Leo to visit the program to speak to the students.

"Like a lot of things in life—you have to recognize what's just happened to you," says Leo today. In the wake of his experience with Sonya Pettus, meeting Marilyn was another revelation. To say that the breakfast went well is an understatement.

Leo was enchanted by Marilyn's description of the program and immediately saw that he was being offered a way to help hundreds of young, potential Sonya Pettuses. He decided to make a large donation.

In the summer of 1996, Leo visited the program—and, for the first time since he'd been released from the hospital, saw Sonya again. Over a dinner of spaghetti, garlic bread and lemonade, both Leo and Sonya told the SMYSP students their life stories. "I think mine was interesting," says Leo, "but Sonya's was compelling. She was an unbelievable role model. I told the students that they were going to change the world. 'If you don't believe it,' I said, 'look at me. Someone like you just saved my life, and now she's on her way home to Fresno to work as a physician.'"

"We met outside," remembers Sonya of seeing Leo again. "It was really surreal. We hugged and then went in to see the kids. We sat in a circle and shared bits and pieces of our lives. It was inspiring to see the kids, the energy in the room. The kids saw that someone like themselves could really have an impact. A couple of the kids there didn't have a mother or a father, and I remember leaving that day feeling that I was very blessed. My mom allowed me to make it. Other people might feel bad about my story, but I feel blessed—I had someone to push and guide me."

Leo remembers the students as "the most engaging, passionate young people. They had a sparkle, an intellectual curiosity, a passion for their communities. I remember one girl who was living in the Mission in San Francisco. She was tiny, 4 foot 8, the most unbelievable girl. She got up at 5 a.m. every day, fixed breakfast for her family, got on the bus, started classes at 7:30 and then went home to take care of her family while her mother worked two jobs. Sonya had a tear in her eye listening to their stories, because they were her stories. It was great for her to see a room full of people coming behind her."

In the years since his near-death in the hospital, Leo has remained the largest individual benefactor of the program and a key part of its survival. "I haven't seen anything comparable to SMYSP," he says. "It's small and individualized and it makes a huge difference in the lives of the people it touches. It is the single best melding of education and medicine I have seen."

pati
ibarra

"God does not hear you if you don't speak."
— Mexican proverb

Pati Ibarra has a calm, contemplative way about her and wears the countenance of someone who has long known who she is and where she's going. Youth sparkles around her, too: it's in the fullness of her cheeks, the way she peppers her conversations with expressions like "That's *dope*," the flair in the cut of her denim jeans. Like so many of SMYSP's graduates, she is a study in contradictions. She has just graduated from Brown University, is an Ivy League alumna who spent her formative years in small rural towns in California's Central Valley.

Pati was born in Mazatlan, Mexico, to a single mother—a remarkable mother who crossed the American border under the cover of darkness and spent years picking fruit and packing chickens to make ends meet and give her daughter a new kind of life. "My mom is one of 10 children, eight girls and two boys," says Pati. "Her name is Francisca. Her family was always really poor, but all of the children went to school. My grandma was of indigenous descent from a little village close to Mazatlan, a city on the coast that's very tropical. My grandpa was of Spanish descent, and I think his father might have been a sailor. My grandpa was a construction worker, and he built the house they lived in: a wonderful, large house that's still in the family. But he had a drinking problem, and that created difficult times."

When she was still a young woman, Francisca met a man, fell in love and got married. The marriage provided a way out of her home, a way to escape her father's drinking. She had two sons, Jesus and Enrique. But her husband, in the end, provided no more stability than her father. When he won the lottery, he left with his winnings; Francisca filed for a divorce.

Pati's grandmother ended her relationship, too. Her Catholic faith was too strong to allow her to divorce, but she left her husband and moved into a one-bedroom home. In many ways, it was an improvement. "My grandma's house was small but it was very friendly and open," says Pati. "We were a very close family."

When Jesus and Enrique were in their early teens, Francisca met a banker, again fell in love and became pregnant. The relationship faltered, but Francisca welcomed her pregnancy; she had been eager to have another child and was hoping for a daughter. She got her wish when Pati was born. The banker, Pati says, "was never a part of my life. My brother Jesus is like my father."

Francisca was working in a pharmacy in Mazatlan, but she couldn't make enough money to support her two sons and her new daughter. She looked north for opportunities for her family. When Pati was 5, Francisca left for the United States. Aware that there was no way that she could work and take adequate care of her children, she was forced to leave Pati and her sons behind until she had carved out a life for them in the United States.

"I remember missing my mom a lot when she left," says Pati. "I went to live with an aunt, and I was very anxious and cried a lot. She lived in a different town, and I missed my grandma and my brothers. Soon I moved back to my grandma's. She was always very active and busy. She would get up at the crack of dawn to do the shopping and then come back and make our breakfast, usually eggs and beans. She was quiet but always there. I felt taken care of."

Francisca and a friend had hired a *pollero* to take them across the border. Polleros make their living crossing people to "the other side" for a fee. It's a risk every time you do it: hire the wrong pollero and you can wind up robbed and stranded—or in the hands of the immigration service. Fortunately, the women were taken safely across the border. They found work picking fruit on a small farm in California and rented a small trailer to live in. Francisca was in her mid-30s, working long, hard hours and making next to nothing. It took her a year to save enough money to send for her daughter.

"I arrived when I was 6," remembers Pati, "and I was really confused. All I knew was that I was going to see my mom, and when I saw her, I was ecstatic. We met somewhere in Los Angeles and drove north. I remember driving near Fresno and asking what all the signs said."

Pati spent her first few weeks in America in the fields with her mother, picking peaches and grapes. After a month, Francisca—determined to see her daughter in school—enrolled Pati in kindergarten. It was a shock. "It was really hard for me to suddenly find myself with people who didn't speak Spanish. My mom tried her best to help me but she was working. I felt very disoriented. I had already learned the things we were studying in school, but I had learned them in Spanish, so I had to relearn everything in English."

The home situation took some getting used to, too. Francisca lived with a man, "but it didn't really feel like a family," says Pati. "He was very strict and serious, while my family is relaxed and carefree. He wasn't used to having a child in the house. And I was a child who just wanted to play and have fun. So I think that clash in personalities made it very difficult to live comfortably. We had this awful little apartment on the outskirts of Fresno, and there were other people living with us. My mom was working 12 hours every day.

"Then we started moving, to different towns in the Central Valley. Some of the other towns were better because there were more Spanish-speaking Mexican kids, but as far as the English-speaking kids went, I was still isolated. Finally, I learned English. TV helped a lot. After a year or two, I could carry on a conversation. And once I learned the language, I began to like school."

The instability at home continued. Francisca left her boyfriend, and she and Pati moved to Madera. "By that time, my mom had moved up from picking fruit to working in the packing and processing houses, but I think she was really struggling," says Pati. "The neighborhood was awful: every other house was a crack house, and our neighbors were selling drugs. They helped take care of me after school while my mom was at work; one day, we saw the cops outside their house arresting people. I was about 8 then." After the arrests, Pati was home alone after school while her mother worked. She learned to cook for herself.

Eventually, with the financial situation in Madera growing worse, Francisca returned to her boyfriend. The three moved to the town of Parlier, where they lived until Pati finished high school. Parlier was California's second poorest community; the median income was $5,000 a year.

"Parlier is a small town, with maybe 10,000 people. It's very rural, full of low-income farm workers. I liked the fact that there were people there who spoke Spanish," remembers Pati. "And they were *very* hard-working people. Nobody worried about crime; everyone was working all the time. Downtown, there was a grocery store and two little restaurants. Outside the town center, there were peach and plum orchards. There were big companies in the area with big names, like Dole and Sunkist. The law is that people working in the fields are supposed to be legal, but the employers look the other way." As for Pati's own legal status: "My mom always told me if I ever got asked, just don't say anything."

The three rented a small house they shared with farm laborers. "There were two bedrooms: the men had one, and we had the other. Everyone shared the kitchen. The men who lived with us were nice, but they kept to themselves." The men were like most of the people Pati had known growing up: people who wanted a better life for themselves and their relatives. Many had families in Mexico and Central America; they'd left to make money to send to their loved ones.

a. Pati at 5 in a park in Mexico. b. Pati in kindergarten in Mexico. "We were celebrating dia del nino, or 'the day of the child.' We dressed up in what we wanted to be. I was a nurse!" she recalls. c. Pati at 8 celebrating Christmas with (left to right) her mother and brothers Enrique and Jesus.

Eventually, the family was able to get a larger house through a program that Cesar Chavez had started for low-income families and migrant farm workers. "It was a three-bedroom house, a simple house, but it was new," says Pati. "It was on a plot of land that they developed into housing. There were 30 or 40 houses that were all the same, with a small bathroom, a small kitchen and a little backyard. My mom went to yard sales and decorated it as well as she could."

Although she was mastering the language, Pati was put into special English as a Second Language (ESL) classes. "By the end of elementary school, my English was fine. But when you're in ESL—even if you're smart—they never notice your progress or your potential. I think I missed a lot of opportunities because of that. For example, I never got into the GATE program for gifted students."

In junior high, Pati began to get a lot more involved in sports: volleyball, softball, basketball. "There wasn't anything else to do," she says. "I wasn't being challenged in school and I was bored, and my friends were doing sports, so I joined in." It sparked a passion that continued through high school, and, had she not been working two jobs through college, would have continued there, too.

When Pati was 13, her brother Jesus arrived. He was 25, and with his help and guidance, things started to look up for all of them.

"Jesus was always supportive and encouraging," says Pati. "He, like my mother, made many sacrifices to better our family. He didn't like the situation he saw us living in, so he decided to stay with us. He left Mexico, his friends, family and even college to help me and my mother. He persuaded my mom to leave the man she was living with, and she finally left for good.

"Jesus is really an inspiration to me. He worked in jobs he hated to support our family. And to me, he's been like both a mother and father. He's always had total faith in me, I think even more than I had in myself. I say he was also my mother because my

a. Pati and Jesus on her first day at Brown. "He was about to go back to California. It was bittersweet because he was very proud of me, but we were sad because we would be so far away from each other," she remembers. b. Pati graduating from Brown with (left to right) her aunts Dora and Martha, her mother, her aunt Juany and Jesus. "It was a very proud moment for the family," she says.

mom had to work, and together with the language barrier, it was very difficult for her. It was my brother who made sure I had everything for school, that I did my homework and that I studied. I don't think I would be at the level that I'm at if it wasn't for his help. He's been my best friend ever since I can remember, and I think that we have just gotten closer as time goes by."

At the same time that Jesus moved north, a law passed allowing immigrants from Mexico who had worked in the fields for a certain period of time to apply for American residency, whether they'd entered the country legally or not. Francisca applied for and received her papers. "After she got her residency, I could apply, too," says Pati. By the end of high school, Pati was a U.S. citizen.

With Jesus' help, the family managed to buy their own home. They'd found a small house in Parlier; it took a year of saving, but they got a bank loan to pay for it. Pati's mom also got a better job, working in a chicken processing plant. It offered more pay than packing fruits and vegetables, but it was still intense work. "It's a very cold environment in the factory; it's all refrigerated. You wear long metal gloves and use a knife to cut up the chickens, which are coming around on a conveyor belt," explains Pati.

219

"The work is fast, fierce. My mom has hurt both an arm and a knee since she started and has needed three operations for injuries she's received on the job."

At school, Pati's classes were easy, too easy. She was comfortable enough with English to have started reading books on her own. In sixth grade, she discovered Nancy Drew books in the library at school and read all the science textbooks she could get her hands on. Her drive to learn was fueled by an innate curiosity and also by her family. "They would keep telling me, 'You don't want to end up like us, working all the time and not even able to have a decent car,'" she remembers. "My mom and brother wanted me to do well, and to do something that made me happy. They never stressed money as a goal, but they did make me understand that it was important. Above all, they wanted me to do something that I liked and not to wind up like them, working for the money and nothing else.

"I had emotional support from the family, but I was really alone in finding out what school was about. My family didn't know the American system, so they didn't know the steps I had to take to ensure a good education. My goal when I was small wasn't to go to college, and even when I started high school, I wasn't thinking about an Ivy League school, it was more like a nursing program or a community college. Even then, it was the family saying, 'We got a letter saying you're a smart kid, so do something about it.' When I was younger, they would create little incentives, like, 'If you do well this semester, we'll take you to McDonald's.' That meant a trip to Fresno."

The student body of Parlier High School is almost exclusively Mexican American, and it numbered about 800 when Pati was there. The school's funding was low and class offerings were minimal. When Pati arrived, there was only one advanced placement class on the roster: Spanish, the one subject virtually every student in the school had mastered. Nonetheless, remembers Pati, there were people at the school to encourage and mentor her.

"My high school principal, Juan Sandoval, was the coolest guy," she says. "He really encouraged and helped me. He was Mexican and grew up in a small town, too. He had very humble beginnings, just like us, but he got his master's degree and then his Ph.D. Even after high school, he was always there for me. He was only at the school for two years, my junior and senior years. He's now running a new education program for the district.

"Still, many students felt limited by the school, not challenged by it. There was a lack of everything. I remember my junior and senior history classes, for the first semester we had to share books. Things like that made it difficult even for the kids who wanted to learn. We had only one counselor for junior high and high school. She had her chosen few students who she thought would make it, and she showed little interest in any of the others. I never went to her. A friend of mine who's a very talented artist and who just graduated from the Rhode Island School of Design went to her, and she told him, 'I don't think you should do that; just go to community college.'"

In her sophomore year, Pati heard about a program called the Ivy League Leadership Project. The program had been started in 1991 by a teacher in the school district, Martin Mares, who was convinced his best students should be studying at places like Harvard and Princeton. He wanted to encourage and empower Latino students, to get them to think about the larger world beyond the San Joaquin Valley, to persuade them that they were smart enough to be at America's top universities. With the encouragement of a locally born journalist who'd graduated from Harvard, Ruben Navarrette, he began to tell students about some of the country's finest colleges and to convince them to apply. Each year, Mares led the district's brightest on a tour of East Coast schools. Pati was intrigued. Her interest was further honed during the summer after her sophomore year, when she was part of an Upward Bound math and science program. "They talked about schools, too. My citizenship papers were being processed. It started me thinking about college a lot."

In her junior year, Pati decided she wanted to tour the schools that Mr. Mares was mentioning. She was interviewed in the local paper, the *Parlier Post*, where she declared her future goal was to become a professional. "You had to fundraise on your own to get the money to visit the schools," she remembers. "I needed to raise $1,000. I worked, and my mom helped me. We made tacos and enchiladas to sell. I sold raffle tickets. We sold pizzas and asked businesses for donations." In the spring semester of her junior year, Pati embarked on a 10-day tour that took her to Brown, Dartmouth, Cornell, Yale, Harvard, Princeton, Columbia and MIT. "There were 30 of us on the tour, all from schools in the San Joaquin Valley. There were 10 of us from Parlier High School. We slept in dorm rooms donated by students to keep the costs down, and the universities donated food."

Pati knew that she didn't want to spend the summer after her junior year working in the fields, "but that was the only summer job you could get in Parlier," she says. She started looking for interesting, college-related things to do. One day, she was talking to an office secretary at the high school when the woman pulled out an application form that had just arrived. It was from SMYSP. "I have no clue how that application got to the school," says Pati, "but I was really interested. At that point, I was curious about medicine and the sciences. My mom had worked in a pharmacy in Mexico, so she knew a little about pharmaceutical drugs. That's how I first got interested in medicine: hearing her talk about that work."

Pati decided to apply to SMYSP and went to the interview at Stanford, which was about 200 miles from Parlier. "We had an old Ford, so we drove," she says. "This was my first interview for anything in my life, so I was nervous. The whole school intimidated me. But the counselors were so nice to me. We talked about my school and why I was interested in the program, about my plans for going to college and how the program could help me decide if medicine was what I wanted to do. When I got accepted, my family was very excited and proud. And it was great how the program opened my eyes. I may not have known anything at the beginning, but at the end, I knew I could apply to schools. It built up my self-esteem. It helped me develop socially and know that there's a bigger world out there.

"The students made the biggest impression. I'd never been in contact with such smart kids before. In Parlier, biology was just a joke. We had no books, no lab equipment, no facilities. So at first I was intimidated by these kids who seemed to know everything. But it was a positive thing because it pushed me to learn, and I did. And I found out that science wasn't really for me. I did my research project on diabetes. I loved the sociological aspects but I was turned off by the biology and the chemistry. And if I'd taken all those science courses in college, I would have hated college. I appreciated the program for helping me to see that.

"SMYSP truly gave me my first shot at an education. The program looked out for my well-being. And by creating an ongoing network for all of the graduates, it continues to help."

Pati spent her senior year as class president. She tutored, played tennis and basketball, and worked hard on her college applications. "I was thinking about East Coast schools because of the Ivy League Leadership Project," she remembers. "I had taken the SAT. I took it twice, because the first time, I bombed. Then I bought a guide on how to prepare, and the second time I took it, I did better." Pati applied to six universities and was accepted at three—Brown, UCLA and UC Berkeley. She decided to go to Brown. "My first impression of Brown was really good," she says, remembering her visit there. "It seemed homey; the students were friendly." It also helped that Pati's friend Elisa, another alumna of the Ivy League Leadership Project, was going to Brown, too. When Pati flew out to the school, Jesus flew with her to help her settle in. While Pati had been in junior high and high school, she'd watched Jesus struggle for a better life for himself. She watched him go to night school every day after work for more than five years to better his English. She knew he was about to begin attending junior college and that he hoped to transfer to a four-year college to get his bachelor's degree. He was the most powerful role model in her life and the perfect person to deliver her to Brown.

But while it was exciting to be at Brown, things were not easy. There were money issues, cultural issues, academic issues. Pati had excelled in her high school, but now she was learning at a whole new level. "I felt, 'I came here to do something; now I have to do it,' and I made up my mind that I was going to graduate," she remembers. "But there were a lot of moments when I wanted to pack up and leave, especially freshman and sophomore years. My freshman year, I had to learn everything from scratch. I had to learn to ask for help. I had to study a lot to pass—forget about getting A's. For most of the students at Brown, it was important to get good grades; for me, it was just important to pass. I wanted to be an A student again, but the reality was that I had a lot of catching up to do, and in many cases there wasn't enough time. It was humbling. I missed my mother a lot, and I doubted whether I belonged. But my mother was always very strong, very helpful and very understanding whenever I would talk to her on the phone. She didn't ask me to come home. She wanted me to get my degree.

"Socially, it was all new, too. I was coming from a small town where everyone spoke Spanish and came from very similar backgrounds. I had never been around so many white people. The majority came from prestigious families and private schools. At first, I was very conscious that we came from different cultures. And so many of them had had better educations than me. Fortunately, after getting to know more people, I found that we did share many things. Education was a commonality. When I was growing up, education wasn't big with my friends. At Brown, I found people who were interested in learning for the sake of learning. There, essentially, we all wanted to go on to do things with our lives and be something. It was important to find a niche at Brown, and in my case, it was through people that I finally felt that I belonged there."

222

To help fund her schooling, Pati worked the whole time she was at Brown, which left her no time for sports or other extracurricular activities. During her freshman year, she worked 15 hours a week at a library; in her sophomore year, she kept her library job and added another in a school cafeteria. As a junior, she worked in a day-care center at Brown's Summer Studies office and counseled students at the local YMCA. "I remember always having to save and work," she says. "I was stuck between the wall and the sword."

Pati spent a semester of her junior year in Barcelona. The year before, she had discovered Spanish studies and been captivated. "I just loved getting the chance to speak Spanish and studying Spanish authors. Of the authors we studied, I found Gabriel García Márquez the most interesting. I loved learning about that whole period when Latin-American writers were coming to the fore. I had had no clue who all these people were—Jorge Luis Borges, Carlos Fuentes, Rubén Darío—and it was really cool to learn about my culture through these writers. I ended up doing a double major of psychology and Spanish studies.

"In Barcelona, I took courses in Hispanic studies, a grammar course, an art history course. The program took us to Segovia, and we traveled to see castles and museums and old monasteries. I was able to relax a bit. And I traveled on my own to Paris, Florence, Rome and northern Spain. I paid for it out of my school loans."

In Spanish studies, Pati found her heritage; in psychology, she found her calling. "I realized I'm interested in peoples' problems and how I can help," she says. "I feel like psychology is a way I can do that. I know how much my brother Jesus helped me just by telling me over and over again that I was special. Whenever I was feeling worthless, whenever I was discouraged—by my SAT scores, by not getting accepted to some of the colleges I applied to—he would tell me that I was smart, that my family loved me and I should keep trying."

When Pati graduated from Brown, her family was there. "Graduation was a tremendous event for us," says Pati. "It meant that I did belong after all. I'd made it. My mother, brother and three of my aunts from Mexico came to join me in the celebration. Having them cheer when I received my diploma was the best. I realized that I probably couldn't have done it without their support and encouragement. The fact that my aunts traveled so far and sacrificed so much just to be with me showed me how proud they are.

"I really valued the friendships I made at Brown. I got close to people I never thought I could get close to. And I got to thinking about where I grew up and how people there need outlets, people to talk to. Parlier has become a very close-knit community, and now we help each other out when things are hectic. Before, when I was small, it wasn't like that. Now there are programs like the Ivy League Leadership Project—but there are still a lot of social issues in the town. There's poverty, and my biggest concern is with the kids. They don't really have much to do after school, and that creates a problem, especially with the teenagers. They have kids, and to me, kids having kids is one of the biggest issues surrounding that community. My high school class had a high percentage of people going to college, but some people dropped out, or the girls got pregnant and left school. The ones who didn't go to college work in the fields, or as mechanics, or maybe as store managers."

Pati is now toying with the idea of moving back to Parlier. She is torn between her desire to live in a large, diverse community and her desire to go home to help the people she knows. "I feel like I have a responsibility to my community and my people, to help them as best I can to achieve their goals, just as they encouraged me," she says. "It's just not true that if you work hard enough, you'll get there. Nobody does it alone."

She feels a responsibility to her family, too. In her junior year of high school, her family lost their house when her brother Jesus lost his job, and, unable to make payments, they were forced to sell. Pati's mom was laid off by the chicken processing plant. Tired and a bit disillusioned, she recently moved back to Mexico after 16 years in California. Jesus, after much hard work and diligence, was accepted to UCLA but found himself unable to afford the school's tuition. He is still in Parlier and is saving to return to school at Fresno State.

Pati, too, is saving to return to school. She is now working as a research assistant and plans to enter a graduate program to earn a master's degree in social work. Last summer, she worked for a bilingual education program designed to help students learn English while maintaining and enhancing their Spanish. Pati visited children's homes to introduce the program, and there, she says, "I met countless Mexican immigrant families like my own, struggling to survive—let alone prosper—in a foreign society and an unknown educational system." The work convinced her that she should become a social worker dedicated to helping, as she puts it, "under-represented populations." Ultimately, she says, she is convinced that she'll return to Parlier. "I want people to know that there are people like me who are available to help. I want justice for people, and I want to help my community. Like Cesar Chavez, I'm always inspired by seeing what people can do."

224

reunion:
together again

On one Saturday each summer, dozens of SMYSP alumni return to Stanford for the annual day-long SMYSP reunion. The event has become one of the hallmarks of the program: a yearly reaffirmation of friendship and shared experiences, a day full of camaraderie and encouragement.

By 9 a.m. on the day of this summer's alumni reunion, the SMYSP house is full of returning students, ranging in age from late teens to late 20s. The graduates who fill the room chart the history of the program: some are already doctors, some are in graduate school, some are in college, and the most recent are just finishing high school. There is much laughter, lots of excited talk about classes, families, careers and lives that are changing. At 9:30, while this year's students are off at their SAT tutoring, the first official event of the day commences: a conversation with medical students who talk about their educational journeys. The first to speak is Peggy, Stanford graduate and past SMYSP counselor. Peggy is a tall, articulate Latina woman whose story is one of persistence in the face of rejection.

"I graduated from Stanford in 1997," she tells the 40 or so people gathered about. "I stayed here to work in 1997, and then in 1998 I applied to medical school. I didn't get in. I had five interviews, and I felt very close to getting accepted, but I didn't get in. So I went to a program designed to help minority students gain admission to medical school. I perfected my personal statement and raised my MCAT scores, and I applied again. And I didn't get in again. I reapplied a third time and was accepted to UCLA. I'm here to tell you: don't give up. In California, there are only 10 medical schools. Every year, 4,000 to 7,000 students apply to each one of those schools. Only 500 to 1,000 students will be asked to come to the school for an interview. And only 80 to 150 of those interviewed will actually attend."

Peggy's story draws a round of applause. The next speaker is Simone, who is just finishing at Stanford Medical School. "I am the most atypical medical student you'll ever find," she tells the students. "I was born in Guyana and moved to Brooklyn when I was 14. I fell in love with science. I loved chemistry and biology. I didn't have any money, but I never believed being poor should hold me back. I thought, 'Being poor is not a crime, but staying poor is, if there are opportunities for me.' I wound up going to Columbia University for college; it was close enough to go home for a pep talk. I knew I wanted to be a doctor, but I lacked friends who knew about medical school. For a while, I felt I was just bumbling along.

"I also knew I had to try very, very hard if I wanted to get into medical school, because I have sickle-cell anemia. During college, I was in and out of the hospital, and it was hard for my counselor to think that I could be a doctor. But having sickle-cell anemia really motivated me. I wanted to find the cure for it, or at least to be the doctor holding patients' hands and telling them they'd be okay. And here I am, I'm now in my final year of medical school. I really believe if you want to be a doctor, you can do it."

228

Throughout the morning, others recount their histories, and the pattern of their stories stays constant: there is hardship, tension and finally triumph. Grace, the only SMYSP counselor this year who is already a medical student herself, has six pieces of advice she wants to give those considering med school: "One, take time off and explore. Travel your own road. Two, find mentors who care about you, and form a connection with them. Three, make sure that you really want to do this. Keep shadowing doctors. Four, if you bump into anyone who tells you that you can't do it, move on. Five, be very inquisitive. And six and most important: do what you love and what makes you happy."

After the panel, there is a barbecue lunch in the backyard. Trays of ribs, baked beans and corn sit on one of the house's picnic tables. Before long, the alumni are each carrying heavily loaded plates of food and looking for spots in the garden to sit and catch up. Joseph, who graduated from SMYSP two years ago and is now finishing his freshman year at Berkeley, is playing the piano in the living room; the theme to *Mission: Impossible* comes wafting through the air as the students begin to eat.

Chor, another SMYSP graduate of two years ago, is sitting on the house's red-brick patio with SMYSP alumnus and roommate Kao Vang and SMYSP alumnus Harpreet. All three are students at UC Davis, and they carpooled to Stanford together early this morning. Soon, other students come over to join them, and the talk turns to the challenges of organic chemistry, to biology labs, to the business of settling into college life. A constant theme of the discussion is how much SMYSP has helped—with specific things like SATs, scholarships and letters of recommendation and in less tangible ways, like making the students feel that they deserve to be in college, that they have just as much right to do battle with organic chemistry as the next guy.

Midway through lunch, this year's SMYSP students return from their SAT tutoring. They fill up plates of food and then—between bites—introduce themselves to the alumni. After the meal is finished, more formal introductions are made: everyone sits in a circle in the living room and says their name, where they're from and what they're studying. Communities mentioned include Oakland, Atwater, Sanger, Hayward and Fresno; majors include biology, neurobiology, biochemistry, ethnic studies, microbiology, cultural anthropology and music. After everyone has had a chance to speak, a panel of alumni takes the floor.

Moises, an athletic-looking man in shorts and sneakers, tells the students, "I'm sitting here talking to you 10 years after I went through the program, and that's a testament to the fact that it helped me as much as it did. I'm very proud to be part of this program. It had a tremendous impact on my life. I came from Mexico, where my parents didn't have the opportunity to go to school, and they could only help me so much. I didn't go into medicine—I studied engineering at the University of Notre Dame—but I have stayed connected. When you are having a hard time, just remember to follow your heart and be positive. You can always count on the people you're meeting here."

229

The final speaker of the afternoon is Diana. She is dressed in a denim jacket, and her long black hair is pulled back from her face. "I grew up in San Francisco and now I live in Oakland," she says. "SMYSP was an inspiration for me. It was an inspiration to see a whole bunch of people of color come into a house like this. Being a part of SMYSP, I saw other people's struggles, and it empowered me to keep on going."

Diana, who graduated from SMYSP in 1999, is now majoring in ethnic and Chicano studies at UC Berkeley. Ardent and aware, she speaks to the students with the fervor of a union organizer. "Think about the bigger picture of health," she urges. "For example, when I hear someone in Oakland say, 'I have asthma,' I think about the fact that a lot of people in Oakland have asthma because of the industry in the city, because of the air quality in the city. Disease is political. Don't lose sight of where you came from and the needs of your communities. Remember that the fact that you got here has to do with years of struggle and people busting their butts to get you here. Now that you're here, find your circle, and support and push each other. After the program is when the real reality check comes, when you'll master financial aid, applications, et cetera. SMYSP will give you a lot of hook-ups in the health field. Know that you'll see these people in the future. Help each other."

german
hernandez

"I never ask God to give me anything; I only ask him to put me where things are."
— *Mexican proverb*

German Hernandez is the chief medical resident at one of San Francisco's largest, most hectic hospitals. A recent graduate of Harvard Medical School, he is still young, but already he has the bearing of a seasoned doctor. An advanced maturity is nothing new for German: even as a toddler, he was independent beyond his years. By the time he was 3, he was walking to preschool by himself along the hot, dusty streets of Iguala, Guerrero, the Mexican town where he grew up. "My parents gave me lots of leeway from an early age," says German. "I always felt that they wanted me to do things on my own—but with their support."

Iguala is a small city set in a dry valley about two and a half hours inland from the Pacific coast, halfway between Mexico City and Acapulco. "When I was growing up, probably 40 percent of the streets weren't paved," German remembers. "When it rained, the streets turned to mud and then the mud turned to dust, and there was dust everywhere." Iguala is a center of commerce, surrounded by agricultural communities where farmers grow mangoes and corn. It is still somewhat of a rural area: people in the surrounding mountains lack basic services like running water and sewers; people in the city who do have water piped into their homes can't drink it without first boiling it, for it is filled with microbes. Still, within the community, German's family lived well. "I was really quite a privileged kid," German says of his days in Mexico. "We had a nice home: a four-bedroom house with three bathrooms, a garage and a big yard that had palm trees and mango, papaya and guava trees. There was even a TV." German's parents ran a store called La Fe (The Faith) in Iguala's central market. It had belonged to German's father's parents; when German's parents married, they bought the store and ran it together. "In Mexico, stores like this are called *tiendas de abarrotes* or 'groceries,'" says German. "We sold dry goods, canned goods—anything that wasn't perishable. The market was adjacent to the bus station, and people from smaller towns would come to buy supplies. I remember loading up dollies with food and taking them to the station. I loved maneuvering them."

German's parents, Ofelia and German Sr., were introduced by Iguala's priest—who just happened to be Ofelia's brother. "My dad is a simple guy, not pretentious, just relaxed," German says. "My mom is a lot more social and likes to be in the center of things. She's always doing something. I think I have a bit of both in me."

German grew up spending most of his time with adults. On Sundays, he was the impromptu bell ringer and offering collector at his uncle's church. "My uncle would give Mass at the town church, and then we would hop into his car and go from village to village so he could say the Mass," German remembers. "I always liked hanging out in the store with my parents. One day, I didn't want to go to kindergarten. They said, 'You have to go to school.' When they were pulling out of the driveway to go to work, I jumped on the back of our truck and hung on. But then the truck started to go faster, and I got scared and started screaming. So they took me to the store, but they made me just sit there and do nothing all day."

While German was fortunate enough to live in a financially stable family, he knew that not everyone was as lucky. "I was always conscious of poverty," he says. "In school, there were kids who didn't have enough money to buy uniforms, or they had old worn-out uniforms. The kids who didn't have enough to eat weren't even making it to school.

"I remember being in the store with my mom, and she had a big file folder of the names of people who had come to the store and written her IOUs. I think when you grow up in Mexico, the notion of poverty is with you from day one. You see people on the street asking for money. You see disabled people pushing themselves on the street in makeshift carts. It's everywhere. But seeing my mom interact with people who didn't have as much as we did taught me a lot about giving and sharing."

German's parents wanted their children to have good educational opportunities: "My mom and dad always felt that because they didn't go that far in school, they wanted more for us than that—although my dad finished high school and my mom finished middle school. My dad had wanted to go to medical school, but when he finished high school, he didn't get the chance. When he was older, he volunteered at the local Red Cross, where they took care of people who had no money. My dad learned medicine just by seeing and doing. He ended up doing a lot of basic trauma care, suturing and such." German would often accompany his father to the local hospital and watch him work.

"Basically, my parents told me that they worked hard so that I could go to school, and that was my responsibility," he says. "They thought that since they didn't have a lot of opportunities, they would give me all the opportunities they could afford. They never pressured me. My parents were very progressive in their thinking, but it was always driven by the goal to further our education."

When German was 5, his parents asked him if he'd like to go to the United States for a couple of years to learn English.

"When they said, 'Do you want to go and live with your uncle and aunt?' I said, 'Sure, whatever.' I remember being very nonchalant about it."

German's parents put him on an airplane bound for the Bay Area. It was another example of his level of privilege, he says, that his parents could get him a visa and afford a plane ticket. "When I came, I didn't speak a word of English," he remembers. "I stayed for two years with my uncle and aunt, Ruben and Liduvina Carreon. My uncle had moved to America in the late '60s. He started as a dishwasher and worked his way up to be co-owner of a restaurant. We lived in San Mateo for the first year, and then we moved to Napa, where the new restaurant was. It was in an old farmhouse.

"My aunt was just wonderful, a stay-at-home mom who was very nurturing and supportive. She sacrificed a lot for me and my cousins. My uncle is the hardest-working person I know. He worked six days a week, and the one day he had off, he spent with us. He was also supportive and nurturing, but much more strict. He only went to school until second or third grade, but he learned to read and write on his own. His parents passed away when he was 7, and he was raised by other relatives and had to fend for himself. He taught me to set my goals high and to work hard to achieve them. After a lot of hard work in his own life, he's very successful."

When he was 7 and now bilingual, German returned to Mexico and started second grade. Ever resourceful, German's father had branched out from the store and started a business selling bleach. "When he was starting his business, he would go to all the bars around town and collect their empty glass bottles to use for his bleach. He would bottle, label and deliver the bleach himself. I would help out. I bottled bleach, and I used to drive the delivery truck. I would go store to store. It was fun," remembers German.

"But then, one of the many devaluations of the peso came, and my dad's business went broke. By this time, he was making his own plastic bottles, but to get the right kind of plastic, he had to pay in dollars because it was all imported from the States. Mexico would sell oil to the United States, and then the United States would sell Mexico back refined plastic. So his business went bankrupt, and my mom took over running the store. Then in '85, we had a big earthquake that ruined the store, so my mom decided to sell. My dad got a desk job in the local school district. Their financial situation now is much worse than it was before. My parents still live in the same house, but now it has a bunch of cracks from all the earthquakes."

When it was time for German to enter the sixth grade, he moved to Cuernavaca to

a. German (far right) at 4, with his cousins from California. "It was after this visit that my parents decided I should live with my uncle in San Mateo so I could learn English," he recalls. b. German at 6 in Napa. "My uncle and my sisters had come up from Mexico to visit," he says. German's uncle is in the back row, second from right. German's sister Yolanda is in the back row, far right. His sister Ofelia is in the front row, far right.

live with his sisters. "Cuernavaca is about an hour south of Mexico City," he says. "My sisters had moved there for high school. I lived with them for two years, and when they were done with school and moved away, I lived by myself for a year." German was 14. "I went to school and I learned to be responsible," he remembers of the time. "I also did a lot of fun and mischievous things. I drove a beat-up 1980 Datsun, and I remember picking up friends to go to school, but sometimes going instead to the river to fish or swim. During that year, I didn't know what I wanted to do next. I had an inkling of medicine, because that's what my dad always wanted to do. But in Mexico, it meant six years after high school, and that seemed much too long to me."

When German finished middle school, he called his uncle and asked if he could come to the States for a year. "And when I came here, things changed a lot," German says. "I didn't cut school or play around, because I'd already done that. I got more serious about doing something with my life. I started to be more involved in community service and helping others."

German enrolled in a high school in Napa. His English was rusty, and, with no friends, he felt isolated for a while. But academically, things were a breeze. "When I got to high school, I found it was basically a review of my middle school education, except for English," he says. "In Mexico, you start studying biology, physics, chemistry, algebra, et cetera from seventh grade on. If you get beyond ninth grade in Mexico, the quality of education is much higher than in the United States, and middle school is designed to prepare you for that. So I wound up signing up for classes like auto shop and photography because they sounded cool.

"I got very involved with the American Red Cross, teaching HIV prevention and going out to talk to migrant workers in the fields. Then I took a Red Cross course to learn CPR, and it got me even more interested in medicine. But I still didn't know anyone who had gone to college in the United States until I got to SMYSP."

a. German at 17 in his junior year at Napa's Vintage High School. b. German graduating from Harvard Medical School. He's pictured with his Uncle Ruben and Aunt Liduvina. c. German on his wedding day with his wife, Lisa Soto Hernandez.

"It was the most amazing thing to live at Stanford for five weeks and hang out in the hospital, the morgue, the operating room and the emergency room. But probably the people who made the biggest difference for me were the counselors who were already Stanford students. It was the counselors who really encouraged me so that the whole idea of doing medicine became real. No one painted a pretty picture. Our mentors and other medical students told us how little sleep they get and how the health care system is a mess."

German worked in the morgue at the Palo Alto VA hospital. "I think I got to do more autopsies there than I ever did in med school," he says. "I remember we did an autopsy on a gentleman who had had a heart attack, and he had so much fat tissue and calcifications in his body. Afterward, we walked to the VA canteen, and all they had left were hamburgers! There were two SMYSP students working in the morgue: me and a guy named Jesus Rodriguez.

"Jesus and I had actually met before, at a science fair at UC Santa Cruz. When we both ended up at SMYSP, it was pretty amazing." Like German, Jesus was born in Mexico but had immigrated to the United States, and he was living with his mother in the town of Madera. The connection between the two has continued. "Jesus is a physician now, too, in family practice," says German. "We did SMYSP together, went to college together, worked in the same lab in college and even roomed together for a while. It's great that he's in family practice: he's a very gentle and calm human being, always with a smile on his face. I am sure he is great with kids."

At SMYSP, German began to think about his own place in the medical arena. "Working in the morgue, I realized that I didn't want to be a pathologist," he says. "One of my mentors happened to be rotating through the emergency room so I tagged along with him. Many patients spoke Spanish, so I ended up translating for them and their doctors. I think it was really the patient contact that drew me into medicine once and for all. There were people in need of help, and I found I could be useful. I was drawn to medicine more by a desire to help people than by a quest for knowledge.

"The biggest thing I took from the program was motivation. I *felt* like a student. I realized that I could go to college and I could go to medical school. My parents came up from Mexico to visit when I was in the program. I didn't know they were coming so it was a wonderful surprise. They were in awe of everything and very proud." German returned to high school with a new understanding about what he needed to do to get into college. "In my high school, there were pre-set tracks: students in honors classes and students in non-college prep classes. I was in-between, taking auto shop but starting to enroll in other types of classes. When I first got here, I was surprised that I had a choice about what I wanted to take, because in Mexico, everyone is at the same level. I had no idea what the difference was between a regular course and an honors course.

"In Napa, there are a lot of Mexican migrant workers, so a lot of the high school students are Mexican. Most of them don't have role models; they come home and their parents don't even understand what their homework is about. There really aren't a lot of high expectations; there's nothing to push the students. And a lot of students get funneled into the armed forces, or into technical or vocational schools or community college—which is great for some people. But who's to tell somebody that that's what they should do because they're not smart enough or because they just did not have the right educational opportunities?"

German took the SAT and aced the math but struggled with the verbal sections. His overall score and his grades were good enough to get him into Stanford. "I was very lucky," says German. "I was applying as an international student, even though I'd gone to high school in California. It was the last year they had need-blind admissions for non-U.S. citizens. After that, you had to have money. There's no way I could have gone to Stanford if I hadn't gotten help. But I got a very good scholarship. My family helped. My French teacher, Mrs. Mary Ellen Boyet, even gave me money. The rest I took in loans and work-study." German got a job in a dermatology lab and encouraged his friend Jesus, also now a student at Stanford, to apply. "I thought working in the lab would help him get into medical school," says German. "He was the main trouble-shooter for the PCR, or polymerase chain reaction machine. I remember once somebody wrote on the board, 'If you're having trouble with the PCR machine, talk to Jesus.'"

Stanford wasn't easy. German's parents didn't doubt his abilities, but they were amazed at how far he'd come. When he told them he'd been accepted at one of America's top universities, they kept asking him to make sure that it wasn't a mistake. German

238

assured them it wasn't—though sometimes he himself wondered. "All my freshman year, I thought, 'Maybe I don't really belong here,'" he says. "School definitely got a lot tougher when I got into college. I remember the first year with general chemistry, the place was packed. Then as the first mid-term came along, the class got smaller and smaller. But I found I could do it. I just worked harder."

German majored in biology at Stanford. He hung out with his former counselors from SMYSP and got involved with the school's Latino community. "I was part of an organization called Chicanos in Health Education," he recalls. "On weekends, we volunteered as translators at a clinic that offered free health-care services to the under-served. We also put on health fairs and tried to reach out to Latino high school students interested in going to college."

During his last year at Stanford, German met his future wife, Lisa, in a class called Group Communications. "She's from El Paso, which is about 90 percent Mexican. She'd never left home before coming to Stanford, so college was a complete life-changing experience for her."

In his junior year at Stanford, German took the MCATs for medical school. It was like the SATs all over again: great scores in science, not so great in writing. German thought a lot about where to apply. He was still in the United States on a student visa, which meant his chances of getting into a University of California medical school were just about zero, since UC medical schools give priority to state residents for their few highly sought-after spots. German applied to private medical schools in the United States and waited. Soon, Harvard wrote to tell him they would admit him—and they were prepared to help him financially.

"Harvard was a great place," he says. "I thought it might be a really stuffy place, but it wasn't. It was very welcoming. It exposed me to a lot of different people—different Latinos, like Puerto Ricans. I continued to volunteer at a clinic. We had the world's best faculty in whatever area you wanted to study. We got our white coats and started seeing patients from day one. What I really liked about Harvard was the amazing ratio of faculty to students. Even though there were maybe 150 students in each class, they divided us into five groups, or societies, with a master who was your advisor throughout medical school. They made it feel small enough so it was nurturing."

While German was in Boston, his fiancée Lisa was in Austin, studying law. The two married just before graduation and returned to the Bay Area. Lisa is now a labor and employment attorney for the County of San Mateo; German is the chief resident at San Francisco General Hospital, a large, public hospital that services patients from all over San Francisco and was one of the first hospitals in the world to recognize and treat AIDS. German chose to work at SFGH, he says, "because its mission is to take care of the under-served. It's where all the patients who don't have insurance go."

"The majority of the Latino population in California tends to have few resources and many are uninsured and live in poverty. That makes it a more susceptible and vulnerable population. A lot of my time is spent taking care of the under-served and I find it extremely rewarding.

"I've always known that I wanted to work with Latinos, because that is where I feel the most useful: I can speak with patients in Spanish, understand culturally what it means for them to be going through an illness. I can understand the subtleties of what they're experiencing or in what they're trying to tell me. Also, I can see that Latino patients relate more to me, so they're more apt to follow through with the plan of care and take an interest in their health."

German and his wife live not far from the hospital in a multicultural neighborhood. Many of the people he treats live near him and he sees them often: when he is out walking, at church or in the grocery store. His presence in the neighborhood only increases his connection to his patients and his desire to help them.

"Working here has made me see the health problems in the Latino community firsthand," he says. "For example, we are seeing an epidemic of diabetes. It's omnipresent and I think that a lot of our patients are hindered by their low levels of literacy and education. They don't understand or know what diabetes is, and therefore, they don't have an interest in taking care of it, or they don't know how to take care of themselves. At the hospital, we try to overcome a lot of those barriers."

German sees no easy answers to improving the overall health of the Latino population. "Increasing everybody's level of education would be a start," he says. "And money is an issue: our health network is under-funded. The work of programs like SMYSP is important to increase the number of minority physicians in medicine. But it's just a small piece of a larger equation.

"I feel very privileged," German says as he reflects on the course his life has taken. "My family is very strong and secure. My brother-in-law, who has an auto body shop, has also been very inspirational in my life. Both he and my uncle have been role models: they came to this country when they were not so young and spoke no English, but they worked their way to success. I thought if they could do it, so could I. That's probably why it was easier for me than many of my friends at SMYSP. I can't compare my situation to the student whose situation is so bad that they fear for their life or their livelihood. Sometimes I wonder if I took a spot at SMYSP that should have gone to someone who deserved it more than I did. My dad would have been completely happy if I had come here and gotten a job in my uncle's restaurant or in my brother-in-law's auto shop. SMYSP really changed my life. I never would have gone to Stanford or Harvard without it. It made me strive for possibilities that I wouldn't have known existed."

bioethics:
the meaning of life

It's 10:45 Friday morning, the last week of SMYSP, and the students are getting ready for their last lecture of the program. It will be given by Dr. William Hurlbut, a professor in Stanford's Department of Philosophy, who has come to talk about bioethics. Dr. Hurlbut is a compact, energetic man with open, clean-cut features. As he sets up his slide projector, the students take a mental break: Michelle and Elizabeth crack open sunflower seeds. Corinne has her head down on the desk, taking a catnap before the lecture begins. Oscar and LaTasha talk intently about their upcoming presentation for their research project on cervical cancer.

"Okay," says Dr. Hurlbut, grabbing the students' attention and launching into his subject right away. "When we look out at the world these days, we're all sort of aware that these amazing advances are coming. Things are slowly building up to a critical mass that's going to change what it means to be human. Key questions are evoked by these changes: Who are we? What do we want to emphasize in ourselves? So much is implicated and there are so many questions: What does suffering mean? Should we treat aging as a disease? We can now induce male breast-feeding, and maybe someday, male pregnancy. So should we? And is there a natural way to know what we should do? Is there such a thing as a 'right' course of action?

"So what is bioethics? 'Bios' means life; 'ethics' deals with values of human conduct, with rightness and wrongness. 'Ethics' is from the same linguistic root as 'ethnic,' which raises the connection between culture and conduct: How do societies affect ideas about what's the 'right' conduct? And what does biology mean to ethics? For example, what about sociopathy: is that purely a biological condition, or do people have some kind of control or choice when they act in a sociopathic way?"

The students are listening intently now; the questions Dr. Hurlbut is throwing at them have got their neurons firing and their psyches spinning. Hurlbut turns off the light and turns on the slide projector. His first image is a vast network of stars flickering through a haze of cosmic gases. "Human existence is located between infinities," he begins, "between the vastness and the minutiae of the universe, between the cosmos and the atom." Hurlbut's tone is authoritative but reverent. Caught up in the startling wonder of life, he is speaking with awed conviction.

"You were once a microscopic cell in a cosmos so full of stars that all the grains of sand on the earth do not equal them in number. There are 200 billion stars in our galaxy alone. Think about it: we are lodged in something truly amazing.

"Our universe is 12 to 15 billion years old. Earth is 4.5 billion years old. Life is 3 to 4 billion years old. Mammals are 200 million years old. Human existence is lodged between the eons of cosmic time and the frenzy of atoms that collide a billion times per second. We are lodged within the infinite range of what is possible, within the miraculous reality that all of the elements that needed to come together to allow for life actually did."

244

Dr. Hurlbut's message is unlike any the students have ever heard in a classroom. This is no you-can-get-it-if-you-really-try pep talk, no motivational homily. His message fills the room with the white light of wonder and says: each one of you, through your very existence, is a revelation.

Hurlbut shows slides of the earth—pictures taken from space and then from the planet's surface, showing its remarkable beauty. "We are formed and fashioned by the earth," he says. "Try to imagine the dawn of the world, when we lived tied to the earth, in harmony with it, constrained by it. Try to picture what it was like to be a human being then: bright sunlight, sunset, rocks and ravines, the night sky, darkness and the howlings of animals, the strangeness of the body. What is the heart? Why breathe? Why menstruate? Imagine the mystery of unseen forces."

Hurlbut's slides now are depictions of early humans clad in furs and skins: hunting, sitting around fires. He tells the story of a skeleton found—a skeleton thousands of years old, of a man born without teeth who lived well into adulthood, who must have had someone who chewed his food for him to ensure his survival. "There never was a time when human beings weren't intelligent and sensitive, compassionate for the sick and the aged," he says. "Perhaps there was even a romantic sensibility and a deep fidelity. All of our earliest records give evidence of a creature who was a creator, who was set apart."

The slide changes to a modern-day urban skyline. "We've gone from the cave to the skyscraper, and now"—he flashes to a slide of cells under a microscope—"to in vitro fertilization, a small doorway to the radical revision of human life. We are now just at the point where we can start screening fetuses for disease, for physical traits. What do you think?" he asks, looking around the room. "Is that okay?"

Jose's hand shoots up. "No," he says, his tone unequivocal. "You shouldn't have the right to choose whether something has the right to live."

Tom's hand goes up next. "There may be an issue with money that wouldn't be fair."

Dr. Hurlbut nods his head. "These measures will probably be used with the poor first, perhaps as part of a welfare package," he says.

Kamille is next. "I really think it's an individual choice," she says adamantly. "For myself, I would keep a child even if, for example, I found out it had sickle-cell anemia."

Ivan throws his hand up now. "I have to say I agree with screening," he says. "By doing it, doctors will be helping to prevent suffering and disease."

"Let's talk about suffering," says Hurlbut. "Is it okay to abort for suffering? And who gets to decide? I knew a 22-year-old woman with cystic fibrosis, and the night before she died, she told me, 'I am so grateful to have lived.'"

"Abortion is not a simple thing, and sexuality carries implied ethics," he says. "You shouldn't be having intercourse if you aren't ready for the consequences of having a baby." Hurlbut has stepped outside the realm of the hypothetical into what sounds like the role of a guidance counselor. "Ethics really have to do with life happiness and with life purpose. With them, you'll be happy; without them, you'll be a mess."

Dr. Hurlbut discusses the results of a survey which gauged the national mood on prenatal screenings for selective abortions. "One percent of the people polled favored abortion for gender. Six percent favored it for Alzheimer's disease. Eleven percent favored it for people who'd have a tendency to be obese." It is a statistic that is too easy to find appalling; the moral ground is firmer than quicksand. But swiftly, Hurlbut is back to the moral mire. "With the new technology of in vitro fertilization, it will soon be possible to grow a twin of ourselves. Is it okay to grow that creature and harvest it for organs and blood cells?"

Corinne, a twin herself, looks horrified. "No," she says firmly, "that is not okay. That other embryo deserves just as much dignity, just as much of an identity."

"But the dilemma of body parts is coming," insists Hurlbut. "What about cloning? Is it okay to clone yourself to get body parts?"

The students debate the issues. There are no easy answers, and their responses mirror those of academics all over the country. Some want to use genetics to lengthen human life and minimize suffering, while others believe life's mechanisms should be left largely untouched.

"Life is changing," says Dr. Hurlbut at the end of his lecture. "What direction will it move in? What images of perfection will guide it? These are the questions we will grapple with in the future. But there are some absolutes: remember that all life incorporates pain and that all life will end. I believe, ultimately, that love sums up ethics. For unless you have some love in your heart, your life isn't worth living anyway."

phuong
vo

"Venture all; see what fate brings."
— Vietnamese proverb

At first, Phuong Vo's smile is a bit tentative, like a young bird taking off. But then it soars, sending an infectious radiance across her face. It is a smile to erase the loss and struggle that she had to deal with growing up in the aftermath of the Vietnam War. "Phuong means 'phoenix,'" she says. "For a long time my name didn't mean that much to me. Now I see that it signifies my life."

Phuong was born in Ca Mau, a small town on the southern tip of Vietnam, in 1972. Her family—like all families in Vietnam—had suffered in the nation's civil war and decolonization struggles. Her uncle had been killed in the '50s, around the time of the battle of Dien Bien Phu. Her father, a foot soldier in the South Vietnamese military, did not support the war, and throughout the conflict resisted promotion in the name of keeping a low profile and staying safe for his family. But as the war dragged on, staying safe was almost impossible, and in 1972, the same year Phuong was born, he was seriously wounded in battle.

Though she spent her first three years living through the war, Phuong has no memories of the conflict, nor of another battle fought inside her own body. When she was 3, she contracted polio. "I had a very high fever and after it broke, my parents were worried because I didn't seem to be getting better or walking," says Phuong. "They took me to the doctor, and that's when they found out I'd had polio. There were others in our town who'd gotten the disease." The polio had attacked Phuong's left leg and left it atrophied; she would walk with a limp for life. And yet, says Phuong, "The doctor said I was lucky because my case was comparatively mild."

In the wake of the North's victory, Ho Chi Minh's forces expropriated a large, two-story brick house in Ca Mau. Once a month, it became the site of a community clinic where the town's only doctor treated patients for free. People from all over crowded in. Phuong, watching the doctor work, wished she, too, had the skills to make people well. She remembered the words of a young friend whose family was bitterly poor: the girl told Phuong that whenever she was hungry or sick, she would sleep to forget the pain. "If I were a doctor," Phuong thought, "I would be able to help her."

But a life as a physician seemed out of reach to a young girl who'd suffered polio and whose parents ran a small business selling household goods and renting billiard tables. Phuong lived with her mother, father, a younger sister and two younger brothers, an aunt, her father's mother and a beloved older cousin who took her everywhere. She worked at the stand, helping her parents, and went to school. She felt carefree and happy, she says, living "an ordinary child's life."

In the mid-'70s, Ca Mau became a hive of smuggling activity and the staging ground for boats bearing refugees eager to escape the country. From 1975 to 1979, more than 300,000 "boat people" left Vietnam, most often bound for Malaysia, Hong Kong, Indonesia and Thailand. Phuong's father, watching the covert exodus around him, did not want to leave.

"My father was hopeful that after the transition from the old government to the new, things would be better," remembers Phuong. "But things kept deteriorating. Eventually, my father decided that he wanted us to have a better life, especially to get a better education. Only a few select people were able to go on to college in Vietnam, and it was based on who you knew. Even if you scored very high on an entrance exam, they would find a way to make it nearly impossible. Even before the end of the war, Vietnam was like that. After the war, it was worse."

The family began its efforts to leave. "The first time," remembers Phuong, "we just went to another town and pretended to be visiting relatives. The smugglers came and took our money but then didn't take us. The second time, the boat came and we went to the river, got into the boat and went out to sea for a while. But the engine didn't work, so we had to go back. The third time, we were out in the boat and women and children started to cry because people said we were being followed. Then there was a shot through the boat and somebody was killed. There were maybe 30 or 40 people on the boat. We were all captured and put in prison."

In the prison, Phuong's tenacious spirit and independence began to emerge. "I was 8. I don't think I was scared," she says. "That was actually a really great adventure. In prison, I learned how to talk sweetly to the cook to get more food for my family. When my aunt came to visit, they let me go out to meet her. So I wasn't restricted; it was just something very different from my normal life. The prison camp was in the country, with a forest and a river on one side. The men stayed in a house with bars on the windows and were kept chained. But the women were free. We would go down to the river and wash. The river was guarded, so we couldn't swim away. We were let out after a month." Phuong's father, however, was confined for a year. After the others were let go, he was transferred to a much harsher prison where, again, he was kept chained. More than two decades later, his ankles still bear the scars.

"After my father got out of prison, we kept quiet," Phuong says, "waiting for another opportunity. When it came, it came unexpectedly. At the time, my sister and I were away visiting family; my younger brothers were at home. When we returned home late one afternoon, my parents said, 'We have to go.' They didn't tell us we were escaping, because we might talk too much. My maternal grandmother was supposed to go with us, so my parents decided that my father would take me and one of my brothers; my mom would wait for her mother with my sister, who was sick, and baby brother, and then catch up with us. We split that way and started traveling to another town, where the boat was. My mother made it there before the boat left, but my sister was too sick to make the journey. My parents decided it was not safe for her to go; they were afraid she might not survive. And my baby brother could not go without my mother; he was only a year old. So that night, we left—my dad, me and my brother. This time the boat made it, but the family was not together.

"I don't remember exactly how long we were at sea. It was about two weeks. We were fortunate that we had enough food and water on the boat and enough oil and gas. It was a fishing boat with a little covered cabin. Once we were outside Vietnamese waters, we could go on deck. There were about 30 of us. I remember dizziness and wanting to throw up and big ocean fish always around us. Sometimes we saved our urine in case we ran out of water."

The boat made it safely to Malaysia. On arrival, the family was sent to a refugee processing center. "We came in the late afternoon and they gave us a place to shower and food," Phuong says. "They gave us clothes and sandals. And then, almost the next day—because so many more refugees were coming in—they drove us to the port and we went on a boat to a small island off the coast that was for Vietnamese refugees." But on the island, the family was further torn apart. The trip had taken a serious toll on Phuong's father, who was still suffering from the impact of prison and the war. He was placed in the camp hospital. Phuong and her brother, then 4 years old, were placed in an orphanage. There, the boys were expected to sleep downstairs, the girls upstairs. Phuong's brother didn't want to leave his sister, so the two ran away to family friends in the camp and refused to go back. The friends took them in while their father was healing.

It was a difficult, unstable time for all three. "Whenever we heard a boat was coming in, my brother and I always went down to see if the rest of my family had made it," remembers Phuong. "But it never happened. We didn't have much money left. We were

a. Phuong, her brother Ky and a friend in a Malaysian refugee camp, at Christmas in 1981 (taken about four months after leaving Vietnam).
b. Phuong, Ky and their father arriving in the United States from the Philippines. "We were really happy, but very exhausted," Phuong recalls.
c. Phuong at 16 in a portrait for her 10th-grade school yearbook.

given a ration of food each week. I remember lying in my bed one day and looking at the beautiful blue sky and I thought how my mom was somewhere else and I was here. And if the sky fell down, I would be in one place and my mother would be in another, and we would never see each other again."

After two months on the island, the family was shipped to another camp, this one in Kuala Lumpur. "It was much better than the island," Phuong remembers. "There was more food: every day, we could get breakfast, lunch and dinner by standing in line. My father was back with us and we had our own living quarters which we shared with other people. I remember they even provided movies for us to watch once a week— gladiator movies and horror movies."

The camp was surrounded by barbed wire, and going outside was strictly forbidden. But Phuong was occasionally allowed to accompany her father to a hospital in the city: "My father was having problems with his eyes and respiratory problems. We went with him to the hospital, so we got to meet people outside the camp. At the time, I spoke very little English, but I could speak a Chinese dialect that some Malaysians speak, so I was able to talk to the nurses." Her father's illness in the camps contributed to Phuong's

252

desire to study medicine. "I hated having things happening that were out of my control," she says. "I was so afraid my father would die and we would be without him. Vietnam seemed so far away—it seemed to be on another planet—and my mother was there instead of with us."

In Kuala Lumpur, Vietnamese families applied for political asylum, then waited until they were granted papers to enter a new country. Phuong's father knew he and his children would be able to immigrate to the United States, because the American policy at the time was to grant an entry visa to anyone who had fought for the South Vietnamese military for at least five years. But before the family would be allowed into the United States, they had to spend additional months in a camp in the Philippines, "to

a. Phuong's mother, father, friend Leo, sister Loan, brother Hai, Phuong and friend Doris. "We were celebrating Leo's birthday," Phuong says, "which we have been doing for many years, at my parents' apartment in Oakland." b. Full circle: Phuong in her hometown, Ca Mau, in Vietnam in August 2001. She's with her cousin Sau in the town's market.

get more exposure to American cultural things," remembers Phuong. After six months in Malaysia, they were sent to the Philippine countryside.

The camp in the Philippines was really more of a village; there was no barbed wire, no fences. There were Laotians and Cambodians in the village, people Phuong was meeting for the first time. There were Americans present to teach English. After three to four months, the family was sent to Manila, the last stop before a flight to the United States. There, Phuong was fitted for a new brace to help her walk more easily. "There was a Filipino woman there who was very kind to us," she remembers. "She took me to therapy and to be measured for my brace. She even got us clothes." In Manila, the family was allowed to go anywhere and explore. The newness was exciting, though Phuong missed her mother greatly as she prepared to start a new life without her. She was 9 years old.

Phuong's family arrived in Oakland, California, in October 1982, 13 months after leaving Vietnam. It was very different from what they knew. "When we first came to Oakland, it was amazing to think that we were in the place where we were going to stay, that we didn't have to move anymore. But it felt lonely. It was mid-October when we came and it was getting cold." Phuong had distant relatives who lived in Oakland, a great-aunt and her family. But the relatives were reluctant to help: "We lived with my great-aunt until that first December, but it was always tense because we were only in-laws. And then they just moved and left us in the house. We couldn't possibly rent it by ourselves, and we had no idea how to find another place. Luckily, the social worker told us, 'With the little money you have, you can share an apartment with another family.'"

They moved into a one-bedroom apartment on 9th Street in Oakland's Chinatown. The other family—a woman and her two sons—got the bedroom; Phuong's family got the living room. Phuong took over her mother's duties, doing all the laundry and cooking for the family. For the first time in a long while, she was happy. Life finally had some measure of security and Phuong had a place she could call home—a place she wouldn't be forced to leave. "I loved the 9th Street area," she says, looking back. "It was a nice place and there were a lot of Vietnamese families who lived in the neighborhood, so right away I had Vietnamese friends. There were so many people like us who were just starting out," she says. "In school, the teachers had a Vietnamese assistant to help us. Learning a new language was difficult, but adapting was not so hard." Phuong worked hard in school. "From the time I entered school in the United States, a determination was planted in my head that I needed to study hard in order to have a better life," she recalls. "It was very different from when I was a student in Vietnam."

Soon after they moved to 9th Street, the family met their greatest friend, Leo Connolly, a just-retired economist for the state of California who was looking for ways to keep active. He decided to volunteer as a tutor and was referred to a Vietnamese woman who worked for Catholic Social Charities. She asked him if he would be willing to help recent immigrants learn English and a bit about American ways. Leo said he'd be happy to.

"I tutored a number of people before I met Phuong's father," remembers Leo of the time. He is in his late 70s now, a friendly man whose affection and respect for Phuong and her family is evident. "It was great fun for me. When I came to their apartment the first night, I met Phuong and her little brother. They would sit at the table when their father was having lessons. I fell in love with Phuong right away—she was like a grand-daughter. Occasionally, I tried to help her with her homework, but she was very independent and wanted to do everything herself.

"I do feel that Phuong's family is like my family," says Leo. "I watched Phuong and her brother grow up. I tried to encourage them to read a lot, and since they didn't have much money, I would take them to the ballet, the opera, the symphony. Phuong didn't like those too much, but she was very appreciative of the books I gave her. I introduced her to Yukio Mishima, and she read *Death in Midsummer* and liked that very much. She still reads some of the Japanese modern classics. And she read some Jane Austen novels and *Snow Falling on Cedars*.

"I think just by being there and getting them out of the house, I helped. Their economic conditions were pretty terrible. I think the main thing was... an immigrant family has very little contact with middle-class, white Americans. I thought it was important that they knew someone familiar with American mores and that they felt someone took an interest in them. There are people in this country who are so hostile to immigrants, and

I don't think they have any conception of what a rough life it is. Not too long ago, I was tutoring at the Chinese community center and I met a man there who'd been a doctor in China. Here, he was training to become a janitor."

Of Leo, Phuong says, "He made us feel he had adopted us. He started taking my brother and me places, like the Academy of Sciences, or the Asian Art Museum. It exposed me to things my father wouldn't have been able to show me. Without Leo, my world would have been very narrow. Just knowing that he was there and that I could ask him for help if I needed—it really boosted my confidence. It was like having money in the bank."

Phuong started high school at Oakland Technical High. Her ninth grade class numbered roughly 200 students; by 12th grade, half of the class had dropped out. Phuong estimates only 30 of her classmates went on to college. Still, she credits some of the teachers at Oakland Tech for their dedication to their students. "A couple of the teachers were very caring: Maryann Wolfe, who taught history, and Marietta Joe, who taught English and history," she says. "They put their own resources into making classes better; they took us to movies and plays and out to eat, too, and paid for it all themselves." Leo's literary influence took hold, and Phuong became a voracious reader. "In English," she recalls, "we read Emerson, Thoreau, Whitman. I liked the transcendental writers and the romantic era. In those classes, we had a lot of opportunities to do critical writing and have critical discussions.

"In high school, I concentrated on getting good grades and took challenging courses. My focus was to do well so I could move on to college and medical school. I read about outstanding students and tried to do what they did. But it was hard with the science programs; they were just not good. We didn't have outings and the classes weren't challenging, and when we had labs, students disrupted the classes."

When Phuong was in the 11th grade, her chemistry teacher, Mary Tomczyk, circulated an announcement about SMYSP; she also made a copy of the application form and handed it to Phuong directly. That was enough encouragement to get Phuong to fill out the forms. "I took it lightly during the application process," she recalls. "I thought they probably wouldn't select me. When they called me to come for an interview, it was exciting. I remember there was a question about a vaccine. It was something like, 'You have only one dose of a vaccine. Who would you give it to—a baby, a middle-aged person or an older person?' And I said, 'Either we all get it or we all die, so we have to share it.' Now that I'm older, my answer would be different. Now I think you'd really have to evaluate the disease in each person as well as their social and mental health. It's still a complex question."

Phuong got into the program and moved to Stanford for the summer. She was homesick at first, but that feeling wore off as she got to know her fellow students and gradually developed a second family at SMYSP. "This was my first time to live closely with people from other cultures and we were all excited to share the program and our dreams," she recalls of the time. "I was very shy, and it was wonderful to learn to interact with different people. It was just what I really needed at that time."

The academics, too, provided inspiration. "There was exposure to a little bit of everything. It gave me an idea of what it would be like once I got to college and medical

255

school. At my hospital job, I talked a lot to the head nurse who was my supervisor; my most enjoyable moments in the program were talking to her about who I was and what I hoped to do. She took me around to patients. One stuck in my mind. There was a young man from San Diego and he had melanoma cancer. We talked a lot about his fear of dying; he was divorced with a young son and he wanted to be with his family. He was the first cancer patient I had ever met, and I could feel how helpless and vulnerable he was."

Phuong left SMYSP with a greater sense of confidence that she could make it as a doctor, and with an even stronger conviction that she could make it in America. And then, two months after the program ended, her mother, sister and younger brother finally arrived in the United States. But while she was happy to see her family after so many years, it took Phuong time to feel comfortable with her mother again.

"For eight years, I had lived on my own," she explains. "So when my mom came, it felt strange to have her there. Sometimes she tried to talk to me and she cooked the food I liked. When she did that, I was not appreciative. I thought, 'I can do all that myself.' My father had always been very strict. When we came to America, many times I was not allowed to do things that my friends did. And many times I wished my mom was there to tell him, 'Oh, it's okay, she can do that.' And when my mom finally came, I wanted her to speak up for me like I had always imagined she would have. But she didn't. And I think part of me was angry for that. That difficulty lasted about four or five years. My mother and I didn't become close, I think, until I was away by myself in graduate school; then I really felt more appreciative of my family."

Phuong, who had spent third grade in a refugee camp learning basic English, was the valedictorian of her class at Oakland Tech High. Leo helped her with her valedictory speech. "I gave her a quotation from Immanuel Kant: 'Adopt those moral principles you want others to conform to,'" he recalls. "That went over big."

Phuong was accepted to UC Berkeley and started there in the fall of 1991. It turned out to be a much more arduous endeavor than she'd expected. "Going from high school to college was very difficult, unlike any academic journey I'd ever taken," she says. "In my freshman and sophomore years, I struggled a lot. I felt very isolated. I tried to believe that if I worked hard, I'd make it. But sometimes I felt that I was at the bottom. I began to feel that maybe I wasn't supposed to go into medicine." A C-minus grade in any science class made it very difficult to get into medical school, and it was all Phuong could do to squeak by with C's. She felt demoralized.

But one thing helped. "During my senior year in high school, Marilyn Winkleby introduced me to the man who had been her public health advisor at Berkeley, Dr. Leonard Syme," Phuong recalls. Syme was world-renowned for his research on social inequalities in health and famous on campus for his enthusiastic support of students. When Phuong was a student at Berkeley, she would visit him. "I think I was very privileged to be able to talk with him," says Phuong now. "I would confide in him about my interests. It was a time when I was struggling with my feeling of failure in the sciences. Talking to Dr. Syme made things seem clearer and more hopeful. He showed me that there were other options. Talking to him, I developed an interest in looking at social factors affecting health."

When she could find time away from school, Phuong focused on her community. She was acutely aware of the need for mentoring in the fledgling Vietnamese student population and with a friend, co-founded a program directed at low-income teenagers from east Oakland. "My friend and I talked about how when we were growing up, we wished for a place where we could be with people who could help us," Phuong recalls. "Eventually, we arranged with a Vietnamese language school in Oakland to advise high school students on Saturdays. At least 10 UC Berkeley students took part each week, sometimes 20. We took students on field trips and had writing and SAT workshops."

As Phuong neared graduation, she wasn't sure what to do next. She felt disappointed that her work at Berkeley wasn't going well and saddened by the thought that her long-cherished dream of becoming a doctor might go unfulfilled. One day when she was talking to Dr. Syme, he said, "Why don't you get a public health degree?"

"That gave me some hope," recalls Phuong. "I was feeling like I'd come to the end of the line." Phuong applied to Berkeley's School of Public Health and then waited to see if they'd take her. They didn't.

Phuong was working with Asian Community Mental Health Services, a job she had gotten during her senior year at Berkeley. She worked with developmentally delayed children and later interned at the University of California, San Francisco, evaluating and promoting breast cancer detection programs. She reapplied to the Berkeley School of Public Health. To be on the safe side, she also applied to other public health programs across the country. Again, she was rejected by Berkeley. But this time, she was accepted at a number of other schools, including Harvard. Phuong decided to go east to study health issues affecting minority populations and economically disadvantaged groups. It was a good match.

"At Harvard, I didn't have the feeling of failure that I'd had at Berkeley," she recalls. "I met professors who took me under their wings. For example, I worked with a professor who studied poverty and looked at how work has changed, especially for women, since the 1940s and how that has changed the family structure and care of children. She focused on low-income people. I helped with one of her research projects, looking at how working parents have to put kids through child care and how that affects the children's health."

Phuong was in a two-year master's program at the school. After her first year, she returned to California for the summer to intern at the Alameda County Public Health Department. There, she thought a lot about her future. "When I was younger, I always wanted to be the best. But as I grew up, that became less important to me," she says. "What has always been important, and what remains important, is how I can help people have a better life: those who are unfortunate, who come from disadvantaged communities. My life's goal is to be connected with people and resources that will help me improve the lives of those who still live in poverty. I know that there are public health resources to help those people, but I want to be able to help people when they get sick and to heal them. So I decided to hold on to my dream of being a doctor."

"When I went back to Harvard, I told my professor, Jody Heymann, that I couldn't give up my idea of medicine. And she helped me. She found ways to improve my application to medical school. She said, 'We'll write a scientific article together.' She thought that would show the admissions officers that I'm capable of doing science." The two co-authored a manuscript on breast-feeding and HIV infection in children.

Phuong graduated from Harvard's School of Public Health in June of 1999, with a master of science degree. She took the test she needed to get into medical school, the MCAT. And then she retraced a journey she'd taken many years earlier: she returned to Vietnam.

She went alone on a public health fellowship to research HIV and gender issues in the Vietnamese community. She did most of her research in Ho Chi Minh City, and there, after nearly two decades, she saw her grandmother, who had been unable to leave on the refugee boat so many years earlier. "Since we left, my grandmother has tried to leave Vietnam and join us many times, but she has not been able to," says Phuong. "My mother has tried to sponsor her, but the United States says that she is too old to come here. She is 88 years old, and she is alone in Vietnam, living with her sister. She was so good to us. When we were trying to leave, even though she did not have very much money, she gave us money to help us. I remember on one of the escape attempts that went wrong, she took my younger sister and me, when my father had to go one way and my mother another, and we were stranded in this town. She was barefoot, but we walked and walked for a long time. She was an old woman even then, but she struggled because she wanted to help her daughter's children.

"It was very emotional to see her. She has accepted being alone in Vietnam, but I wanted to be with her again, to be there to return some of the love she'd given to us. I want her to stay alive so that I will be able to return to Vietnam and spend time with her."

While in Vietnam, Phuong also journeyed back to Ca Mau. "I went back to visit my aunts," says Phuong. "On the way there, traveling through the countryside, a lot of memories came back. People still live in thatched-roof houses and are very poor. I thought how lucky I am to have the opportunity to travel the world. These people never wander outside of their hamlets. But I like the sense of connection that people there have: they go out in the evening and eat at the food stands and talk together, and they leave their doors open all the time."

Her project completed, Phuong returned to the States, ready to apply to medical school. But her MCAT scores were lower than she'd hoped for. She applied to five schools nonetheless. When rejection letters came back from all five, she refused to give up. She heard about a special year-long program at the University of California at Davis that is designed to help older students from low-income backgrounds who have an interest in medicine. The program offers an intensive exposure to the sciences; it is designed to compensate for poor science programs in under-funded schools—just the sort of help Phuong had been looking for. She is now nearing completion of the Davis program and will take her MCATs again soon, this time for the last time.

"I wanted to give myself one last chance, to see if it really was me or if it was the preparation. And now that I have been in this program, I have achieved one thing: I'm much more confident in my abilities in the natural sciences," Phuong says. "Now I know that I can do medicine. If I had gotten to medical school last year, I wouldn't have had the confidence that I really understood the science. Now I do. At Berkeley, I studied with closed eyes. Now I study and think, 'Oh my goodness, that's not so hard.'"

"I feel very fortunate. If I hadn't been to SMYSP and met Marilyn, who introduced me to Dr. Syme, I don't think I would have found the public health field and had the opportunities I've had. Dr. Syme has played a pivotal role in my career. When I was at

Harvard or in Vietnam, I often thought how grateful I was that he had seen where my interests and passions lay and suggested the public health field.

"When I was younger, I thought things were clearer, that I could travel one path. But life's not like that. Things are not so simple. When you're young, you don't see all the complexities. When you do, you just have to keep going, anyway.

"The older I get and the more rejections I get, the more inner peace I have. I've reached another level. Before, I felt, 'I'm not smart enough.' Now I'm able to see that rejections allow me to redo something, to see more clearly if it is the right thing to do. Marilyn's Christmas card last year mentioned the redwood tree and how it's strong because it grows slowly and well. I read that and I shared it with my housemates at Davis. I said, 'You guys, I think we're redwood trees!' We have faced difficult life situations and haven't had a lot of guidance, but we have our dreams. We grow slow, but we're strong."

Phuong Vo

NO
FOOD OR
DRINKS

graduation:
rite of passage

The last day of SMYSP, a Sunday, is graduation. It is always the most emotional day of the program—the culmination of work, the time for saying thank-yous and good-byes. Living and studying together, the students and counselors have gained so much intimacy so quickly that it is hard to believe that this is the last day they will all spend with each other. The uncertainty of whether and when they will see one another again fills the air, and throughout the day, there are many, many hugs and promises to e-mail and call.

The night before, at their final Todos Time, the students were reflective, sad to be leaving but full of a new-found confidence. They talked about their futures, their new goals, their new dreams. Tom declared that he'd decided to become a biochemical researcher. After five weeks at the VA, LaTasha was more convinced than ever that she wanted to be a physical therapist. Enrique talked about how he'd loved the OR. "I definitely found out that I want to be a cardiac surgeon," he said. Anthony declared his intention to do genetic or pharmaceutical research. Lien pledged to become a pediatric surgeon. "I like surgery and I love babies," she said.

"All of the doctors were so nice and so uplifting. They told me so much," said Dy'esha. "I remember the first time I smelled flesh being cauterized, I thought I was going to pass out. Now I'm like, 'Oh, flesh.'" Marcus laughed. "The other day, I heard someone behind me say, 'Excuse me, doctor,' and I turned around on instinct," he said. "Has that happened to anyone else?" Marcus is planning to become an OB/GYN doctor; in fact, he said, he, Kamille and Elizabeth are planning to all be OB/GYNs and open a practice together.

But not everyone is still convinced they want to work in the medical field. "I'm not sure I could be a doctor," said Jerome, "having to wash my hands every hour." "It made me realize I have *a lot* of work to do to be a doctor," said Yeshe. As the conversation traveled around the room, others talked about how the program had helped them in non-medical ways. "It's taught me that I want to work with people," said Vivian. "It's helped me think in new ways, and it's helping me get started in life," said Corinne. "My mentors are wonderful," said Quyhn. "My life is shifting. I need an anchor, and they are my anchor right now."

The students spend their last night sleeping under the same roof, and by 7 the next morning, graduation day has dawned clear, bright and warm. The ceremony will be held across campus, in an auditorium near the university's famed Memorial Church. Family members are making their way toward Stanford for the ceremony; many leave their homes in Sacramento or Stockton before daylight to make sure that they reach campus before the ceremony begins at 10 a.m.

262

At the house, the students dress in the finest outfits they have. Most of the boys wear their one suit; the girls are all in dresses. Some of them wear their white lab coats over their outfits. By 8:30 they are downstairs, fine-tuning the presentations of their group research projects. The presentations are the heart of graduation, the students' way of showing their families how much they have learned and how professional they have become. The students begin working on the projects at the start of the program. They divide into groups of three and pick a medical topic to investigate, then they write a 10-page paper and put together a slide presentation. The projects are comprehensive: students use the Internet and Stanford libraries to do research and often interview Stanford doctors and scientists. They revise drafts of their projects with the oversight of a counselor. The eight topics this year are diabetes, hepatitis C, smallpox, disassociative identity disorder, the Ebola virus, cervical cancer, the science and psychology of twins and kwashiorkor (a medical condition resulting from malnutrition).

By just before 10, the graduation auditorium is full of parents, siblings, teachers, friends, mentors, medical students, Stanford faculty and hospital staff who have come to know the students over the course of the program. The students arrive and file into the auditorium. They wave at family and friends as they head to their seats near the front of the stage. They look nervous about their presentations.

As the ceremony begins, Erik Cabral rises to give the first speech. "You've all heard my phrase," he begins, and pauses. The students giggle and call out, "Back in '94!!"

Erik smiles. Throughout the program, he has shared the story of that year in his life, when he was at the crossroads, deciding between a life of violence or one of education. Now, standing at the podium in the auditorium, he is a picture of confidence and conviction. "Every day at a university is a first day," he says. "Although this is a final day, it is a first day. Today, you can call yourselves alumni of SMYSP. You can congratulate yourselves for that. But it also brings a responsibility, because now all of you are ambassadors. You have gained many skills, and with those skills comes the responsibility to go back to your communities and teach others about the things you've learned here. You have gained a responsibility to reach out and help other people understand what the college process is like.

"As alumni, you leave here with people who care for you very much. I encourage you to use any means necessary to stay in touch. I hope all of you will come to the alumni reunions we have each year. In closing: keep in touch and remember that you have new roles. The program works. You *will* go to college, you *will* become a professional, and you *will* make your parents proud. For myself, I know that I will go on to medical school and become a physician. If that's your dream and your goal, you will do it, too."

After Erik's speech, each counselor rises to recognize and pay tribute to a few of the students; by the end, each student has been singled out for praise. Nnenna talks about Yeshe, the "quirky Ethiopian princess." Kahea describes LaTasha as "an amazing person whose passion comes out through her involvement in social justice activities." Khalil says Oscar "is very inspirational to all of us. He is one of the most humble, compassionate young men I've ever met." Nkem recognizes Marcus, who "came in 16. Now he's 41

263

and wears a tie every day." Marcus blushes and smiles as the audience laughs. Erik pays tribute to Jose for showing "a tremendous sense of leadership. He was the guy to make pancakes for everybody, was the first to offer to vacuum the living room. He will be an excellent ambassador for the program." Tamara recognizes Michelle as "the daughter of the program. It's inspiring to see how she treats people and how she respects the program and her family."

After they have all been introduced, the students receive a standing ovation. The lights go down, and a slide show of summer moments begins: Enrique and Erik playing soccer, Dy'esha and Kamille grabbing breakfast before class, Ivan on the phone, Thu in the morgue, Tom about to throw a water balloon, Oscar coming down the steps on his crutches, everyone on the beach for a Fourth of July picnic, Jose playing basketball, Marcus and Elizabeth in anatomy lab, Candi on a lunch break in the VA hospital cafeteria. The students laugh and cheer as the images flash across the screen, reliving the events that have brought them together. Then the lights come back up and it's down to business. Group by group, the students walk up on stage to present their research projects. They are still teenagers, but they have changed: they stand a little straighter and speak with more authority. They have learned so much in the last five weeks and met so many new people. But their greatest change seems to have come from within; they have challenged themselves and discovered new strengths and abilities. They believe in themselves more than they did five weeks ago. They trust their place in the world a little more. Presentations done, they accept their diplomas with self-assured poise. They congratulate one another, hug family and friends, pose for pictures. They smile. And it is clear: they are on their way to college.

Postscript — *A number of the students profiled in* Healing Journeys *have continued on their educational paths since the book was completed. Erik Cabral began attending the Stanford School of Medicine in the fall of 2003. Masud Basel is currently attending the Touro University College of Osteopathic Medicine in Vallejo, California. Pati Ibarra began a master's degree in social work at the Columbia University School of Social Work in the fall of 2003. Phuong Vo began attending the Georgetown University School of Medicine in the fall of 2003.*

conclusion

Adolescence is a time of growth and challenge, a time for developing an independent identity and making decisions about life. The majority of students who have been a part of the Stanford Medical Youth Science Program have already contended with adversities far beyond the common confusions of youth. As these students looked to the future, they faced the same issues that many low-income students in America contend with: a lack of information about the world of higher education, a sense of alienation from that world and few role models. For many students, the decision to attend college means leaving families and peer groups behind; for some, it creates feelings of social and cultural isolation.

As they make decisions about the future, these students need support to foster the resilience that will carry them through college and into professional life. The students who come to SMYSP arrive at a critical age. They are intelligent, capable and committed, and SMYSP exists to assure them that they can thrive, even in the country's finest universities. All of the students who have completed SMYSP, like the 16 profiled in this book, have dealt with hardship. They relied on their intellects and self-discipline. They took risks. They chose education as a path. They stayed resilient and flourished. But they didn't succeed alone. At key points, they found people who gave them support and love, and made them feel talented and worthy. They had friends, mentors and teachers who encouraged them to become independent, responsible and altruistic.

All of the students profiled in this book had at least one mentor who changed their lives. With Kao, it was his fourth grade teacher; with Leonard, his high school history teacher; with Katrina, her high school counselor; with Destinee, her sixth grade teacher; and with Pati Ibarra, it was the Ivy League Leadership Project. All 16 went on to study at some of the best colleges in the country: six at Stanford, six at University of California campuses, three at Ivy League schools and one at Northwestern. Thirteen of the 16 chose careers in health. Those who did not, chose law (Leonard), academics (Xavier) and engineering (Khalil).

These 16 students will now go on to inspire and mentor others. The hope they generate will manifest itself in ways that no one can foresee. It is an act of faith to invest in another person's future. When Sonya Pettis' mother supported her daughter through college and medical school, she had no way of knowing that Sonya would help save Leo Hindery's life and help ensure SMYSP's survival.

Families, teachers, friends—those who are committed to youth—are among the most important benefactors in our society. We have enough research to know what students need to achieve educational success. They need family and institutional support. They need people to believe in them and to give them time and energy. The question is not whether we will be able to help the next generation of students, but whether we are willing. The issue in our society is one of commitment.

SMYSP is a small program. It accepts only 22 to 24 students a year. Its merit and relevance come from its success, not its size. Of the 333 students who have attended SMYSP from its inception in 1987, through 2002, 147 have graduated from college, and 131 are currently attending college. Only three of those who began college have had to leave to take full-time employment. Fifty-two, the most recent SMYSP graduates, are finishing high school.

Of the 278 students who have attended college, 47 percent have attended a University of California campus (usually Berkeley, Davis or UCLA); 31 percent have attended Stanford, an Ivy League school or a private university; 14 percent a state university; and 8 percent a community college. The academic majors of the 147 students who have graduated from college show an emphasis in the basic sciences: 58 percent have majored in the biomedical sciences, 11 percent in the physical sciences and 31 percent in the social sciences and liberal arts.

The careers of our college graduates also emphasize the health professions. Eleven percent are in or have completed medical school, and 21 percent are employed in health-related jobs. Thirty-two percent are in or have completed graduate school, 22 percent are employed in non-health-related jobs, and the remaining 14 percent are homemakers or are engaged in other activities. The numbers of students pursuing advanced degrees and health careers will surely grow as more alumni complete their undergraduate degrees.

We wrote this book because we believe that SMYSP offers a model of how to reach students and help them further their educational goals. Through 15 years of the program, we have learned a tremendous amount from our students; they have taught us about their cultures, their schools and their communities. In turn, we have learned what helps students succeed and what nourishes them.

SMYSP offers students five free weeks on a university campus with a peer group that celebrates education. The small structure builds a sense of community and guarantees that students will form lasting friendships. The program's annual survey and long-term advising ensure the continued presence of SMYSP in students' lives. Through continued guidance, SMYSP is designed to support the students long after the program is over. SMYSP alumni, in turn, support the program by advising younger students, promoting the program in their schools, serving on advisory boards and meeting with benefactors.

SMYSP offers a model that can be recreated in any community with a willing university and altruistic donors. It offers a model that can be duplicated in other disciplines, such as law, business or education. We hope that other universities will establish programs like SMYSP. But we realize that most of you who read this book will not create an entire program. We hope the message that you take from the book is that there are thousands of students who can benefit from your support. We encourage you to be involved with the young people in your communities. As the stories in this book attest, you will be sowing the seeds of hope and change.

— Marilyn Winkleby

acknowledgments

SMYSP would like to thank the following for their support of the program: Va Lecia Adams, Tom David, Les DeWitt, John Doerr, John Dolph, Leo Hindery, Jr., Jeanne Kennedy, Alana Koehler, John Malone, Judith Ned, David Perry, Dolly Sacks, Mailee Ferguson Walker ■ Stanford University, Stanford Hospital and Clinics, Stanford University School of Medicine, Palo Alto Veterans Affairs Hospital ■ Avant! Foundation, The California Endowment, The California Wellness Foundation, David and Lucile Packard Foundation, Ed Littlefield Foundation, Flora Family Foundation, Genentech, Howard Hughes Medical Institute, The James Irvine Foundation, Joseph T. Garrett Charitable Foundation, Kaiser Family Foundation, MacDonnell Foundation, May and Stanley Trust, Orr Family Fund, Raychem, Roberts Foundation, Syntex, Valley Foundation.

Funding for *Healing Journeys* was provided by The California Endowment, The California Wellness Foundation and The James Irvine Foundation.

Proceeds from the sale of the book will go to SMYSP to fund student scholarships.

If you are interested in contributing to SMYSP, please contact: Dr. Marilyn Winkleby, Stanford Prevention Research Center, Stanford University School of Medicine, 211 Quarry Road, Stanford, California 94305-5705.

Marilyn Winkleby dedicates this book to Lorene Winkleby and Mike Fischetti, who lead lives of caring and giving; to Desirae, Chris, Diana and Juanita, who are members of today's resilient youth; and to all SMYSP participants, who inspire the youth of tomorrow.